GIZEH AND RIFEH

RIFEH. POTTERY SOUL HOUSE. TYPE L. IX-XII DYNASTY.

102

GIZEH AND RIFEH

BY

SIR W. M. FLINDERS PETRIE

WITH CHAPTERS BY

SIR HERBERT THOMPSON, Bart., and W. E. CRUM

DOUBLE VOLUME

OXBOW | books
Oxford & Philadelphia

This edition published in the United Kingdom in 2024 by
OXBOW BOOKS
81 St Clements, Oxford OX4 1AW

and in the United States by
OXBOW BOOKS
1950 Lawrence Road, Havertown, PA 19083

Paperback Edition: ISBN 979-8-88857-081-4
Digital Edition: ISBN 979-8-88857-082-1

First published in 1907 by the British School of Archaeology in Egypt
Facsimile edition published in 1977 by Aris & Phillips Ltd

Oxbow Books is grateful to the Petrie Museum for their collaboration in bringing out these new editions

Printed in the United Kingdom by CMP Digital Print Solutions

For a complete list of Oxbow titles, please contact:

UNITED KINGDOM
Oxbow Books
Telephone (0)1226 734350
Email: oxbow@oxbowbooks.com
www.oxbowbooks.com

UNITED STATES OF AMERICA
Oxbow Books
Telephone (610) 853-9131, Fax (610) 853-9146
Email: queries@casemateacademic.com
www.casemateacademic.com/oxbow

Oxbow Books is part of the Casemate Group

Front cover: Reproduction of a wooden model boat, funerary, with separate figures of rowers and equipment attached from Gizeh, Early Middle Kingdom Petrie Museum UC75868. Image courtesy of the Petrie Museum of Egyptian and Sudanese Archaeology, UCL.

CONTENTS

CHAPTER VII

THE XIIITH—XVITH DYNASTIES. RIFEH.

CHAPTER VIII

THE XVIIITH—XXTH DYNASTIES. RIFEH.

CHAPTER IX

THE CLASSIFICATION OF THE POTTERY.

CHAPTER X

SAITE AND LATER PERIODS.

CHAPTER XI

THE DEMOTIC PAPYRI.

BY SIR HERBERT THOMPSON, Bart.

CHAPTER XII

THE COPTIC MANUSCRIPTS.

BY W. E. CRUM.

LIST OF PLATES

WITH PAGE REFERENCES TO THE DESCRIPTIONS

(Plates with lettered numbers are only issued in the Double Volume)

The plates of tomb inscriptions referred to as Pl. XIII F on p. 11 are not yet published.

On plate XXI the house below 130 has lost its number, 30.

PREFACE TO THE 2024 EDITION

In the 1970s, a much-anticipated new series of publications illustrated objects and themes related to the excavations of the archaeologist William Matthew Flinders Petrie (1853–1942) in Egypt, and aspects of the collection of University College London's Petrie Museum of Egyptian and Sudanese Archaeology. A young couple setting up in business in the early 1970s, Aris and Phillips published these works, written by members of the UCL Egyptology Department, in their *Modern Egyptology* series. Building on Petrie's own observations, the authors of these volumes aimed to complete the great task of publishing the Petrie Museum of Egyptian and Sudanese Archaeology's vast collection, and to present some of the research that Petrie himself was not able to address in his own published works during his lifetime. As the current Curator of the Petrie Museum, it is a great privilege for me to support Oxbow Books in their mission to republish the series, which remains a key source of information for all those interested in object-based approaches to the study of the ancient world.

The Petrie Museum, part of University College London (UCL), is home to one of the largest and most significant collections of Egyptian and Sudanese archaeology in the world. Free to visit, this extraordinary collection tells stories about the lives of ordinary people who lived along the Nile Valley thousands of years ago. Originally set up as a teaching collection, the Petrie Museum comprises over 80,000 objects housed together with an internationally important archaeological archive. It is a collection of world firsts and 'oldests': the oldest woven garment; the oldest worked iron objects; the first known depiction of loom weaving; the oldest known written document about women's health, the earliest veterinary treatise; the oldest will on paper. The Museum has Designated Status from Arts Council England, meaning that it is considered to have outstanding resonance and national cultural significance. The collection has a substantial, visible international reputation for research, supporting hundreds of researchers every year, both remotely and in person.

The Petrie Museum is named after Flinders Petrie, who was appointed in 1892 as the first Professor of Egyptian Archaeology and Philology in the UK at UCL. Over three-quarters of the material in the Museum comes from excavations directed or funded by Petrie, or from purchases he made for university teaching. In 1880 at the age of 26, Petrie travelled to Egypt to survey the Great Pyramid. For the next five decades he was at the forefront of the development of archaeology in Egypt and later in Palestine, and his detailed methodological approach continues to shape the discipline today.

Petrie worked at more sites, with greater speed, than any modern archaeologist: seeing his life as a mission of rescue archaeology, Petrie aimed to retrieve as much information as possible from sites that were shrinking dramatically in size as Egypt modernised during the late 19th and early 20th centuries. He published a large part, but not all, of the finds from his excavations in his illustrated typological volumes, arranged according to object types and themes. Today, much of the Petrie Museum's collection is displayed and stored in a way which reflects these publications: for example, several storage cupboards are dedicated to the material illustrated in the 'Objects of Daily Use' volume, and objects in the drawers are arranged according to the order of the published plates. This offers a unique opportunity for researchers to engage with Petrie's typological and methodical approach to archaeology, as well as with the history of museum collections.

The first catalogue to be published in the *Modern Egyptology* series was *Amarna: City of Akhenaten and Nefertiti* in 1972 by Julia Samson, Petrie Museum Honorary Research Assistant. As official publishers to the UCL Egyptology Department the series went on to produce facsimile reprints of eight of Flinders Petrie's most important site reports and many of his object catalogues, originally published through the British School of Archaeology in Egypt. The substantial annual royalties from these reprints were paid into the 'Petrie Fund' at the time, which provided special grants to students in financial need.

In many ways, the new reprints of this classic series can be seen as the latest layer in a vast 'publication stratigraphy' of the thousands of finds from Flinders Petrie's excavations, which now live in museum collections around the world. On reading these volumes, I hope that readers will also be inspired to learn more about the Petrie Museum collection and its fascinating history.

Dr Anna Garnett
Petrie Museum of Egyptian and Sudanese Archaeology,
University College London
January 2023

PUBLISHER'S PREFACE

Oxbow Books is pleased to present this title in our *Classics in Egyptology* series. This series of facsimile re-issues is comprised of two sub-series. The first consists of 16 typological catalogues produced by W.M. Flinders Petrie based on his massive collection of Egyptian artefacts. Mostly excavated by Petrie during many seasons of campaign in the last years of the 19th and early decades of the 20th century, they now reside in the Petrie Museum at University College London. Published between 1898 and 1937 and long out of print, the catalogues were re-issued in facsimile by publishers Aris and Phillips in the 1970s. These were followed in the next 15 years or so by publication of a number of newly commissioned titles, based on more recent examination of elements of the Petrie Collection by contemporary experts, under the name *Modern Egyptology*. A selection of these additional titles forms the second component of our own series.

The archaeology of Egypt continues to fascinate. Multi-disciplinary investigation and research continues unabated, encompassing methodologies, scientific and data processing techniques, theoretical approaches, and even whole paradigms that were unheard of in the 1970s and undreamt of when Petrie was working in Egypt. Yet all the titles included in this series continue to be invaluable sources of basic data, providing an unparalleled resource that can easily be cross-referenced with the actual materials they describe and discuss. They remain within the Petrie Collection where they may be accessed and re-examined as new research flourishes. As historic documents, the Petrie catalogues stand as exemplars of the craft of typological classification, the backbone of modern archaeology – much of which, though refined by absolute dating and another 100 years of research, still stands the test of time.

A note on presentation

The facsimile titles of Petrie's catalogues re-issued in the 1970s were produced from scans of the original publications. Scanning technology at that time was not of the standard or resolution of today. The scans are no longer available, nor has it been possible to obtain, and in doing so destroy, original copies of the Petrie catalogues. These titles have therefore, of necessity, been rescanned from the 1970s re-issues. Where necessary the pages have been digitally enhanced for clarity of reading and to ensure the good quality of the plates, though inevitably a few are not of the standard we might wish, because of the quality of the previous scan, and occasional blocks of text are not precisely 'straight' or evenly situated on the page. However, some pages in the 1970s re-issues had been inserted in the wrong order and this has been corrected. The originals were produced at a folio size. The pages have been reduced slightly to standard A4 for ease of shelving and because this has the effect of slightly improving the scanned images. In some cases, illustrations were presented to scale and the original scale is given on the plate. There were also no digital files available for titles included in the *Modern Egyptology* series, so these too have been scanned from printed copies.

GIZEH AND RIFEH

INTRODUCTION

1. THE work of the British School of Archaeology in Egypt, during the past winter, lay partly at Gizeh, and partly in the district between Asyūt and Sohāg. The reason for this division was that only a small part of Gizeh was available, not enough for a season's work, the whole of the pyramid region being already occupied by American and German claims. A large and speculative district in Upper Egypt was therefore also occupied by the School, and the greater part of the season's work was carried on there. The whole party began work at Gizeh on December 1. Mr. Ward and myself explored the western desert, from Asyut to Sohag, December 24 to 29. I returned to Gizeh, and then went back to Mr. Ward to begin work at Rīfeh on January 10; Mr. Rhoades left Gizeh and began work at Deir Balyzeh January 18, and was joined there at the end of the month by Mr. Mackay, who had finished packing at Gizeh. At the end of February Messrs. Mackay and Gregg went to Deir el Ganádleh, and Mr. Rhoades joined us at Rifeh. By March 11 the whole party was reunited at Rifeh; March 17 I left, and the rest of the party gradually diminished till Messrs. Rhoades and Mackay finally closed the packing on April 2.

The importance of Gizeh in the IVth dynasty is known to every one by the three pyramids of the kings; but discoveries of late years indicated that there had been an earlier cemetery to the south of the pyramid region. Half a mile south of the Great Pyramid a ridge of rock rises from the plain, above the Arab cemetery and a group of trees, which form a well-known landmark in many pictures. This ridge runs south for half a mile, and is riddled with tombs, especially at its southern end: it was this cemetery which we examined during December. In the plain beyond it lay two patches of pottery and stone-chips; the nearer was around a tomb of the Ist dynasty, which had been opened by M. Daressy for the Cairo Museum; the further or southern patch was of the age of Ramessu II, and had apparently been a monument of his son Kha-em-uas. The division of the work was that Mr. Ward, Mr. Mackay, and Mr. Rhoades took charge of the workmen, and began to measure up work and keep accounts, and Mr. Mackay also took some photographs; Mr. and Mrs. Firth did much of the drawing; while I organized the work and also did drawing and photographing. I have to thank Dr. Reisner for kindly allowing our cases to be deposited at his camp, between the close of the work at Gizeh and the end of the season.

2. At Deir Rifeh our work extended from the well-known Coptic village by the ancient tombs, at about six miles south of Asyut, for about three miles southward to beyond Zowyeh. The finely sculptured rock-tombs, now in possession of the Copts, were not touched by us, as Mr. Griffith had carefully copied them twenty years ago (*The Inscriptions of Siût and Dêr Rîfeh*); but I copied some remaining painting in two other of the great tombs. In front of these we searched the banks of chips, and found a few unopened tombs of smaller size with fine burials; and the whole of the small rock-tombs were cleaned out, but very little was found in them. Our principal work lay in the cemeteries of graves dug in the plain below the cliff (see Pl. VIII). Here we found burials from the VIIth dynasty down to mediaeval times, but mostly of the XIth, XIIth, and XVIIIth dynasties. Our huts were built by the side of the modern cemetery just south of this ground; and south of us lay another cemetery, of the Hyksos age. Going further to the south we pass a cemetery of the XVIIIth dynasty near Zowyeh, entirely plundered recently; and the next group is a small cluster of burials of the VIth dynasty at the mouth of a valley, and another group out in the plain a little further to the south. Some eight miles south of our camp is another small cemetery of the VIth dynasty at Zarāby. The work at Rifeh was mainly superintended by Mr. Ward, while I was engaged in drawing and photographing.

Mr. Rhoades afterwards joined us, while Mr. Ward did part of the packing. Mr. Mackay worked the cemetery at Zaraby, and afterwards finished the packing at Rifeh.

3. All along the western desert are innumerable Coptic settlements on the cliffs. These are all of one type; in each case a quarry-cave of Roman age has served for a refuge for the Egyptians at the Arab invasion; walls were built in the great rock caverns to divide them into houses; as peace became established the buildings extended out over the foot-hill in front of the quarry-cave; lastly, at any time during the past eight centuries, one or another of the old strongholds has been abandoned, and the Copts have settled in villages on the edge of the cultivation, leaving their old refuges with little or no regard. These settlements are usually known as Deirs, called after the nearest village. In our district there were the following: (1) at 4 miles south of Asyut, Deir Dronkeh, now recently deserted and a new village built on the slope below it; (2) at 6 miles, Deir Rifeh, still fully occupied, but with many new houses below it on the slope; (3) at 8 miles, Deir Zowyeh; a little early settlement on the cliff at the mouth of a valley, appears to have been attached to a large square fort-like Deir on the edge of the cultivation, now fully occupied; this great Deir or Coptic village must be early, as it is surrounded by a wide stretch of rubbish mounds which go back to Roman times; (4) at 11 miles, Deir Balyzeh, a large settlement high up on the foot-hills with quarry-caves, dating from about the VIIth to Xth century A.D., now entirely deserted; this was largely excavated by Mr. Rhoades first, and then by Messrs. Mackay and Gregg; (5) at 19 miles, Deir el Ganadleh, a large quarry-cave full of walls, paintings and inscriptions, and considerable buildings outside of it. Half a mile south of it is a later Deir, in which a modern screen has been added to the sanctuary, and service is occasionally held; the doors stand open, and there is an immense circular well in front of it, about 20 feet across and 160 feet deep. Thirty miles south of this we reach the well-known Red and White monasteries, Deir Abu Bishai and Deir Amba Shenudi, which are original Roman buildings before the Arab conquest.

We have to thank Dr. Alexander, and the staff of the American College at Asyut, for help to our workmen, and facilities in other ways. They relieved us of the need of transporting duplicate pottery and the skulls found at Rifeh, by accepting them for the collection which is being formed at the College.

CHAPTER I

THE Ist DYNASTY. GIZEH.

4. In 1904 M. Barsanti found, and M. Daressy excavated, for the Cairo Museum, a tomb of the Ist dynasty, in the plain about a mile and a half SSE. of the Great Pyramid. The account of the work is published in the *Annales du Service* vi. 99. The brief description there given need not be repeated, as a much more detailed account follows here. But some statement of the objects discovered is valuable. Pieces of charcoal of the roofing remained in the ruins. The southern chamber contained fourteen flint knives, some of the type of the first on pl. IV, beside broken fragments, and some scrapers. The next shallow chamber contained long jars of the type shown in *Abydos* i, vi, 13. The deep burial chamber contained more pieces of jars and eight large conical seals, apparently of the type 126 (*Royal Tombs* ii, xvii) from a piece which I found: also pieces of alabaster and hard stone vases, including about sixty cylinder jars; small sketches of nine types are given. A few pieces of ivory also appeared. In the two northern chambers were pottery jars, of the types in *Royal Tombs* i, xlii, 35, 55 and 78. As the objects remain in M. Daressy's room at the Museum, and he was away when I passed through Cairo, I could not draw them for complete publication as I had wished.

5. The structure of this earliest tomb of the Memphite region is important, as showing how far the Abydos type was followed in the new centre. The form of the tomb may be seen in Pl. VI. The middle chamber surrounded with piers is the deepest; the two chambers at each end of that are about half the depth; and the whole of these subterranean chambers were covered over by a brick mastaba with panelled sides. These various parts we now describe in detail.

The burial chamber is over 35 feet long (426 inches E., 422 W.) and over 18 feet wide (221 N., 220 S.); it was over 7 feet deep originally, but is so much broken at the top edge that it is hard to trace the roofing. The best indication of depth is that of the northern chamber where the roofing beams were traced at 33 inches over the floor, which is 60 inches over that of the burial chamber, or 93 inches altogether, and this agrees with the height of the top of the wall in the north-west corner where it is preserved. In the south-west corner the floor is rather lower, and the highest plastered face is 96 inches over it.

Within this chamber was a wooden lining, which rested on a footing beam ; and the space between the lining and the wall was divided by the brick piers. Such is exactly the arrangement of the tomb of king Zet, contemporary with this at Abydos. These brick piers—as at Abydos—were built in after the wood lining was in place, as the ends abutting on the wood are bare brick, while the sides are plastered, and the mud mortar has been squeezed out against a vertical face at the end. The corner pier is shown on Pl. II, where the groove of the footing beam can be seen running into the pier, but met by the beam at right angles before entering the brickwork. A strange feature is that the upper part of the piers has a hollow shell of one brick thick, the wall was plastered behind this, and then the hollow was filled up with bricks, as seen in the photograph.

The purpose of these piers was not merely to subdivide the space, but also to embrace and steady the upright posts which carried the wooden lining. In each pier is a circular hollow, shown at ground level on the plan. These hollows are 5 or 6 inches across, and slope forward as they rise. The best preserved, at the north-west corner, are 5 to 10 inches from the lining face at 62 up, 8 to 13 inches at 42 up ; therefore it would lean forward to touch the lining face at 95 up, or exactly at the level of the roof. These posts doubtless carried a long beam to which the wooden lining was attached.

The wooden chamber inside was about 356 × 164 inches, according to the traces of the base beams and posts. There is no trace of a wooden floor either in the burial chambers or in the shallower chambers at the ends. In the southern chamber a line of wood along the floor was part of a box about half an inch thick. The clearing out of the chamber by the Museum workmen may have removed traces of the flooring and fittings, as they had certainly taken out large jars, which were standing in place. Though the chambers were partly burnt, the floor beams had survived till much later times. Across the burial chamber is a skew wall roughly built of bricks, some burnt red, others crude black, side by side, showing that it was built from the burnt ruins of the tomb, perhaps in Roman times. Through this wall the floor beam ran intact, and has left a hole six inches high and five wide. In other parts the places of the floor beam were five inches high and four wide. The extent of burning varied up to partial vitrification ; probably much of it was due to the unguents.

The end chambers were evidently for offerings, being only 33 high ; traces of jars remain along the side of the southern chamber. The walls average 39 inches thick (38-41) ; and the chambers are about 220 from east to west, like the burial chamber, and 104 (101 to 107) from north to south. The sides have been greatly cut away recently, apparently in clearing the tomb, so that it is difficult to trace their real place.

6. The existence of a mastaba above the chambers was not suspected until we cleared the ground. The best preserved part of it is shown by the view in Pl. II ; the plan in Pl. VI. The panelled brickwork is of the same plan as that of the tomb of the queen of Mena at Naqada, and the great mastaba on the top of the hill at Gizeh shown in Pl. VII. The faces of the brickwork were all coated with white plaster, and the floors of the bays likewise whited. In two places a pot was left in the bay, before being covered over by the coating wall, 22 to 25 inches thick ; this wall is seen in the view, Pl. II, on the right hand of the panelling. The extent of the mastaba was proved by a row of bays on the west, by a fragment of a bay on the south, another on the east, and by the inner face of the wall on the north ; for the dimensions see sect. 13. The general position of the missing bays is roughly indicated by the rounded outline on the plan.

On each side of the mastaba, at a short distance from it, was a line of graves, see Pl. VI ; on the west side they were joined together, being formed by two long parallel walls with cross-walls between, shown in Pl. II ; on the other sides the pits were built separately. All of these graves were lined with brickwork, mud-plastered, and roofed by wooden poles a few inches apart, covered with brushwood. The only difference between these and the Abydos graves of the royal retainers and officials, is that all the graves were there joined together as only the western row is here. The graves vary from 78 to 102 inches long ; but twenty of them are between 86 and 89 inches, seventeen are longer and nine are shorter. The breadth is about 52 inches.

7. At the south-east of grave 12 the top of the lining-wall was at 45 inches over the floor of the grave ; thence up to 63 inches was a bed of marl thrown out in excavating the graves. At about 60 inches up was brick rubbish from building the grave, and at 63 in the loose sand which covered it were some broken pieces of coloured stucco. The original built paving over the grave was at 69 ; and thence up to 83 was blown sand and mud rubbish

over it. These pieces of stucco were thus on the old surface around the grave, but below and outside of the brick paving which covered the grave. The pieces (see Pl. V E) had formed a stucco coat which had been put over a raised grave structure. This building had been ribbed with blue stripes, sunk in a white ground; and had a plain battlemented dado around it, from which the round-topped tomb had sprung. Then at a later date the whole had been replastered, covering the dado and top all in one uniform coat with stripes. The stucco found was this coating, bearing on one side a cast of the older structure, and the face of the newer on the other side. This section and view of the inner side is shown on Pl. V E, with the restoration sketch. The ribbing was in the same place on the inner and outer coats; but in parts it obviously slanted. The original tomb and the new coat had been coloured blue on the same bands. The bands measured were white 4·4, blue 5·8, w. 4·0, b. 3·2, w. 7·4, b. 3·1, w. 3·8, b. 5·9, w. 4·6. It seems then that there was a broad blue of 5·9, with a narrower of 3·1 on each side. The whites between averaged 4·2 wide, and a broad white of 7·4 parted the groups of blues. The whole group was 28 inches. The dado spaces are 13·2 high and 15·2 low, or 28·2 inches for the group. The bands therefore keep pace with the dado, though not centred over the battlements. The curvature of the stucco indicates a breadth of about 103 inches; but as the Egyptians used a parabolic arch, the actual breadth would be rather less.

The original size of the built-up tomb was probably adapted to the grave below. The nearest of these graves that could be measured was 126 inches long including the end walls. Now if there were the number of battlements that are shown in the restoration sketch they would be 126·4 long, or exactly the length of the grave and its walls. If there were the number shown on the end, the breadth would have been 98·4, agreeing with the breadth of rather under 103 shown by the curvature; the grave with its walls below was about 84 wide over all. As the stucco was found between graves 11 and 12, and grave 11 had contained a very rich burial, it seems probable that this decorated tomb was above grave 11.

8. The burials had all been disturbed, and about half of the graves were empty; two graves with bones remaining are shown in Pl. III A, the former is grave 38 and the latter is grave 39. As regards the direction, the bodies remaining in four N.—S. graves were all with head north, face east. Of the E.—W. graves, three had head to east and four had head to west, but all with the face to the north. Thus evidently the head to north and face east was the normal position of burial. All the bodies had the knees sharply bent, where the position was preserved. At Abydos the royal retainers lay with head north in five cases, south in one other; and facing half to east half to west; but the graves in the town of the Ist dynasty are contrary in direction, eight having head to south, one to north, and one to east; and all lay on the left side, that is usually facing west. Hence the royal retainers at Abydos and the Gizeh burials have the same direction; while the Abydos town burials are reversed.

The sketches of the plans of graves are shown in Pl. VI A. It seems that the graves were plundered while the roofs were still in place, as in some cases the alabaster jars had evidently been thrown one on the other in a corner and broken on the floor of the grave. The contents of the graves were as follows. The cylinder vases are all drawn in Plates V, A, B; the bowls in Plates V, C, D; the pottery in V, E.

Grave 000. Flint knife, Pl. IV; large ivory spoon, rotted; 1 cylinder jar; 1 bowl.

1. 1 bowl; 2 large jars.
2. 2 bowls, one with *uas* sign.
3. 2 cylinder jars; 1 bowl.
4. 2 large jars, 2 egg-shaped jars, bowl, pottery.
5. 2 stone bowls.
6. 1 cylinder jar.
7. 6 bowls.
8. 2 bowls.
11. 2 ivory cylinder jars, III; IV; V, 15, 16. Ivory ibex, IV; V, 9: circular boxes, IV; V, 19–21: 2 spoons, V, 31, 32: hair-pin, V, 26: hand, IV; V, 25: bull's leg, IV; V, 28: disc foot, V, 27: bit of cup, V, 24: slip, V, 18: covers and slates, IV; V, 10, 11. Gold needles, IV; V, 13, 14. Copper lid, IV. 2 copper tools, V, 22, 23. 4 small stone vases, III; V, 1, 2, 4, 5. Lazuli vase, III; V, 3. Bit of flint armlet, V, 29. 6 cylinder jars; 13 bowls.
12. Copper bowl. 6 cylinder jars. 5 bowls.
13. Ivory cylinder jar, V, 17; long spoon, V, 34. Glazed disc, IV; V, 35. Adze at hand and at knee, III, A. 2 ivory pins. Cylinder jar. 2 bowls.
14. 2 pieces of flint bracelets, cylinder jar, 2 bowls.
15. Vases as in Pl. II. 3 cylinder jars, 6 bowls, 3 pots.
16. Cylinder jar.

17. 3 cylinder jars.
18. Cylinder jar, 4 bowls.
21. Bowl.
23. Ivory gazelle wands, IV; V, 6, 7. Comb, IV; V, 8. Lid, V, 12. Flint armlets, III. 4 pots.
36. 2 pots.
38. Pottery. See view Pl. III A.
39. Bowl. See view Pl. III A.
40. 2 cylinder jars. Box coffin.
41. 2 cylinder jars and stand. Flint scrapers.
42. Trace of box coffin.
44. Trace of box coffin.
51. 2 bowls.
56. Slate palettes, III. Copper chisel. Inscribed flint, III A. Flint flakes.

9. The stone vases are drawn in the Pls. V, V A, V B, V C, V D, and some photographed in Pls. II and III. The types are well known in the Ist dynasty (compare *Royal Tombs* ii, Pls. xlvi. to liii G). The cylinder jars of alabaster have the wavy line in only two examples, and such belong to the beginning of the dynasty; but the cord pattern is closely notched as in the first half of the dynasty, and not coarsely as in the second half. The small trumpet-mouth vases belong mainly to the tombs from Mena and Zet. The slate, syenite, and alabaster bowls are of the types from Zer to Den. Hence as this tomb is dated to Zet by the sealing (III A), it does not seem that there was any perceptible lag in the styles between Abydos and Gizeh. In Pl. III the four cups and the barrel vase are from grave 11, the upper necked vase from grave 13, and that at the base from a tomb on the hill.

As regards the materials they are closely like those used in the royal tomb of Zet. The total numbers for comparison are 60 vases recorded here, 85 from the tomb of Zet, and 752 from all the royal tombs. Reducing these to percentages of each kind of stone we have—

	Gizeh	Zet	Abydos (total)
Crystal	1	5	8
Basalt	3	3	5
Syenite, &c.	7	10	11
Volcanic	1	5	11
Serpentine	1	3	3
Slate	19	7	8
Dolomite	11	15	14
Alabaster	47	28	18
Coloured limestone	4	20	13
Grey "	0	3	5
White "	6	1	4

The predominance of slate and alabaster at Gizeh is due to the forms having been more exhaustively drawn, whereas a great mass of duplicate examples at Abydos were not registered. On the whole the Gizeh tombs seem poorer in the rare stones, which might be expected as they are only the tombs of retainers and not of a king as at Abydos. The vase fragments found for the Museum in the main burial at Gizeh are not published in detail, and I could not refer to them as the official in charge was away when I enquired.

The exact similarity of a remarkably fine bowl of metamorphic rock to one from the tomb of Zet (*Royal Tombs* ii, l, 153) suggests that they came from the same workman. Altogether there is no local difference of any importance between the objects used at Abydos and at Gizeh, and this shows the unification of the civilisation at the time.

10. In one grave, 56, at the east end of the south line, two slate palettes were found, indicating that the scribe or artist was buried there. These are shown in Pl. III; each has one pan covered with black and the other with red paint. From the size of the pans it is clear that they were not for small quantities used in writing, as the colour would dry up too quickly; nor were they for colour-washes on walls, as they would not hold enough. The use of them seems to have been for painting scenes on the flat, or for colouring statues; and certainly a small brush was used, as shown by the streaks of colour on the edges of the larger palette. Such a palette is shown hung by one end over the shoulder of a scribe, on the panel of Hesy; and this larger palette has a hole in the end for hanging it. The size of the larger palette is 10·94, 10·98, 10·76 long, 5·45, 5·48, 5·50 wide, the pans 4·60 across; the lesser is 4·14, 4·11 long, 2·17, 2·18, 2·20 wide, the pans 1·72 to 1·74 inches across.

The accounts of this scribe were found in the grave written on a slip of flint, at about the position of the hands. This is photographed on Pl. III A. The numbers on it are written much like the piece of accounts from the tomb of Zet (*Royal Tombs* i, xix, 11), and we read the numbers 78, 103, 40 and 60.

In the same grave, 56, a much corroded copper chisel was found beneath the large palette, lying upon the pelvis. In another grave, 13, on the west side, two copper adzes were found; the better preserved is shown on Pl. III A. The body was in a box coffin about 49 × 28 inches, with the knees sharply bent; one adze lay before the arms, the other was set upright between the knees. These are exactly the same form as the copper adze of king Zer, *Royal Tombs* ii, vi, 23. A copper bowl, rather crushed and corroded, was found in grave 12; it was like that from the tomb of Semer-khet, *Royal Tombs* i, xii, 11.

The flint-work was much like that of the same period elsewhere. The first knife on Pl. IV is like a curved tip of one found in the tomb of Zet; and the second knife is like the fragments found in the tomb of Zer, see *Abydos* i, xiv. The pointed flakes resemble those of Zer and Zet, and the round-ended flakes from grave 41 are like those of Zer, Zet, and Mer-neit. Thus the style of flint-work, both detailed and rough, agrees with that at Abydos, and shows that there is not fifty years of difference either way between the work of the southern and northern capitals.

The flint bracelets, Pl. III, were found on the right fore-arm of a body in grave 23. They are like those found in the tombs of Zer and Zet.

11. The toilet objects are shown in Pls. IV, V. The little circular ivory dishes with lids, are not known before. The two loops at the sides are doubtless for a hinge-pin and a closing-pin: the decoration on the sides and lids is by rows of drilled spots. They were probably for containing eye-paint. Below these in the photograph is a carved hand from a statuette. Next is an oryx couchant forming the handle of an ivory lid, of which a piece of the edge lies below. At the right hand is a bull's leg from a casket. At the base of the photograph on the left are two ivory covers for kohl slabs, and one slate slab; such small slabs and covers belong to the time of Zet (see *Royal Tombs* ii, xxxviii, 2, 50, 51). In the middle is an ivory comb, of the same form as one from the tomb of Zer (*R. T.* ii, xxxiv, 26). Below it are two needles of gold; they have only been found of copper before. At the right is a copper cap from a jar, and a cylindrical jar of ivory.

The two ivory wands, Pl. IV, with gazelle heads were found in grave 23; they are finely carved, and were doubtless used by a dancer for marking time, as in the scene in *Deshasheh*, xii. Below is a disc of blue glazed pottery, now faded white, with holes for suspension.

The spoons were frequent in graves, but are always found broken up in the plundering. The various forms are drawn in Pl. V. A similar bowl was found in the tomb of Zer (*R. T.* ii, xxxiv, 81). They differ from prehistoric spoons in having the curious bend of the handle turning down to the under side of the bowl.

12. The bracelet of hawks, Pl. III, is of blue glazed pottery. It is a cheap imitation of the type of gold and turquoise bracelet found in the tomb of Zer (*R. T.* ii, i), and pieces of the same form are known in ivory and in lazuli (*R. T.* ii, xxxv, 81). In this case the backs of the pieces are plain, and therefore it is seen that some faced one way and some the other way, unlike the royal bracelet where they all looked the same way. At least three have been lost, there are eight facing to left and only five facing to right; the extreme left-hand one in the photograph is reversed. The pieces have two threading holes running through each; and as some small glazed ball-beads were found with them, twice as many as the hawks, it seems that the beads were threaded between the plaques. The two thread-holes run into one in the terminal rings, by which the bracelet was tied on. The long beads of similar blue glaze were doubtless a necklace; they were found in the grave with the bracelet pieces.

13. The measurements of the panelling of the brickwork of the mastaba are regular, the successive portions being (in inches)—

	Projection	Bay	Group
	108	71	179
	106	72	178
	109	70	179
	107	76	183
mean	107·5	72·2	179·7

These are in the proportion of 3 to 2, $107·5 \div 3 = 35·8$, and $72·2 \div 2 = 36·1$. In the projection the panels and the flat wall average exactly the same width, 15·3.

On continuing from the southern remaining panel to the fragment on the south face, the distance is 354 or 2 groups of 177; and from the northern remaining panel to the north face was 540, or 3 groups of 180. Thus the fragments of the ends fall very closely in their right place. The total length was 1897 and breadth 831; deducting the 108 repeat of the projection, this gives 1789 for 10 groups, and 723 for 4 groups; or 179 and 181 for the average group of side and end. It can hardly be questioned that the bay is 100 digits and the projection 150, the group being 250. The true diagonal digit of the 20·6 inch cubit is ·728, and 250 of this would be 182 inches for the group. We find in the IIIrd dynasty mastaba (sect. 18), on the contrary, that the customary digit, of

28 to the cubit, was used. Some other dimensions, such as the distances to the outside of the east and west graves, and length of the brick chamber, seem to indicate cubit measurements; but as co-ordinate measures do not agree with this, it is best to leave these out of consideration.

CHAPTER II

THE IIND AND IIIRD DYNASTIES. GIZEH.

14. ON the top of the south end of the ridge facing the cultivation, looking down on the site of the tomb of the Ist dynasty, we found the remains of a tomb of the IInd dynasty. It had originally consisted of a sloping passage, closed by two successive stone portcullises, beyond which was a funeral chamber. Later one portcullis was drawn out upwards, the other was broken, the chamber was cut to pieces by a deep shaft passing through it, the contents were scattered, and a mastaba of the XXVIth dynasty was piled up over the site, with the fragments of early vases in the filling of it. The precise period of the tomb is given by impressions of five different jar-sealings of king Neter-en (Pl. V E), which were found thrown into a small well.

The limestone portcullis now lying on the surface is 118 to 120 inches long, 48 to 55 wide and 11½ thick: it must weigh over 2¼ tons. The grooves for the portcullises are 57 inches wide, and 24 to 25 across: the depth in the rock is 143 inches, or not much more than the length of the block. The two pairs of grooves were 34 or 36 inches apart.

15. The stone vases had been all broken; some of them remained in the chamber, but the greater part had been thrown out and mixed with the later filling of the mastaba. As being well dated to a reign of which hardly any vases were known (*Royal Tombs* ii, viii, 12, 13), they make a welcome addition to the history of vases. The forms are mainly dishes (21), and a few bowls (4) and cylinders (5); but there were many more too much damaged to restore, and therefore the numbers are not exact. The material was nearly all alabaster (26), with gypsum (2 drawn and many others broken), limestone (1), and pink marble (1). It seems then that hard stone had been entirely given up, and the flat dish was by far the commonest form. A pottery jar like those of Perabsen (*R. T.* ii, vii, 31) was also found here.

16. On the top of the hill further back, due south of the Great Pyramid, is a large mastaba, marked on the plan of Lepsius, which was opened and traced round by Mr. Covington and Mr. Quibell. The plan here given, Pl. VII, is due to measurements taken by different members of our party; and as discrepancies exist about the details of the chambers, I regret that we cannot entirely depend upon it. The general arrangement and position of the chambers beneath the mastaba is sufficiently certain for comparison with other remains. It is of the same type as the mastabas of the kings Hen-nekht (or Sa-nekht) and Neter-khet, of the beginning of the IIIrd dynasty (Garstang, *Mahasna*, vii, xviii); and these all differ so much from the royal tombs known down to the close of the IInd dynasty, and those of the end of the IIIrd dynasty and onwards, that we must regard the Gizeh tomb as nearly contemporary with the beginning of the IIIrd dynasty. Unfortunately no name has been found on vases or on sealings; indeed no sealings could be found in it, although I offered a large reward to the workmen.

The outside of the mastaba is panelled on exactly the same pattern as the mastabas of the early Ist dynasty, under Mena (Naqada) and Zet (Gizeh). It seems hard to believe that the detail of such a pattern had continued in use for five centuries without change. The only alternative would be to regard this mastaba as a work of the Ist dynasty, with a reconstruction of chambers of the IIIrd dynasty. But against that is the fact that this is on a hilltop, whereas all the Ist and IInd dynasty tombs are in low ground; and also that there is no sign of alteration in the body of the mastaba. There is therefore no apparent escape from accepting the long continuance of the precise detail of a pattern for so many centuries.

The wall coating round the mastaba is 12 inches from the face of it, and 56 inches thick: and outside of it is a smooth slope of 174 inches wide, rising 40 inches up to the base of the wall. This covering wall is much more important than in the earlier examples.

17. From the inside of the mastaba there were obtained hundreds of fragments of stone vases; but as most of the larger pieces had been removed before, and are now lying in boxes in the Cairo Museum, it seems useless to attempt drawing or restoration till they can be re-united. Two or three forms are shown on Pl. VI D. Beside these there were found many stone balls or marbles for a game, in the well which led from the subterranean chambers to the still lower funeral chamber. These marbles are shown of the actual size in Pl. IV. There were 2 of carnelian,

1 of brown agate, 9 of hard brown limestone, 52 of white quartz, and 59 of white limestone. The red carnelian were ·42 and ·50 inch diameter, the brown stone ·46 to ·56, the quartz ·41 to ·64, the limestone ·38 to ·58 inch.

At the top of the same well is a ledge cut in the rock, and on clearing this our men found a polished slab of chert, about a foot long and two inches wide. This is figured in Pl. III A, lighted from the back to show the translucency. It is not a knife, as there is no edge to it; though thinning towards the circumference, it is bounded by a uniform polished band around it, about a sixteenth of an inch wide. No such object is known before, so it is now in the Cairo Museum.

A lump of small tools or models made in copper, was found in the tomb; the types which can be distinguished are drawn in Pl. VI E. They are similar to those from the tomb of Neter-khet and Sa-nekht (*Mahasna*, xvi, xxiii).

18. The total size of the mastaba as measured by Mr. Mackay is 2160 inches on E., 2184 on W., 1114 on N., 1112 on S. The projecting parts of the face average 77·8 inches and the bay between 69·4 long. There are 14 bays and 15 projections in the length, 7 bays and 8 projections in the width. If we subtract the final projection from the length and breadth, they are 2082 and 1035, or 100 cubits and 50 cubits, divided into 14 and 7 similar portions, each therefore of 200 digits. On examining the subdivisions of the projecting part we find that the average of the flat faces is 11·8, of the recesses 10·2 inches; while if we take the mean digits of the whole length, ·7415 inch, 16 digits is 11·86, and 14 digits is 10·38. These being spaces of 16 and 14 digits, the whole projection is 106 digits and the bay 94 digits. Within the bay the average width of the wide recess is 29·8 ± ·4, and 40 digits is 29·7; hence the bay is a recess of 40 digits with 27 on either side. These dimensions are not based on the pure digit (of which 40 is the diagonal of the square cubit), but on the customary digit of 28 to the cubit; and the cubit here averaged 20·76, which is rather a long value.

It should be recorded that we also cleared around a large stone platform on the east side of the mastaba just described; the appearance of it is shown on Pl. III A. On the top it had no continuous stonework, the blocks being only the basement of the walls, which are now destroyed. A pit in the middle of it was cleared, but led to nothing. From being exactly in front of the mastaba I supposed that it might have been the base of a stone temple, for the king buried in the mastaba, but nothing was found bearing on this. On the west side toward the north, and on the north side, some stone bowls were found, three of syenite and four of alabaster, which are figured in Pl. VI D.

A tomb shaft was found just below the great mastaba on the east; and two bowls of black porphyry, four of diorite, one metamorphic, and four of alabaster were found, which are figured in Pl. VI E.

CHAPTER III

THE IVTH—VITH DYNASTIES. GIZEH.

19. THE great buildings of the pyramid kings stand to the north of the ground which was open to the work of the British School. But in searching the ridge of hill south of the Sphinx we found that the face overlooking the cultivation had a row of rock-tombs cut in it, and many small brick mastabas. The mastabas did not yield any objects, the chambers had been rifled long ago, and the stone lintels had been removed, perhaps by Lepsius. The rock-tombs, though entirely plundered, had the inscribed stone lintels yet remaining. These were photographed in position, and afterwards carefully taken out. The views of them in both states are given in Pl. VII A, and other views of the tombs without inscriptions are in Pl. VII B. I should have wished to plan and explore this hill more completely; but the inexorable necessity of finding work on a very limited ground for a hundred workers brought from a distance, who could not be temporarily dismissed, and the loss of their wages on unprofitable work, compelled me to start digging at Rifeh sooner than I had wished.

The general plan of this cemetery as made by Mr. Firth is given on Pl. VII C. It will be seen that the tombs are all quite separate in design, and do not form part of a group on one system. Where rock-chambers are cut into the hill, it is usual to have a court of brickwork built on in front of them. In other cases the rock is dressed flat, false doors are cut on the face of it, and burial pits are sunk in the rock behind one or more of the false doors. Or else we find this imitated in brickwork with a mastaba face, and pits behind it, as on Pl. VII B. Inside the rock-chambers there is sometimes a shallow burial pit with a little chamber at the bottom; in other cases there is a rough false door, never inscribed, but built of blocks, and on removing these a grave is found cut in the rock, and roofed over with slabs of stone. One such was quite intact. I examined the skeleton, of which some bones were displaced ; yet it did not seem that there was more disturbance than was due to falling apart, nor any clear evidence of dismemberment. The head was to the north.

The plain between the hills to the west of this ridge, three-quarters of a mile south of the Great Pyramid, was also examined. The whole surface is covered for many feet deep with broken stone-chips from quarrying. As it is too remote to have been used as a ground for the waste from pyramid building,—such waste being wanted to bank up the pyramid platforms,—the only solution seems to be that a bed of good stone existed here, which has all been quarried out for the pyramids, and only the quarry-waste left on the ground. Yet a difficulty remains in there being many pieces of red granite, and some of other stones, scattered about the west side of the rocky ridge, as if some costly building had existed in this region. No ground for such a building could be traced, although we looked over the whole area.

20. The inscriptions of the cemetery belong to the Vth or VIth dynasty. On Pl. VII A, at the top, is the lintel of "The royal sealer of the granary Ne-ptah-nofer-her; his wife Nofert ; his children the interpreter of records Amgesa, Khut, Ka-em-redui, and Kakaa. The necropolis man Pepa is satisfied with the contract which has been made with him." Below that is the roll over the doorway, with the inscription for the husband alone. "Give an offering to the king, and an offering to Anup who is in Ta-zeser, for a burial in the cemetery for the lord of devotion to the great god, the royal sealer of the granary Ne-ptah-nofer-her." The meaning of the *suten hotep da* formula has been somewhat cleared by the construction of it at Tell el Amarna, where the crystallized tradition was broken, and the grammar of it can be gleaned from the variants. The possible meanings to be considered in the usual form are: (1) may the king give an offering to a god for favour to the deceased, or (2) may the king and a god give an offering for the deceased, or (3) give an offering to the king and to a god that they may favour the deceased, or (4) a royal offering given to a god for the deceased. Now in the tomb of Huya (Davis, *El Amarna* iii, xxii) there is "*suten da hotep* of thy bread and beer of thy house, &c." The sense (1) is impossible as no God is named ; (2) is impossible as the estate of the deceased furnishes the offerings ; (3) or (4) are left as the only meanings. Again in the same tomb (D., *E. A.* iii, xix) there is "*Ankh suten du hotep* O Ua-en·ra . . . king of south and north Nefer·kheperu·ra" and "*Ankh suten du hotep* O 'He who is great in duration.' I give praise to thy fair face . . . Akhenaten." This will not agree to the sense (1), nor to (2) as there is no person named but the king, and he is not asked to offer to himself. The sense (3), "Give an offering to the king," followed by his titles, is perfectly sound. And the prefix of *Ankh* before *suten*, shows that *suten* is the king, and not as (4), the adjective "royal" applied to the offering.

Below is a roll from another tomb inscribed "Royal friend, the skilful (maker) of date wine of the king, superintendent of the farm stores, Akhet-ab."

Next is a view of a tomb door, and of the lintel apart, reading "Give an offering to the king, and an offering to Anup in his divine house, for a tomb in the mountain of the west, for the lord of devotion to the great god, the ship's captain, the reckoner of the treasury, the royal friend, Per-en-ankh."

At the base on the left is a lintel, "Give an offering to the king and give an offering to Anup lord of Ta-zeser for his burial in the underworld of the royal friend, the superintendent messenger of the judges, the superintendent messenger of the palace, companion in the palace, the lord of devotion to the great god, Er-du-ne-ptah." On the roll below is "His wife Ymeryt."

The last group is a lintel reading "The royal friend, companion in the palace, Er-du-ne-ptah. His wife Ymeryt. He says the necropolis man is to bring these things for a sacrificial offering, never may there be a diminishing therein." And on the drum below is "Er-du-ne-ptah, Superintendent of physicians (?) Er-du-ne-ptah. His child, of his body . . ."

On Pl. VII B is an altar slab inscribed "Give an offering to the king and to Anup within Ta-zeser for a good and great burial in the western mountain of the underworld for the lord of devotion to the great god, and a house of offerings of bread, beer, and cakes to him on the festivals of the new year, of Tahuti, of Uag, of the *sad*, of the great feast, of Pert, and of *saz*. The royal friend, devoted to the great god, the royal purifier, Ra-hapef." I have to thank Dr. Walker and Miss Murray for light on these titles and phrases.

CHAPTER IV

THE VITH DYNASTY. ZARABY AND ZOWYEH.

21. THE cemetery at Zarāby is on the western desert about two miles south of Abutīg. Mr. Mackay excavated it and recorded the details of 126 graves. The objects all belong to the VIth dynasty, according to the graves of that age found at Hu (*Diospolis Parva* xxviii). The principal stone vases and three burials are shown in Pl. VII E, and the pottery in Pl. VII F. From the notes we can classify the characters of the burials in the following details.

The position of the bodies was always with head to the north and face to the east: and this agrees with the direction found both at Dendereh and Hu in graves of this period. The bodies which remained in the graves were not uniformly treated. There were 22 laid at full length, 18 with the knees somewhat bent, 16 with the knees sharply bent and the body contracted, like the early dynastic and predynastic burials, and 4 dismembered burials all protected by large stones laid over them. These dismembered bodies are important as the latest of such a class of burial; the details are as follow. Grave 83, the skull lay parallel to its natural position but in front of the hands, and an alabaster jar (VII E lower line of small vases, left end) was placed where the head should have been: the grave was eight feet deep and was protected by piling big flints upon it, with 2 feet deposit of sand and gravel over the flints. Grave 86 contained two burials together, the head of one separated six inches from the body; the grave four feet deep, protected by piles of stones, and buried under a foot of sand and gravel. Grave 97 contained two burials; the skulls lay at the north end, one facing downward, one facing west; the ribs and vertebrae lay in a heap in front of the skulls; only a leg bone and three arm bones remained from the limbs: the grave was four feet deep, protected by large stones, and covered over with six inches of sand and gravel. Grave 121, had the skull lying base up facing north, with jaw beneath it; only the pelvis and legs sharply bent were found, but they were in excellent preservation; the grave was three feet deep and protected with large stones. Each of these examples seems due to dismemberment before burial, as the large stones placed over the grave were still in position. Beside these there are other less certain cases, as follow. With the body perfect there is grave 20, skull 3 inches off; grave 39, skull 4 inches off; grave 51, skull 2 inches off; grave 60, body face down, skull 4 inches off, with jaw on top of it; grave 67, skull 2 inches off; grave 118, only a jaw, no skull, six feet deep with large stones over it. With no trace of a body, there was grave 15 with a skull and a jaw on the top of it. With bones piled up in a heap, and two burials mixed together in the grave, there were graves 42, 43 (see photographs Pl. VII E), and 81, the last with the two skulls on the top of the heap. With the previous clear instances of dismemberment in view, it seems most likely that these latter cases are really due to ceremonies before the burial, and not to being pulled about by plunderers. Such are the latest cases known of ceremonial separation of the body.

22. The positions of the stone vases were at the ends of the graves. Five at the north end, two at the NW. corner; four at the south end, and two at the SE. corner. The forms shown in Pl. VII E are all well known at the close of the Old Kingdom. It may be noted that the larger forms, those marked 3, 5, 37, were all found at the south end of graves. While the long tubular vases with collars, 35, 45, 57, were all at the north ends.

The positions of the pottery were nearly all at the north end of the grave. The examples are NE. 35, N. 23, NW. 7, W. 1, SW. 1, S. 2, SE. 3, E. 5. Hence three-quarters of the pottery was at the north or north-east; usually it was raised on a ledge above the head. The forms are given in Pl. VII F, and are the same as those of the Old Kingdom at Dendereh.

23. The mirror was found in four cases at the north-east, that is before the face, in two cases it was beneath the head, and in two cases at the south-east corner. A copper adze was the only other metal work.

In two burials button-seals were found at the neck; and in 23 graves beads were in position on the neck. The types of these were what are known from Hu and other places, of the VIth dynasty.

The burials at Zowyeh were partly in a small mound of stream-laid debris at the mouth of a valley (see Pl. VII E), and partly in the plain in front of this. The graves had mostly been plundered, and but few objects were obtained. The best was a string of carnelian amulets of the usual VIth dynasty style, found in the valley mound. The pottery found is here marked Zow in Pl. VII F.

CHAPTER V

THE VIITH—XIITH DYNASTIES. RIFEH.

24. THE cemetery of Rifeh is not absolutely dated by kings' names, except in the XVIIIth and XIXth dynasties. But by the style of its contents it largely belongs to the XIIth dynasty and earlier times. Nothing has been found in it distinctive of the VIth dynasty, like the pottery and amulets of Zowyeh or of Zaraby. For the dating of the pottery the best guide is *Dendereh* Pls. XVI—XVIII; as the numbering is continuous in those, they may be referred to as D. 1 to D. 195. And for the pottery certainly not earlier than the XIIth dynasty, see *Kahun* XII, XIII, called K. 1 to K. 111. The type which seems to be the earliest is the finely formed libation vase, as D. 5, 7; and though this was not found beyond the VIth dynasty at Dendereh, it must have lasted later here, as it is associated in graves 38, 53, 55, 112, 321 with forms which belong almost to the XIIth dynasty. The distinctly intermediate forms are the coarse libation vase D. 109, 124 of the XIth dynasty found in graves 101, 117, 255, 322, and with soul houses 35 (H), 68 (L), 140 (F), and 143 (E). The globular pot with a narrow cylindrical neck, usually in bistre-brown ware, is of the XIth dynasty, as D. 61; and it occurs in graves 86, 92, 99, 150, 228, 254, 256, 331 to 4, and with soul house 61 (H). Coming to the XIIth dynasty the globular developed into the drop form, as in D. 189, K. 16, found in graves 93, 335, and house 142 (H); the thin brown cup comes in now, as K. 1-3, in graves 107, 116, and with houses 46 (J), 44 (M), and 93 (J). The scrabble patterns of this age, as K. 39-45, are in graves 61, 62, 130, 251, and with house 53 (M). It is hardly needful to point out other connections; these abundantly show that the cemetery is certainly as old as the XIth dynasty, and very probably began in the VII—Xth, while it extends well into the XIIth, but shows nothing between that and the XVIIIth dynasty.

25. The rock-tombs of Rifeh extend for a few hundred yards, as shown on the map Pl. VIII, at about a third of the whole height of the cliffs. Those furthest north, now occupied by the Copts of Deir Rifeh, I merely visited, as Mr. Griffith had copied all the inscriptions twenty years ago, and there were other matters more important than making a facsimile copy.

The tomb of importance nearest to the Deir is a large unsculptured group of three chambers, with three burial pits, see XIII E. It appears to be of the XIIth dynasty by the style of it, but the only records in it are ink-written figures and inscriptions of a re-use of it under Ramessu III, copied in Pls. XXVIII—XXX. Beside these inscriptions in the first hall, there are traces on the chamber wall at the back of this. The courtyard is 215 inches wide and about 400 long; the passage 101 wide, 171 long; the hall 292 N., 283 S., 474 E., 470 W.; the back chamber 204 N., 203 S., 208 E., 210 W., the recess 46 × 62; the side chamber 130 S., 103 E., 102 W., the recess 39 wide. The cubit shown by the principal dimensions averages 20·55 inches.

Further south is another and much larger tomb, which has never been finished, see XIII E. It consists of a single hall, supported by six pillars, and with a pit in the middle. The design is really with the pit central, and four pillars around it; but it has been enlarged by cutting further into the north side, where two more pillars are unfinished, with large masses of flinty limestone left projecting unworked. The form of this plainly shows that it was a tomb, and not merely a quarry; yet the manner in which the unfinished cutting has clearly been done for the sake of the stone, shows that the tombs were also quarries. This explains the immense halls of the rock-tombs of this age at Beni Hasan, Asyut, Rifeh and elsewhere. When a ruler of a nome built his palace for this life down in the plain, he so managed his quarrying as to form a palace for eternity in the cliff. He made his work serve for both worlds; and the labour which we wonder at in the vast halls represents so much solid masonry down by the Nile for palaces which have long since vanished. The hall of this tomb is 85 feet long by 49 feet wide, and lofty in proportion; probably some 4,000 or 5,000 tons of stone have been removed. The dimensions are, west of pillars 320 inches, pillar 50, between pillars 300, pillar 65, in front of pillars 293, total E.—W. 1028 inches. Across, north of pillars 66? pillar 60, between 114, pillar 51, between 78, pillar 67, south of pillars 130, total N.—S. 586 inches.

The southernmost great tomb is that of Khnumunofer. The engraved inscription is given by Mr. Griffith in *Inscriptions of Siût and Dêr Rifeh*, pl. 16. The copies of the drawings yet remaining are given here on Pl. XIII F and following. These are on the north wall; on the west are the colossal figures of the man and his son, also a false door painted and traces of a scene of the deceased seated with inscription above it, but the deep well before it was too dangerous for ladder work on the wall. On the south are traces of ships, and short phrases. The west side of the chamber is 389, the north 458 inches. The south-east corner is entirely cut away, owing to Roman quarrying. Also the whole floor has been lowered from about three to ten feet by quarrying, thus rendering it more difficult to reach the painted parts. For long work upon ladders I found it best to make a very wide splayed ladder, so that it was abundantly firm sideways; to have a long top bar, projecting on each side; and then to make a sling, of an old sack with rope tied at each end of it, the ropes fastened over the top bar, and the sack passing between the legs. Thus the whole weight can be put sitting on one thigh, the feet merely steadying the body, and both arms can be used quite freely without any chance of tilting over. Many hours can be thus spent on a ladder doing careful copying, without much strain, and with entire safety. The tracing paper was attached to the wall by small spots of seccotine; the rolls of paper were hung in a bag, and the drawing board, measure, and brush were all hung to nails on the ladder. It is not worth while to transport well-made ladders about the country; a couple of bars three inches square, which can be bought in any town, and some sawn strips of board for steps, fastened with big nails, make an excellent ladder in a few minutes.

Beside these great tombs there were hundreds of small chambers cut in the rock. These had nearly all been plundered anciently, and scarcely anything remained in them; the wooden head, Pl. XI, is the only noticeable piece left. But a few unopened tombs were found, as described below.

26. The tomb of Nekhtankh son of Aa-khnumu was the richest. It was at the east end of the south side of the courtyard, of the tomb with the inscription of Ramessu III. A descending slope led to a small chamber barely large enough to hold the funeral furniture, 80 inches long, 70 wide at the south-east back and only 50 in front. The positions of the objects are shown in Pl. XIII E. The heads of the coffins were toward the opening of the tomb. The finest coffin was that next to the canopic box, see the upper one in Pl. X A. It contained (lying on its side) the beautifully decorated body coffin with the name of the *ha*-prince Nekhtankh, the second on X B. In it were two figures of the deceased, see Pl. X E. The second coffin and body coffin are much inferior, and are for the brother, Nekht. In it was the figure wearing a wig (Pl. X E). The canopic box, Pl. X D, was in the corner of the tomb; each side is similarly decorated. Inside it is divided to half-way up by cross boards of wood. Each compartment has a soft packing of fibre placed in it; and on that is a pottery canopic jar, painted yellow and inscribed. Each jar has a carved wooden head, all human, stuccoed and painted. Upon the box stood a pan containing stalks and leaves. In front of it was a jar with similar stalks and leaves. Before that stood the two boats, Pl. X C; the one for sailing up the Nile, with the men gathered to pull the rope raising the yard; the other with the mast laid down, and the sweeps out for rowing down the Nile. With these stood the two female figures of servants carrying offerings. The whole of the funeral furniture and the larger coffins are as fine as anything known of this period, as will be seen from the photographs.

27. A little south of this along the edge of the rock terrace was the untouched tomb of Khnumu-hotep. This contained four coffins, in a rock chamber only just sufficiently large to hold them. There was no furniture beyond the coffins, and most of them had perished by white ants, although half a mile from the cultivation and about 200 feet up the solid cliff. The first (331) was a square box coffin, painted red, with blue bands, and yellow inscription, much decayed; in it was a finely made white body coffin with gilt face, see lower part Pl. XI, of Khnumu-hotep son of Ketu. The next (332) was a box coffin, white, with yellow bands and blue hieroglyphs, of Khnumu-hotep daughter of Sit-anhur; all greatly decayed; in it was a finely made coffin of red, with elaborate diaper pattern (see X F) on a red ground, the face covered with silver foil, and the wig striped blue, green and red, top Pl. XI. This coffin was so greatly decayed, that parts only could be saved, by the greatest care. Inside there was a scroll-pattern scarab on one finger (Pl. XIII E), a string of small full blue beads on the neck, and a little armlet of lighter blue on one arm.

Next was a finely painted box coffin, white ground with doorways on the sides (Pl. X F) greatly decayed; the name had been painted out, and so this was not its original purpose. In it was a female body in bandages, with a cartonnage headpiece, like that of Pl. XI, but in worse state. Tied on to one finger was a scarab with a twist pattern and two *nofers* (XIII E); also two carnelian beads on the wrist. Furthest in the tomb was a box coffin (334), dark yellow with blue hieroglyphs, not well painted; inscribed for Ankhet daughter of Atha. In it was a female body in bandages, with the cartonnage headpiece shown in Pl. XI. On the neck was a small amethyst ball bead between two little silver beads. The bodies of all these were mere yellow dust, inside the thick wrappings; but the bones were beautifully preserved.

Near by, on the south, was a small tomb, with a box coffin, painted red, with yellow bands and blue hieroglyphs, roughly done and the name lost. The body was that of a young girl, and had on it a gold shell pendant, an inch across.

One other tomb contained a thick plain box coffin of earlier style, with blue inscriptions on bare wood, which had been yellow-washed, without any stucco. The inscriptions are given on Pl. IX; the name is Kheti. A vase of globular form, with very tall expanding neck, was with it; see Pl. XIII B.

28. The main quantity of burials were in the gravel shoal in the plain; see Pl. VIII. These were all in graves about three or four feet deep originally, with the head to the north. Later washes of gravel over the shoal had buried them all about two feet; so it was only by trial, and best by trenching east to west, that we could find them. All had been plundered, and hence no gold work was found; but many strings of beads, and some fine objects, were obtained. The graves are also described in connection with the soul-houses in the next chapter, sect. 34. The only pottery usually were two jars placed on a ledge above the head.

29. The most important figure found was the grey granite seated figure of Khnumu, Pl. X. This lay at about six feet down, below a burial at the bottom of a grave; some green ball beads, the size of peas, of regular XIIth dynasty type, were found in the grave. The surface of the figure had been considerably painted with black, apparently on the whole of the flesh. The work is best in the expression, and the muscles of the back and arms, which are as good as most of the earlier art. The faults are a lack of proportion, the legs being too large, and coarse work in the hands and wig. On the belt is an ink-written inscription, with a name ending in *u*, and only one sign before it, apparently *khnum*; as Khnumu is a divine name sometimes found used personally, it is probably so here. The whole reads, "Khnumu brother of Henthotep *maakheru*": the sister's name is on the base in front of the feet. The prominence of the god Khnumu in this region is due to his being the god of the town, Shashotep.

Some wooden figures of this age were found, but all had lost the colour, and were somewhat injured; and none were of much merit. The head in Pl. XII is on a larger scale than the other carvings. A small seated limestone figure is fair in detail but lacks proportion, the head being too large.

The group of monkeys, Pl. XII, is cut in limestone in the usual style of such figures, and barred with stripes of red paint. The subject is fresh to us; the female ape is holding her young one, while the male turns his back on them and is preparing to drink from a large globular pot.

The ivory wand, Pl. XII, is an unusually large and fine specimen of this class. It was found in a grave without any other objects. The type is as usual, the lion's head at the root end, the jackal at the tip. There are 21 neb signs, and nine mythological animals with knives.

30. About seventy alabaster vases were found of the XIIth and XVIIIth dynasties; those of the earlier period are shown in Pl. XI A. With these should be compared the dated forms found at Hu (*Diospolis Parva*, xxix, xxx). None of these are of the VIth dynasty types, or of the degraded forms of such attributable to the VIIth—VIIIth dynasties. But of the types assigned to the Xth dynasty there is 194 like *D. P.* xxviii, Y. 250; the wide foot vase, last beyond 215, like *D. P.* xxix, W. 157; and the gold disc like *D. P.* xxviii, 98. The evidence of the vases then would show that the cemetery dates from about the Xth dynasty, but was mainly used in the XIIth. The taller round-based vase, 243, is of blue paste like *D. P.* xxx, 188, 461, and was found with the two alabaster which are on either side. The almost cylindrical vase below it, 215, is closely like the vase *D. P.* xxx, Y. 34, and that at the base of the plate found with a group at Gizeh. The other two cups of 215 are like the form *D. P.* xxx, 349. The spouted tray 70 is a usual type of the XIIth dynasty, as in *D. P.* xxx, Y. 448. The general forms of the kohl vases are well known in the XIIth dynasty.

31. The beads were of the usual types of this age. None of the VIth dynasty amulets or the button seals were found. The earlier strings had the bulls' heads in carnelian or amethyst, the hawks in amethyst, and other reminiscences of the Old Kingdom. But the greater part were purely of the XIIth dynasty style of ball beads of blue or green glaze, carnelian, or amethyst. A few strings of small garnet beads were found; and mud beads well blacked and polished to resemble haematite, with poorer imitations down to mere rough mud. A feature here was the frequent occurrence of a fish of carnelian in the centre of a necklace.

32. The weapons found are shown on Pl. XII, and the outlines on Pl. XIII, which show further detail and some larger wooden forms. The dagger is in perfect condition, the blade showing portions of the polish, the ivory handle and ebony inlays being complete with the silver studs which fastened them. The narrower dagger blade is probably rather earlier, but both belong to the XIIth dynasty. The two axe blades below are shown with their fittings in the drawing, like that from Hu (*Diospolis*, xxxii, 1). They are deeper than those of the Vth dynasty shown at Deshasheh, but not so deep as in the XIIth dynasty at Beni Ḥasan. Probably they might be dated about the Xth dynasty. Two little cakes of colour, red and black, and a piece of ivory, were found with 194. The thin edge of copper inserted in a stick, Pls. XII, XIII, is seen better in the drawing where the binding holes are clear. This is an early form of weapon, much like that of the Vth dynasty (*Deshasheh*, iv); it is very rare, and is now in the Cairo Museum. The narrow-waisted axes are of the early XVIIIth dynasty; and the hard wood handle does not belong to the axe blade, but fitted one of exactly the same size of haft. On XIII, 11, the drawing shows the place of a copper band, which has been removed. The long curved stick, Pl. XIII, 10, is like that in the hand of the chief seal-bearer Baqt in the tomb of Khnumhotep (*Denk.*, ii, 127, top line). A broken throw-stick, 12, was found in the cemetery of the XIII—XVIth dynasties; that of ebony, fig. 13, is of the XIIth dynasty.

33. The pottery has been discussed in sect. 24 on the age of the cemetery. The most remarkable piece is the bowl from grave 61, shown in drawing, and also in photograph Pl. XI A; the three animals upon the brim are a lion, a crocodile, and apparently Taurt with hippopotamus head and a crocodile on her back. By the scrabble pattern on the brim this belongs to the XIIth dynasty. Of an earlier date are the pottery stands, Pl. XI A, with holes in them to support libation vases: there are two, three, or four holes, almost always in one line but sometimes in a square. These accompany the later narrow-based type of libation vase, and were intended to hold such in a row, like the vases in the *khent* sign. They are found with the earlier type of pottery and soul-houses. The well-formed cups with stems found in graves 52, 53, 323 are a fresh type. A curious form reappears here, the circular pot with a head and stump arms, and with two birds incised on the body, Pl. X F.

CHAPTER VI

THE SOUL-HOUSES. RIFEH.

34. For many years past, pottery trays of offerings have been known from Upper Egypt, and a few have been approximately dated in recorded observations (*Dendereh*, 26). But they have not been very common; only 15 were found in the whole cemetery of Dendereh, and only 10 existed in the Cairo Museum. Occasionally more elaborate models of dwellings appeared, but none of these had any record of the discovery or date. Further, many forgeries of intricate models were made, and complicated the question.

This year's work at Rifeh has now produced about 150 models of dwellings, more or less complete, beside trays of offerings. It is possible from these to trace the order of development, and the purpose and use of this class of models. The cause of such models having hitherto been rare, is explained by their position upon the surface of the ground over a grave, which we now find to have been the case. And the reason that they were preserved at Rifeh better than elsewhere, is because the graves were made in a growing shoal of gravel, which continued to grow and so gradually buried the models, until the present surface is usually about 20 inches above the level of the model. Thus they have not been exposed for more than a few centuries, and though mostly cut by sand-blasts, and partly broken, yet there was far more preserved here than elsewhere. The more distinctive are published here in thirteen Plates, XIV to XXII, which show about a hundred examples, beside various details of fragments.

Regarding their position they were at various levels, but much the greater part were from 20 to 25 inches below the present surface, and 35 to 40 inches above the floor of the grave. This was therefore probably the depth of the grave when cut. It will be seen in the diagram on Pl. XXII E that there is a tendency to group, so that the depth of grave below the soul-house is inversely as the height of soil above it. That is to say that the soul-houses were occasionally put on a pile of earth 10 inches high (at the SE. corner), or in a hollow 10 inches deep (at the N. end); but not a quarter of them were thus irregular, the great majority having been just placed on the ordinary ground level. That they were gradually buried by washed soil, and not intentionally buried at first, was clear from their condition. The majority were well preserved at the base, but greatly weathered above;

also many showed the successive lines of storm water concreting the blown sand at higher and higher levels as they gradually became buried, absolutely proving that they had been long exposed on the surface.

The position around the grave, and the direction of face, are shown in the other diagram, Pl. XXII E. It will be seen that two-thirds are at the north end of the grave, a few east or west, and very rarely to the south. The face is so placed as to look inward to the grave in more than three-quarters of the instances, and only one in ten stood with the back to the grave. As they were doubtless shifted about somewhat during centuries of exposure, we cannot lay any weight on the exceptions to the general rule, which is evident. That they were not oftener placed on the east side, and facing the east, like the ordinary tables of offerings of earlier times, shows how greatly they had departed from the original conception, and how they had become dwellings for the soul rather than places of sacrifice for the living.

35. The origin of such pottery trays of offerings is obviously in the stone altars of offering which preceded them. In the earliest dynasties a mat was laid on the ground, on the east of the tomb, and a vase of offerings was placed upon it. These have been actually found (see *Deshasheh*, 35), and the *hotep* hieroglyph was formed from such a group as early as the time of Mena. To this mat and vase succeeded the stone altars of offerings which are familiar to us in the Old Kingdom. These were imitated cheaply in pottery, and gradual elaboration transformed them into the models of houses for the soul. These have been here classified into consecutive types lettered from A to N. It is not certain whether the *ka* or the *ba*—the ghost or the spirit—were supposed to use these. On one hand we see that the formula is that a *hotep* is for the *ka* of a man, on the other hand the food and drink provided in the cemetery by the sycomore goddess is always taken by the *ba*. To avoid this uncertainty we may simply call these models "soul-houses." The initial motive for such dwellings may perhaps be seen in foreign influence. The hut-urn was usual in early Italy, and the button seals, which came in after the Old Kingdom, point to Mediterranean immigration.

36. How far were they models of actual houses, or how far merely an expansion of the *hotep*? Obviously we cannot suppose that joints of meat usually lay about in the courtyard of an actual house. Yet on the other hand we have what is an exact copy of an actual house tank on a stone altar of offerings in the Vth dynasty, with the different levels of water at different seasons inscribed upon it (Cairo Museum). Thus even the stone altar had begun to borrow actual features from a house, before the rise of the pottery trays. If the tank is thus represented, can it be supposed that a house usually had a tank in its courtyard, as shown in these models? If we look at actual Oriental houses, even as copied in Alger and Spain, we see that a tank in the courtyard is the essential in any superior house. In Egypt we see the tanks painted in the middle of each hall at Tell el Amarna under the XVIIIth dynasty (*Tell el Amarna*, ii). In the XIIth dynasty at Kahun a tank was placed in the middle of the courts of the mansions (*Illahun*, xiv, xvi). When we look at these models we see that the channel or drain from the tank in the earlier examples is often covered over by the threshold, a form which would be absurd if it had no reality, but which is obviously useful in an actual doorway (Pl. XVI, 1). Also there are often the holes for posts to support a canopy over the tank, to screen it from the sun (Pls. XIV, 8, 9; XV, 100; XVI, 1; XX, below 46); such is obviously copied from an actual tank and screen, and would not be invented for the soul, which was supposed to come out at night for its sustenance. From these actual examples of the use of tanks, and the points of the models copied from working details, we must regard the court and the tank as copied from forms really in use. The portico, which seems essential to these houses, is seen copied in the rock tombs of the VIth to the XIIth dynasty, with a pole roof over it; and it was as constant a feature of every temple, which was the house of the god. That the court may have actually had a low front to it, as in these models, is suggested by the example where the portico is not closed at the end by the side walls (*i.e.* without *antae*), a feature which would hardly be made in the trays if without actual precedent. We must conclude then that probably all the features of these models are copied from actual houses, excepting the offerings lying about; and these gradually disappeared in the later models, which became houses pure and simple.

37. The date of these models can only be inferred from the pottery; and the forms of that are dated by the examples found at Dendereh. The upright libation vases are one of the most variable types. In the VIth dynasty they are well formed, slightly curving out at the base (*Dend.* xvi, 5, 7, 22); in the Xth and XIth they are straight and coarse (*D.* xvii,

124), and they are not found in the XIIth dynasty. Comparing these and some other forms, we should be led to class the models with which they were found as follows:—

Date	Nos.	Type
VIth dynasty and later? .	126	A?
	100	B
	133	E
Xth—XIth dynasty . .	33	E
	35	H
	61	H
	101	J
	68	L
	78	M
XIIth dynasty	45	J
	102	L
	46	M

No doubt the pottery styles, and also the types of models, overlap each other's stages, and do not begin and end at a word of command.

The general order of the types of models goes well in accord with the dating of the pottery; but in view of the other evidence we can hardly place the beginning earlier than the IXth or Xth dynasty, while the end lasts well into the XIIth. The trays probably continued to be made as the cheaper forms throughout; and the examples that could be dated at Dendereh, run from the IXth to the middle of the XIth dynasty.

38. The general characteristics of each of the successive periods of these soul-houses may now be stated. The summary of all the actual examples is given in Pl. XXII A, and the register of each example in detail is in Pls. XXII B, C, D. Here we only state the main points which serve to distinguish one class from another. Some technical terms are used here for features which are the same as those in modern Egypt; the *satáh* is a roof enclosed by a dwarf wall, which is a usual safeguard on Oriental houses; the *mulqaf* is a hood to catch the wind and drive it down into the house; the *'eshsha* is a screen from the sun, supported on poles.

Type A. A shelter with pillars in front, or portico, no *satáh*.
" B. A portico with *satáh* on top; with or without a stairway.
" C. A hut at the back with portico before it.
Type D. A chamber with portico, but no *satáh*. Generally 3 doors to it and 2 *mulqafs*, with or without *'eshsha*.
" E. Two *mulqafs*, with *satáh* between.
" F. From two to five chambers, no *satáh* or *mulqaf* or stairway.
" G. *Satáh* across the *mulqafs*.
" H. 3 *satáhs*, on and between the *mulqafs*.
" J. 2 *mulqafs* across the whole, each with *satáh*.
" K. Closed door, no *mulqafs*.
" L. No *mulqafs*; beginning of furniture.
" M. Court enclosed with high wall; furniture.
" N. Four stripes on the wall; furniture.

39. *Trays of offerings*. Pl. XIV. The earliest style of tray found is a massive corner of a thick slab of pottery, No. 1, with polished drab face; it has the corner of a tank-hollow on it, and several holes as if for sticks to carry an *'eshsha*. It is obviously an imitation of a stone table of offering. No. 2 is a slab rather less massive, with two tanks on it and a rude trace of offerings, apparently ribs and a haunch. No. 3 is a fragment showing a tank, haunch and ribs, with a border around, and holes at the corners, apparently for an *'eshsha*. No. 4 shows the bull's head but no tank; the ten little cups around it are peculiar to it. In nos. 5, 6, 7 we see well modelled figures of the bull's head and other offerings, apparently made before they had sunk to mere conventions, and while there was some sense of the art of the Old Kingdom. Nos. 8, 9 show two tanks, with bull's head, haunch and ribs, and holes for the *'eshsha* over each tank. Nos. 10, 11 have no *'eshsha*; apparently a long-necked bird is shown sacrificed on 11. The nos. 12 to 15 are very degraded forms, which probably belong to a late period. We never find here the two parallel water channels, which often occur at Dendereh, and on those in the Cairo Museum from near Erment; that seems to be a more southern type.

40. Type A. *Shelter without satáh*. Pl. XV, 106, 5. The number attached to each example was placed on it in the order of discovery, merely for the sake of identification and registering. Perhaps the earliest type of shelter is 106, where the roof is stretched up by two posts, much like a Bedawy tent, from which it almost seems copied. The more usual form of this type, 5, is as a plain portico along the back of the tray; but without any roof edging or *satah* on the top. Sometimes the columns have plain disc bases to them. A curious type, which does not agree with any other, is the little hutch, 126; it has

some slight lumps that may be intended for offerings inside it, but never had any tray of offerings. It seems like a soul-shelter invented independently, apart from the traditional tray or altar.

41. Type B. *Shelter with satáh.* Pl. XV, 31, 148, 86, 72, 96, 100. This type has two, three, or four columns. In 148 the portico is open at the ends. There may be a stairway to the *satah*, as in 86. The tank in 100 has holes for an *'eshsha* over it, and these are marked by bits of stick put in them for the view. There is no order in the offerings of bull's head, ribs and haunch; they are found on either side of the tank. The *satah* wall may be worked as a cornice over the portico, as in 100.

42. Type C. *Hut chamber.* Pl. XVI, 7, 21, 1, 147. Here a hut is added beneath the portico. In 7 the sides are broken, but the bases of columns remain in this order :··:, showing that a roof was carried across; but it seems only to have joined the side walls, as the back wall has a smooth top at half height. In 21 and 1 it is obvious that the roof was continuous above the hut. The apparent abacus on the column in 21 is not original, but merely a prop to hold up the broken roof for the view. In each the top of the hut is complete in itself, either rounded as in 7, or with a cornice to it in 21 and 1. In 7 (and another instance not figured, No. 91) a chair is placed in the hut. The *'eshsha* in 1, and the covered channel in front, are both early features, and agree to this hut type coming near the beginning of the series. No. 147 is a curious modification, where a long chamber has been started, swallowing up the portico, and without any columns before it. There was a central door, and probably two windows in front. Such windows are very unusual, but some may be seen in upper floor chambers, at the top of Pl. XX.

43. Type D. *Chamber with portico.* Pl. XVI, 115, 12, 116, 10; Pl. XVI A, 151, 82, 87, 122. This type has a *satah*, unless the *mulqafs* are at the ends, as in 116 and 10. There may be three *mulqafs* as in 82, 87, or two as in 12, or more as in 115, 151. The number of pillars is nearly always four; but sometimes there is no end wall to the portico, as in 12, 151, 122. The flying stairway at the end of the portico is seen in 151, 122. Three tanks are never seen except in 82, where only the bases of the columns remain. In 122 notice the column inside the chamber, seen through the door.

44. Type E. *Satah between mulqafs.* Pl. XVI A, 19, 98, 13, 25; Pl. XVII, 150, 67, 74, 29. There are always two *mulqafs* in this type, and sometimes two more beneath the *satah*, as in 67. The closed door appears for the first time, in 29; though perhaps XVIII, 80 may be an earlier example as being more natural, and not reduced to four scores as here. It probably represents a door made of stems of maize plastered with mud, such as may be seen still used. The portico is usually of four columns, rarely of only two, and it is never open at the ends. The stairway is sometimes flying, sometimes winding round the side wall; but often it is absent, showing that the roof was not much regarded. There is in some a definite opening from the portico roof into the *satah*, as in 74. This is one of the commonest types, nineteen having been photographed.

45. Type F. *Several chambers.* Pl. XVII, 95, 69; Pl. XVII A, 69, 55, 65, 3. This type approaches more nearly to the actual house plan, and may perhaps be spread in period over that of other types. The two models with most detail, 95 and 55, are also given in plans on Pl. XXII E. The chambers are sometimes a row along the back, as in 95, 65, 3 and 11 (no view). Or they may be on three sides of a hall, as in 55. Or the hall may have a central pillar, and a square portico in front of it, as in 69.

46. Type G. *Satah across mulqafs with shelter.* Pl. XVII A, 85. This type is only known by one example, which is apparently the first house with a shelter on the upper storey. There is an opening leading from the portico roof to the *satah*, and a little shelter on three columns at the back.

47. Type H. *Satah divided in three.* Pl. XVII, 35, 128; XVII A, 142, 92, 153, 121. The roof is usually empty, but 35 shows a development of the example of G, with a little cloister along the back of the *satah* between the *mulqafs*. The closed door is also well shown here and in 153. No. 128 is a fanciful design, with corner porticoes projecting; a stairway leads up to the left portico, stairs from each side portico to the main portico, and a stair from that to the *satah*. There are two main *mulqafs*, and two others between those, as also in 121. 142 and 92 are small cloisters from the roof, similar to that in 35.

48. Type J. *Two mulqafs with satahs.* Pl. XVIII, 42, 101; XVIII A, 71, 93, 4. This is shown best in 42, where the difference of level, and a little opening between the *satahs*, are seen. The roofs are usually well domed. The developed upper storey now begins, with 101; and a form with a dwarf colonnade in front of the *satah* is seen in 4. A barred window is on the side of 71.

49. Type K. *Closed door.* Pl. XVIII, 80, 84, 107; XVIII A, 16. This type also extends in other instances from E to L; and these here shown probably belong to other types, which cannot be distinguished owing to the loss of the tops. In 80 the door is well made (by the side of the open door), closely ribbed, and representing a door of maize stalks. 16 is coarser, and 84, 107 are very rude; the latter is curious for having two closed doors and none open. This closed door is in various positions, three times on the right, four times in the middle, and twice to the left. It is apparently intended for the store-room.

50. Type L. *No mulqafs, furniture begins.* Pl. I Front, 102; Pl. XVIII, 44, 118; XVIII A, 20, 59, 2; XVIII B, 97, 68, 124. A large change takes place at this stage; the upper storey is universal, the mulqaf disappears, and models of couch, chair, water-stand, and corn-grinder begin to be inserted. No. 44 hardly belongs to this class, but it would be difficult to place it with any other type; the long chamber over the portico has only a doorway, and no stair to the *satah* on the top. In no. 118 the courtyard wall has advanced, and enclosed part of the front, while it forms the side of the stairway. Beneath the stairs is the constant position for the woman grinding corn; in this example there is a water-jar behind her at the foot of the stairway. The upper storey has generally been destroyed by weathering, but a few instances remain fairly complete, as 102, 20, 59, 2, similar to J. 101 excepting the *mulqafs*. At this period the columns begin to have palm capitals, as in 59, and as shown separately in Pl. XXI. The furniture begins with a chair in the colonnade of the upper floor, and a couch with head-rest in the colonnade of the lower floor. This inversion of the order that we should expect, was probably due to the upper air being cooler during the day, and the lower air cooler at night. The finest example, in the frontispiece, shows this arrangement very clearly; this is now in the Cairo Museum.

51. Type M. *Closed court.* Pl. XVIII B, 83, 22, 32; XIX, 32, 66, 43, 79. In this we reach the form of a fully developed house, with high wall around the court and doorway to it; and the abolition of the offerings and generally of the tank, as being unsuited to a high-walled court. The most complete front is that of 66, but other doorways similar to that may be seen in Pl. XX. Unfortunately the upper storeys of all these houses have been destroyed, partly owing to their being higher in proportion than the earlier types, and so longer exposed before being buried. The fragments show that they were finished with serrated walls as seen in 32.

The windows are found in the side, as in the view of 32 on Pl. XVIII B, and in the back, as in 32 on Pl. XIX. The two views of 32 are taken also to show the couch on the upper floor (XIX), and the stairway (XVIII B). The two views of 43 are to show the couch and fireplace (?) in the chamber, and the cornice of the door and corn-grinder. There is another (46, not figured) which also shows the two ridges on the floor, which seem to be intended to hold in the fuel and to support a cooking-pot, like the modern fireplace in Egypt.

52. Type N. *Stripes on wall.* Pl. XVIII B, 103, 119; Pl. XIX, 77, 58. This type is a rather coarser variant of M, except in one detail, the presence of four raised stripes or bars on the wall. They are first found between the doors, either alone, as on two pieces below the columns in Pl. XXI, or as in 58 with the bull's head beneath them. No such offering is known; nor could the ribs, which they might be supposed to resemble, be thus stuck on the wall. It seems as if they had originated in a misunderstanding of the closed door, as degraded in XVIII, 84, where it appears as four marks on the wall between the doors. Later the stripes appear on either side of the head, as in 77, and then shifted to the side wall of the court in XVIII B, 103, 119. No type is found which can be classed as later than this.

53. Having now described the different types that may be distinguished among these models, the next study is the consideration of different parts of the structure. The walls sometimes retain their original painting, of white with red bands; they were copied from mud-brick walls, colour washed as the custom is at present. In the later models the tops of the walls are always serrated, as in the pieces on Pl. XXI, 53, 54. It is noticeable that the tombs in the modern cemetery close by are similarly serrated or crested, as shown in the view above these pieces. It seems that this system of finishing a wall has survived in this district, though not general elsewhere. The arrangement of walls shown in 54 is apparently copied from an actual dwelling, though it is only part of the roof of a house. The entrance was at the top left hand, where a hole seems to be the door socket; the T-shaped wall in the middle divides the area, and makes a private enclosure in the right-hand side, where the corn bin stands in the corner. This is

much like one of the enclosures put up in the fields, for the peasants to guard their cattle by night, during the pasture season.

The roofs are usually flat in the earlier models, doubtless copied from the roofs of palm-stick and plaster, or of maize-stalk and mud, which are usual in the country. But in type D, evidently arched roofs are intended; and in later types, especially J, the domed roofs are obvious (XVIII, 42). In the piece of roof, XX, 160, the ribbing of the arches of brick-work is shown below. And the side of a house shows the ground-floor roofed with a barrel vault, and the same for the upper colonnade, and upper chamber. It should be noted how the lower arch is flat, owing to the weight on the abutments allowing of a thrust; while the upper arch is high, where the thrust needed to be less. The stairway led up in the floor of the colonnade.

Another mode of roofing and flooring is shown by the fragment 26, on Pl. XX. Here a long square beam (now half bare) ran beneath the first floor, and apparently carried it without any columns.

54. The stairways are varied in form and connection. The simplest run up either side of the courtyard to the roof, as in XV, 86. But the flying stair is so often represented that it must have been very familiar, as in XVI A, 122; XVII, 128; XVII A, 85. And this would show that the actual houses had mere low walls round the courts, and not high walls which would have carried a stairway, as in XIX, 43. Sometimes the stair curves in the court, at other times it takes an abrupt corner. For access to the roof of the upper storey the stair is sometimes all in one length, as in Pl. I, or else in two lengths as in XVIII A, 2; or the two lengths may be disconnected as in XVIII, 42. The stairway is twice as often on the spectator's left as on the right hand.

The mode of entrance on the upper floor also varied. Usually it was quite direct, as in XX, 18. Rarely the stair was at right angles to the usual place, running parallel to the front of the portico as in XVIII B, 22. Otherwise it came up under the floor through a trap-door opening, as in XX, 26, and XVIII, 42, 80. And this opening had occasionally a hood over it, as in XX, 38.

55. The windows were usually barred for security, as in XX, 46, where the bars cross. In XVIII A, 71, the window at the side of the house is closed with upright bars. Or else they were very small if on the ground-floor, and high up as in XVII, 69; XX, 64. On the upper floor the windows were larger (XXII, 36), and in two cases just over the couch, as in XIX, 32. The side window in the same model, XVIII B, 32, has a projecting course like a hood-moulding over it; and the same is seen in two other windows on Pl. XX. This is a curious feature to find as it is not needed in a rainless climate. The position of the windows is at the sides in 22 cases, at the back in 19, and in front in 5 cases.

The doorways likewise have a moulding, as seen in the same group, and in XIX, 66; and in one case a cavetto cornice, of which one end is shown. This same projection was also used on inner doors, as in XIX, 43, 77, 79. Some models had hingeing doors, of which one is shown on Pl. XXII.

56. The columns are usually made as mere cylinders; but a base of a disc form is usual in well-made early examples, XVI, 1, 10; XVI A, 82; XVII, 150, 74, 29; XVIII A, 153; XX, below 46, and others. Such a base was usual at the time, as seen at Kahun. The capital is never represented by an abacus alone, nor is the shaft fluted, as at Beni Hasan. But palm capitals are found in many late instances, sometimes alone, sometimes with an abacus above, as in Pl. XXI, and XVIII A, 59.

57. The tray of offerings has a square spout to begin with, as in XV, 5, and others; and this is general till type J, but almost vanishes in M. A rounded form is occasionally found early, as XV, 106, but is not numerous till type L. The spout altogether disappears in M and N when the court was enclosed with high walls.

In some early forms the floor is whitened, and then marked round with a broad black line, see XX, below 46.

The tank is absent in 28 cases, single in 62, double in 13, and there is one instance of three, and one of four, tanks. There is an open channel in 49 models, and it is covered over in 7 cases.

The offering of the bull's head is as often on the right as on the left side, and but rarely in the middle. It is rather more often at the side than in the front corner of the tray. The haunch is at either side, but one in six is in the middle. The ribs are at right or left or in the middle equally often. There does not seem to be any intention in these positions of the offerings. The triangular cakes, XXII, 60, are shown on wooden models of offerings from El Bersheh, and there coloured black. They also appear in the cake-making in the tomb of Khnumuhotep at Beni Hasan.

58. The upper parts of the later houses having all been broken off, we have only fragments to show

their arrangements. In the piece of a late house with serrated wall, XXI, 54, the corn bin in the corner of the roof is seen. Many such corn bins or granaries were found, as shown on Pl. XXII, sometimes two together; and one has a groove round the mouth for a sliding lid.

The figure of the corn-grinder is only placed beneath the sloping stairway (XVIII, 118; XIX, 77, 43; XXII), but the figure is rather unusual, and only found in late times. Other figures shown on Pl. XXII are of the master seated, as 36 and 134; among the detached pieces are two upright figures, one with its back to a column, perhaps servants.

59. The furniture is only found in the later stages, L, M, and N. The couch (see Pl. I) is distinguished by the head-rest placed at one end of it. It is usually on the ground at first; three-quarters of the cases are thus; but later it was put on the upper floor. It is more usually to the left or in the middle than to the right. The head is almost as often to the left as to the right. The chair (see Pl. XXI, 130, 40, 123) is usually in the middle (12 cases), seldom to the left (5), and rarely to the right (2). It is on the ground floor in two-thirds of the cases; but this predominance is partly due to so many models having lost the upper parts. Sometimes a figure is seated in the chair, see XXII, base. The water stand with jars occasionally appears, as in XXI, 130, 30, 123; XXII, 57, 60. In one case there seems to be a drain hole in a back chamber. A fireplace formed of two ridges of bricks, to support the cooking pot, is shown in XIX, 43, and occurs in another case. The forked stool (XIX, 77) in a bed room seems as if it might be for easing (compare Exodus i, 16).

We have now a far clearer view of the arrangements and details of the ordinary Egyptian houses than has hitherto been obtained from any of the actual remains, and we see how closely they resemble in most respects the dwellings of the present time in that land.

CHAPTER VII

THE XIIITH—XVITH DYNASTIES. RIFEH.

60. To the south of the other cemeteries a rise of desert gravel was used for burials during the XIIIth—XVIth dynasties. The graves were irregular pits, mostly five or six feet deep. They had all been plundered, and it was only the fragments that we could recover. There were none of the shallow pan-graves such as were found at Hu belonging to this period. Yet many of the burials were of the same class of invaders as those of the pan-graves, as is shown by the red and black cups, the scratched basket patterns, and the skulls of oxen and goats painted with red and black. The date is shown by the re-use of alabaster kohl pots of the XIIth dynasty, and by a scarab of Shesha, the Hyksos king Assis, of the XVIth dynasty.

61. The principal contents of the graves were leather work and matting. The leather was used for bags of various forms. One was of checkers of red and white leather about an inch square. Another elaborate bag had a row about three-quarters of an inch long of white shell beads, with occasionally blue glazed, inserted like a piping along a seam, alternating with equal lengths of leather fringing. With this was some rough-scratched pan-grave pottery, and bits of a small wooden box, and of ivory with a row of circles as a pattern. Beside strings of the shell beads characteristic of this age, there were also some of the bracelets made of strips of shell pierced at each end. The matting varied in style, and occurred in most of the graves, showing how general the material was in the daily life of these people. One of the more perfect mats is figured in Pl. X F, along with a more closely woven and softer piece, and one of the basket-work lids which are frequently found here. Weaving was also done, as is seen by a weaver's slay next to the mat, which is worn along the edge by the threads of the loom. Next to that is a pair of copper tweezers, and beyond is an arrow point of hard wood, another arrow which has been tipped with flint and still has a flint barb, and two arrow butts with notch, and feathering still in position. Above these is a neck of a black incised pottery flask of Hyksos age; resting on the handle is an armlet of plaited leather, and above are pieces of a horn armlet incised with a plait pattern.

In half a dozen or more of the graves were skulls of animals. Some bulls' heads had very fine horns, and the frontal bones were painted with spots of red and black. The same was done on some goat skulls. But these were not found in large quantities, as at Hu. Beside these foreign remains there were purely Egyptian kohl pots, worn and old, and in one very shallow grave were pieces of a painted box of wood, Pl. XXIV, which had probably been a toilet box of an Egyptian. The figures of Taurt, Bes, and various animals are roughly done in red and yellow, and the hyaena in blue-grey. The heraldic shading is used in the copy here. The position of the fragment placed as a horn to the front animal below is doubtful; by the side pattern it seems to belong to the lower edge of a scene, but cannot be fitted to any such here, nor to the very indistinct subject of Taurt and Bes which was upon a piece of the end of the box.

Two fine scarabs were found in this cemetery; one was of Shesha, the other was of the royal sealer Har, of whom many such scarabs are already known; it was found with the alabaster kohl pot XI A, 24, and a hemispherical cup.

62. The pottery in this cemetery belongs to three classes—the purely Egyptian, the pan-grave barbaric pottery, and the fine black incised pottery brought in by the Hyksos, perhaps from Syria. The Egyptian ware is like that already known of this age, especially the series from Tell el Yehudiyeh (*Hyksos and Israelite Cities*, pl. x).

The different graves may be classified by comparison with the styles of dated pottery. The earlier are distinguished by the types of the XIIth dynasty being continued; as the wavy line in graves 73 and 40, Pl. XXV; in grave 33 is a barbaric square dish like that in 73; grave 58 has a well-made bowl on stand; graves 45 and 48 have the "salad-mixer" type like *Kahun* xiii, 50, 52; grave 49 has the fine type of ring stand, and 50 accompanies this; and grave 59 has the turn-out lip to the cup. All of these seem to be the earlier types, and the graves are placed together here; but the square barbaric dish shows that the intrusion of the pan-grave people was already beginning. The limit of this style may be gathered from the varieties of the ring stands and the jars. The tall stands and straight-sided jars, which belong to these graves, are found at Tell el Yehudiyeh with scarabs of the same style as those of the Hyksos of the XVth dynasty. These graves then probably belong to the XIIIth to XVth dynasties.

The next stage is shown on Pl. XXVI, where the later styles of pottery probably date from the XVIth dynasty, during the Hyksos decadence, when southern influence was increasing. The graves with the strongest barbaric connection are 66, which contained goats' heads with red and black spots, the pottery given in Pl. XXVI, 61, 67, 73, 80, a worn alabaster kohl pot, and a piece of black incised pottery (XXVI, 94) which may be dated to the middle of the XVIth dynasty, about Shesha; grave 71 which contained a bracelet of shell strips, and green glazed and shell beads alternate on a necklace, with pottery XXVI, 80; grave 73 with a shell-strip bracelet, blue glazed and white shell beads alternate, and pottery of northern type XXVI, 92; also grave 79 with goats' heads covered with red and black spots, and a pan as in 77.

Below the Egyptian pottery on Pl. XXVI, and the barbaric which is linked with it, there are the examples of the barbaric pottery found alone. 95 to 97 belong together, grave 47. 99 from grave 71 shows that such bowls belong to the middle of the XVIth dynasty. The incised or scratched ware differs from what was found at Hu, especially in the notched brims, and it extends our view of the varieties then used. The black incised pottery which was brought in by the Hyksos through Syria is of the first importance for the history of this age, as it is dated by the styles of scarabs found with it, which are in their turn dated by the styles of the Hyksos scarabs. This results from the work at Tell el Yehudiyeh last year, as published in *Hyksos and Israelite Cities*, pls. vii, viii, li, pp. 10, 11, 67, 68. The bearing of it upon the dating here has been noticed above.

CHAPTER VIII

THE XVIIITH—XXTH DYNASTIES. RIFEH.

63. It will be seen on the plan, Pl. VIII, that there are three cemeteries of the later age in this district. The northern one was largely of the XIXth dynasty; the middle one was mostly of the early XVIIIth dynasty, especially about the time of Tahutmes III; the southern one by Deir Zowyeh had probably been of early XVIIIth dynasty, but was so plundered by dealers recently that nothing could be settled. The middle cemetery was the main site of work; the tombs were cut in a bed of soft grey marl with white streaks, and were overlaid by a late Roman and Coptic cemetery of shallow graves.

The tombs were of one general type. A stairway was cut descending from the north or north-west about two feet wide at the top, and widening somewhat as it descended; it was about 12 to 20 feet in length, and descended about half that in depth. At the end a small doorway, about two feet wide and three feet high, gave access southward to a chamber about four feet high and seven or eight feet wide and long. There was sometimes another, lesser, chamber at the east or the south sides. As every one of the tombs had been plundered anciently, we could not observe the manner of burial.

64. Very little stone carving was found. The only stele (XXVII N) was broken; four pieces were recovered, the rest could not be found. It was in a Ramesside tomb in the northern cemetery. At the top is a figure of "the keeper of cattle of the temple of Ramessu-mery-Amen, in the house of Ra, Huta" offering to "Osiris lord of the land of the west, the great god, prince of eternity, Isis the divine mother, mistress of heaven, and Hat-hor mistress of heaven and princess of east and west." Below were figures, probably of the son and daughters of Huta offering to him, with names Horaa and Aset-nefert.

As illustrating the difficulty of recovering broken pieces we may notice the group on Pl. X F. The head and shoulder were found in a tomb with the Pasar shabti, Pl. XXVII, while the rest of the block was in a tomb a hundred yards away. The work is careful and as good as most Ramesside carving. Unfortunately there were no inscriptions on it.

The Pasar shabti, Pl. XXVII, is fairly worked, and of the close of the XVIIIth dynasty. The feet were also found with it, but the legs were missing. As we shall see below, the mixture of styles found in the tombs suggests that much of the funeral furniture was re-used, and had been robbed from tombs two or three centuries older.

An unusual carving is that of the Hat-hor head, Pls. XXVII B and N. It is a massive block of hard silicified limestone, of between two and three hundred-weight; it is roughly broken below, and plain on the back. The rounding of the top precludes our supposing that it is the capital of a Hat-hor column, and the purpose of it is unknown. It is now in the Cairo Museum. The inscription is the usual formula, naming Khnumu of Shas-hotep as the god; the persons are Aah-ger son of Nebsenuy priest of Khnumu and his wife . . . . art; Nebsenuy being son of a chief of police Nenur and his wife Sen-ankh-tef.

65. In the northern cemetery a great variety of shabti figures were found. The differences between those placed together suggest that they had not all been made directly for the burials with which they were found. Those on Pl. XXVII C are selected to illustrate the variety of types; double of this quantity were also photographed, but scarcely add to what may be traced in these. The numbers on the plate refer to all that follow them, up to a fresh number: Group 305 shows a large coarse limestone figure, small limestone figures with carefully finished heads and coarse pottery figures. 304 shows two types, the overseer with a sleeved gown, and the ordinary workman. In 151 a large limestone figure was with a small coarse one of pottery. Further on are carefully cut limestone figures in 242, along with coarser ones, and very rude pottery reliefs on a broad background. In 211 is another mixture of limestone, pottery with red bands, and pottery with rude ink painting. The type in 226 is rare, if not new: the figures are of girls, without any of the usual swathing or clothing of a shabti, the face painted red, and black for the hair; with them were a few housekeepers wearing a kilt, which is not usual for female figures. Hieratic inscriptions have been put on the backs of those in grave 175. Other such inscriptions will be seen on Pl. XXVII L. Some interesting varieties are seen on the right hand, at A. The moulded face is used for two different figures, and it was probably the source of the moulds for the last figure in 175, and the last of 279. The group 223 shows tablet figures with a wide background, along with rudely scratched work and the coarsest lumpy features.

66. Of funeral furniture not much had remained. A few pottery coffins were found, but they were not nearly so usual as in the Delta cemeteries, or at Gurob. One of these had the lid, comprising the head and chest, of far better work than usual; it is shown on Pl. XXXVII, and is the only artistic head that I have seen in such a position. As a contrast may be noticed the rude head and lid in Pl. XXVII B. The small faces of plaster, attached to the cloth wrapping, and gilt, which we found here and at Hu (*Diospolis*, 51, 53) are descended from the cartonnage of the XIIth dynasty, see sect. 26.

A folding stool with leather seat was found broken up in a tomb; the parts are replaced together in the photograph XXVII B. By the side of this is half of another stool, the legs of which end in ducks' heads. Some plain wooden head-rests are shown in Pl. XXVII F and J.

Only one set of canopic jars was found. These are large ones of alabaster (XXVII B), the fourth was broken by the ancient plunderers, but can be re-united. The inscriptions are only written in ink.

In one tomb was a triple blue glazed kohl tube (XXVII B) of about the reign of Amenhotep III. With it was a toilet dish guarded by a lion, carved in wood, and three wooden wands with hands. Another very fine wand of ivory, Pl. XXVII, may belong to the XVIIIth dynasty, judging by the very slender hand, resembling the wand of queen Aahmes

(*Student's History* ii, fig. 32) and one found at Gurob (Univ. Coll.). The elaborate network over the arm is a design not known before on wands; this is now therefore in the Cairo Museum. A few fragments of a fellow wand were found with it.

A limestone figure of a woman on a couch (Pl. XXVII B) is one of the largest such found, 13 inches long. It shows a yellow girdle and yellow earrings.

Some baskets of usual forms and work were found; and the basket and lid which were best preserved are shown in Pl. X F.

67. Many alabaster kohl pots and vases occurred in the tombs of the XVIIIth dynasty. These are all shown in Pl. XXVII A; those between repetitions of the same number are all from the same grave. The forms are of the sharp-shouldered and clumsy type of the later period. Among the larger ones, some belong rather to the XIXth dynasty, as 144 222, 504. 120 was found with some beads clearly of the XIIth dynasty, so this might be early, but the evidence of the form is against it; more probably the beads were re-used from an earlier grave. A whole group from tomb 21 is photographed together, showing the variety of alabaster vases, the green pottery egg-shaped balls, ribbed rings of copper, and three strings of beads.

68. The pottery was abundant in the tombs, and all the varieties of forms have been drawn, in order to enable a study of the changes to be carried out, in connection with the tomb-groups. These are given on Pls. XXVII D to L; and as these appear in the double volume, the discussion of them must be taken in a later chapter.

Some special examples of pottery are shown in Pl. XXVII. The fish is of the very thin smooth light brown ware in which such animal figures of the XVIIIth dynasty are made. They are clearly of Greek origin in both the clay and the style; but the source of them has not yet been found. The piece of a pottery figure of a dog is probably northern in origin. The three vases below from tomb 20 give a dating for a type of Aegean pottery not hitherto found in Egypt. The neck is most like Cypriote forms, but the exact source is not certain. The double vase below is of a thin pottery with polished drab facing; and such a style belongs to the reign of Amenhotep III, and this certainly does not extend as much as a century on either side of that period. The Syrian flask at its side agrees with this age.

The pottery figure of a camel laden with water-jars was found in a tomb of the XIXth dynasty in the northern cemetery. There were no traces of a later re-use of the tomb; the style of the figure is of the rough fingered pottery of the XIXth dynasty, and quite unlike any of the moulded Roman figures; and the water-jar is of the XVIIIth—XIXth dynasty type and not of a form used in Greek or Roman times. Hence it is impossible to assign this to the age when the camel is familiar in Egypt, and it shows that as early as Ramesside times it was sufficiently common to be used as a beast of burden. Two examples of the camel's head at about the time of the Ist dynasty should be taken in connection with this (*Hierakonopolis*, lxii, mis-named a donkey, and *Abydos* ii, x, 224). Reference should be made to a memoir in the early history of the camel by M. Lefébure in the XIVth Oriental Congress, vol. ii. The main facts that he brings forward are: (1) a glazed figure of a camel with painted water jars, found at Benha, referred by Freiherr von Bissing to Ramesside age, while a date before the XXVIth dynasty is indicated by the black painting on the blue glaze; and (2) the use of camels in the Delta about 700 B.C. (*Student's History of Egypt*, iii, 323). Both of these examples belong to the Delta, and are probably later than the present example, which shows the camel in Upper Egypt about 1300 B.C.

In the graves of the XVIIIth dynasty were found dozens of rough Nile-mud models of vases, Pl. XXVII A. Those of grave 12 were with red and black line pottery, of the age of Tahutmes III; in grave 29 there was pottery with blue lines, of the close of the dynasty. Some of these imitate cups, others two-handled amphorae. Some are closed with caps of mud. In many there were remains of barley grain and barley mash; it seems then that they represented beer jars. It may also be noted that the use of the large conical bowls with a hole in the bottom is now explained. One contained a pressed cake of barley mash and grains; they were used then to squeeze out the fermented beer from the grain, the cake being sufficiently tenacious not to break through at the hole.

69. The large rock-tomb, No. ii, Pl. VIII, though obviously of the XIIth dynasty (sects. 25, 26), was re-used in the time of Ramessu III. The remains of scenes painted in black outline I copied as far as practicable, and issue here in Pls. XXVIII, XXIX, XXX. Unfortunately the bats have rendered all the upper part of the inscription illegible, and only a very long washing could possibly bring it to light again. At the extreme left is an altar piled with offerings;

before it are Amen, Hor-akhti, and Ptah. Then comes a figure of the deceased adoring the king, and supported by his servants. The attitudes of this group, which are known in other examples, suggest the paralyzing effect of the adoration of a Byzantine emperor, hinted by Gibbon, and elaborated by Scott in *Count Robert of Paris*. The connection with the previous figures is shown by the edge of the counterpoise of Ptah. In front is seen the baboon of Tahuti adored by the king; but these were figures carved and mounted on a portable stand, and probably they were made of wood and coloured or gilded. Beyond that is a table of offerings piled up with a vase, an incense-burner, cakes and flowers. Within a building appears Ramessu III in priestly dress performing sacrifice. The nature of the oval object before him cannot be distinguished, but it is painted red all over, and from being placed on an altar it seems as if it were the subject of sacrifice. Unfortunately no more of this curious scene is preserved; even much of what is drawn is invisible at first sight, owing to the roughness of the surface and the faintness of the lines.

70. Of this age may be noted some results from a field of chips on the desert at Gizeh, about a quarter of a mile south of the Ist dynasty tomb. This ground was turned over by us, and we found some limestone foundation-blocks of a building, some pits about ten feet deep filled with sand and rubbish, and many shabtis. Most of these were for private persons, some were for Kha-em-uas, the son of Ramessu II, and one of queen Nefertari-mery-mut. There were also the small model bronze hoes and baskets, such as were found with shabtis similarly scattered on the Heq-reshu hill at Abydos (*Royal Tombs* i, 33). It must not be concluded that because shabtis, and it is said also a canopic jar, were found here, that therefore Kha-em-uas was buried here, as has been supposed (Maspero, *Struggle of the Nations*, 426): similar shabtis and a jar made by Kha-em-uas were found along with the Apis burials at the Serapeum. In turning over all the ground down to native soil we did not find any trace of a great tomb pit, such as would be made for so important a burial, nor is it at all likely that in the XIXth dynasty a royal tomb would be made on the flat plain of the desert edge. It seems rather that this was a place of deposit of shabtis and funeral articles, like the Heq-reshu hill. I carefully looked over the low hills above it to see if there were any trace of a great tomb behind, which would account for the devotion to such a spot, but nothing could be discovered.

CHAPTER IX

THE CLASSIFICATION OF POTTERY.

71. THE groups of pottery of the IXth to XIIth dynasties, from graves at Rifeh, are hardly sufficient in number, or large enough, to form a sequence of types. But they are a better series than those of Dendereh, which have so far been our best material for this age. So they are here arranged in the best sequence that can be traced, Pls. XIII A—D; and with the open forms on the left, and the closed-in forms on the right. The best general clue that we have is the degradation of the libation vase, Nos. 4, 5, 29, 30, 32, 33, 39, 42, 47, 75–78, 83, 89, 108–9, 135–6, 138, 143, 153, 161. There are examples of the VIth and XIth dynasties (*Dendereh*, xvi, 5–7; xvii, 124) showing degradation; and though small differences may well have been local, yet if we take one site alone it is probable that the degradation will give a fair clue to the order. As a first step, therefore, we arrange these.

Pl. XIII A. The tall cups 3, 8, 13, 19 are found with the best libation type, and so come at the beginning. These carry with them the forms in the same groups, distinguished by the written numbers at the lower corner. In order to indicate the various forms found together, the right and left ends of each group have small arrows pointing to the rest of the group. The wide vase with white spots dabbed on by the finger, No. 20, in group 104, is shown to be early by the cup, 19. This carries with it the date of Nos. 24 and 25. The cups are allied to the bowls Nos. 23, 26, and hence group 85 is early.

The references with H refer to the numbers of the soul-houses; for instance, Nos. 28–30 are H·100, found with the house 100, which is at the bottom of Pl. XV. Hence another means of classifying comes in by the connection with the types of the houses; and though the types were to some extent contemporary, yet as a whole they followed from A to N in order of time. To aid in following this connection, all pottery found with soul-houses has the letter of the class of house put opposite to it at the left margin, with the reference to the house number. Thus on Pl. XIII A at the left margin there is B, the class of the soul-house, and the reference to H·100, where on the same level are three vases found with house 100.

Nos. 34, 35 are hollow pottery objects without any openings; they seem to have been the stoppers for libation jars, completing the form as it is represented in drawings. The age is only suggested by the resemblance of No. 36 to 21. Nos. 37, 38 are connected to similar scraped pottery of the early XIth dynasty (or before) at Dendereh.

72. Pl. XIII B. The group 54, Nos. 43–49, shows the relation of the libation type to the Kheti vase No. 54. And this gives some indication of age; as the Kheti coffin, Pl. IX, is more like those of the VIth than of the XIIth dynasty (*Deshasheh* xxviii, xxix), and yet by the name it cannot be before the IXth dynasty. Probably early in the Xth dynasty is the earliest date to assign to it. And this seems to be the age of the commonest type of soul-house, E. The group 310 is only placed by the resemblance of Nos. 51, 61, 62. No. 500 is used for any isolated pottery from the rock tombs, and only implies a locality and not a single group. No. 70, though found with H·146 of type L, is also found in group 323, which joins to type E with No. 79; hence it only implies that No. 70 is a common form which runs through from E to L.

Pl. XIII C. The round-bottomed bowl seems to begin at this point; and it afterwards deepened into the cup 117, 184, which passed on to the XIII–XVIth dynasties, see Pls. XXV, XXVI. The groups are placed partly by the libation types, and with some regard to the house type. The carnelian button, No. 105, is a very rare object; a broken one of the same form was also found, and I have bought studs of carnelian. This may be an Egyptian development of the earlier carved buttons of foreign origin. The wavy outlines vases, 110, 115, 121–2, are linked to a good form of libation vase, 108; but as that is found with the latest type of soul-house, M, it cannot be placed earlier. The round pot No. 123 is of thin red ware, unlike most of the others of this form, which are of soft brown pottery. No. 139 is a form which lasted long; it occurs with the early group 6 to 10, and here with No. 138, a later form, and a house of type H. The bottle forms 144–5 are associated with a debased type of libation vase, 142.

73. Pl. XIII D. The pottery stands, for libation jars, 154, 167, Pl. XI A, are common at one period, and they must belong to the debased shape with a pointed base and no widening to a foot. With this shape 153 goes a curious cylinder jar with a splay mouth, 152, 158. This, in turn, goes with the bulging pot with holes around the neck, 162. And in 155 B this is found with a house of type L. These links thus all agree in age. The scrabble pattern on 170 and 181, the fanciful addition of vaselets, 168, and of animals on the brim, 171, Pl. XI A, the roll out of the lips, 180, 191, 193–4, 196, 298, all seem to belong to the later developments of the XIIth dynasty.

74. The pottery of the XVIIIth dynasty is very abundant at Rifeh, and larger series were obtained from some of the tombs than are often to be seen. As over 400 drawings were made, registering over 600 pots (besides duplicates in one tomb), this is a good opportunity to attempt a separation into periods. The ground that we have for classing this pottery is a group of 10 forms dated by a ring of Hatshepsut, and two groups of over 30 forms which give a very large body of types clearly rather earlier than the Hatshepsut group. From outside sources there are the published groups before Tahutmes III (*Hyksos and Israelite Cities*, xii A), of Tahutmes III (*Illahun*, xxvii; *Hyk. Cit.*, xii B, C, D), of Amenhotep II (*Six Temples*, v; *Hyk. Cit.* xiii), and of Tahutmes IV (*Six Temples*, vii). Unfortunately there is no large body of Amenhotep III or later, but only a few small vases in *Illahun*, xvii, xviii, xix; nor has any been published of the excellently dated pottery of Hatshepsut from Deir el Bahri.

Starting with the large series from tombs 21, 22, which are clearly contemporary and before Hatshepsut, all the other tomb-groups were sorted in relation to these statistically; and any group which had links with 21, 22 was examined whether any forms would carry it later to the Hatshepsut age. All that seemed earlier were then put together and form the *corpus* of pottery down to Tahutmes I, Pls. XXVII, D, E, F, G. Probably this extends from the late XVIIth dynasty onward, but we cannot yet separate the earlier stages. The next section was made of all groups which seemed contemporary with Hatshepsut and with Tahutmes III, but before Amenhotep II. As a general rule it may be said that none of the forms hold together well after Tahutmes III; the necks are too long, the lower parts too bulging, as may be seen on comparing 331 with 358, 248–255 with 349 to 354. But we cannot discriminate the close of the Tahutmes IV period: only what seem later forms are put together at the end, 406 to 429.

The colouring is a useful guide to age. The red and black lines are all as early as Tahutmes III, and the use of black line by itself disappears later. The red colour is shown here by vertical shade, see 66,

141, 165, 169, 170, 296. Blue has not yet been certainly dated before Amenhotep II, but in one case here it seems that it must be as early as Tahutmes III on the vase 296, as so many as 18 forms not later than Tahutmes III were found with it. In form 404 the evidence is strong for the tomb 240 being as early as Tahutmes III (see 12, 27, 67), and if so a free use of blue arose in this reign. Yet as a mixture of two dates in one tomb is not impossible once in some hundreds of cases, we cannot be certain of this point. The red polished face is very usual down to Tahutmes I, and is marked "red" on the plates. It may just reach into the time of Tahutmes III, though it is possible that groups 5, 205, 209, in which it occurs, are really before his age. The red face on the foreign long flasks 314–6 is quite different. The polished drab facing used characteristically on the forms 308, 374, 391, 413 belongs probably to Amenhotep III, but may be earlier.

75. The pottery may serve as a guide to the age of the other things found in the tombs. The wooden head-rests are of Tahutmes I and III. The figures of girls on couches, tombs 162, 211, of Tahutmes I. The plaster faces which were stuck on the outside of mummy wrappings are of Tahutmes I and III. The clay models of vases, Pl. XXVII A, are mostly of Amenhotep II, but one group is early and one late. The ushabtis, Pl. XXVII C, I much hoped to be able to date, as the styles of badness vary greatly. But in the first place it was seen that a great variety of styles were usually found together, limestone, pottery, all sizes and shapes. And, on looking to the dates, they belong indiscriminately to Tahutmes I and III. Taking them in the order on the plate, XXVII C, 303, 211, 223 are of Tahutmes I; 242, 151, 226 of Tahutmes III; and 173, 175 are late. We must suppose that many different makers had each traditional patterns, and that the stocks were pooled by dealers, and purchasers selected some of each style so as to suit the *ka* in any case. It is difficult to imagine any other causes which could produce similar mixed lots in different reigns. The alabaster vases on Pl. XXVII A of Tahutmes I, 147, 22, 176, 2, 26, 21, 161, 21 group below, show fairly good forms of kohl pot, rather sharp in the shoulder. Those of Tahutmes III are 8, 140, 242, 144, 222, 242, 120; including the two large pear-shaped vases, the figure bearing a jar, the jug with handle, and one very flat kohl pot; altogether the vases are commoner than the kohl pots. Of the Amenhotep II age are the banded dish 262, the decayed kohl pot below it, 257, and the coarse cylinder, 257, with a braid pattern up the side, from the same tomb; while probably later are the small pot, 13, and the tall jar neck, 175. The resemblance of the style of the small beads in group 21, to those of the XIIth dynasty, shows how the early style of things had not yet passed away under Tahutmes I.

The index page, Pl. XVII M, serves to show all the forms found in each tomb; the references are placed in columns, according to the date given to the plates. Thus in Tomb 1 were found six forms which are drawn in the earliest group of plates, three belonging to the Tahutmes III group, and two of later age. These were probably all contemporary, the forms continuing in use across several reigns; but they have been here classed according to their general connections with other dateable forms. The tomb is probably of the age of Tahutmes III, and hence the numbers in that column are underlined.

76. We may here note some minor matters which are additional to the preceding chapters.

A very finely drawn fragment of a painted coffin found in one of the rock tombs of the XIIth dynasty shows minute red lines dividing the spaces for the hieroglyphs. As some of these spaces are equal, and they bear relations one to another, it is evident that they were set off from a measuring scale. The actual measurements from one end are 0, 1·04, 1·32, 2·085, 2·878, 3·142, 3·940, 4·200, 5·756, 6·032, 6·640, 6·860, 7·940, 8·232, 9·794, 10·026 inches. And among these we find intervals as follow: 1·558, 1·556, 1·562; 1·04, 1·045, 1·077, 1·058, 2·660, 1·080, 2·086; ·280, ·264, ·260, ·276, ·220, ·292, ·232. These average 1·559, 1·055, ·260, which are evidently in proportion of 6, 4, and 1. The unit intervals are far more irregular than the others. By the lengths of 1·559 the unit is ·2598; by those of 1·055 the unit is ·2639, or by the whole ·2650. Four of this unit as used here, or 1·04, is obviously the decimal division of the cubit. And the cubit, from these different values of the unit, will be 20·78, 21·11, or 21·20. As the 20·78 is derived from the most accurately marked spaces, and is nearer the normal cubit, we should accept 20·8 as the cubit here, with some variation higher, and divided into 80ths. The decimal division of the cubit is known elsewhere (see *Pyramids and Temples*, 180), but is a rare form.

77. A few additions should be made to earlier pages here, partly in consequence of the double volume plates not having been prepared before the earlier text was printed.

On p. 12 the great tomb group of Nekht-ankh is not only published in the Pls. X A to X E there referred to, but all the inscriptions are given on Pls. XIII F, XIII G, XIII H. These copies are not facsimiles, but hand-copies retaining the general style and the detail of the signs. The degree of exactitude may be seen on comparing the photographs on Pls. X A, X B with the copies. On the coffin plates the lid is placed at the top; and the letters put at the top corners of the sides show how they join up. On Pl. XIII H the lid of the canopic box is above; the jars are lettered with initials of the four genii, and the corners of the box in which they were found bear the same letter. It will be seen that they were not put in quite regularly. Amset and Hapy should have been exchanged in order to be next to the names as written on the outside of the box. Along with the jar of Kebhsenuf was a flat lump of embalmed material in the division; each jar also contained embalmed viscera, which will be examined in future. The whole tomb-group is now in the University Museum, Manchester. In the account (p. 12) note that on Pl. X B the body coffins have been transposed by the printer, hence that of Nekht-ankh is the first and not the second. Also, the statuette in the priest's coffin was the middle one on Pl. X E, and not that with a wig.

Some further references may be given. On p. 7 the plans of the tomb with sealings of Neteren is on Pl. VI B; the drawings of the vases from that tomb on Pls. VI C, D, E. On p. 9 some small stone altars are here published on Pl. VII D. The Pls. V A, B, C, D, were partly drawn by Mr. and Mrs. Firth, the tomb numbers being entered in the bottom left-hand corners of each figure; and partly by myself, with tomb numbers in the right-hand corners.

78. A piece of hieratic papyrus was found in one of the graves of the northern cemetery at Rifeh. Mr. Alan Gardiner has studied it, and favoured me with the following translation and account.

The fragmentary papyrus ($6\frac{1}{2} \times 4\frac{1}{2}$ inches) from tomb 120 is given in transcription on Pl. XXVII O; the hand is a literary one of the ordinary Ramesside type, and in spite of the differing contents of the *recto* and *verso*, is due to one and the same scribe. The *recto* starts thus: "Beginning of the Instructions given by the hereditary priest Neter[mer, the mouth that pleases in (?)[1]] the entire land, the *sem*-priest in charge of [all] *shento*-loincloths, . . . (the name is lost). [He spoke] to his children: I tell what I have pondered over (?); hearken [ye] . . . for (to do so) brings to revered old age." The promise of this exordium is hardly fulfilled by the very ordinary hymn to a solar deity with its hackneyed phraseology, that follows:—" Praise to . . . in the course of the day Rejoicing is created for him . . all people (?). He is Re, by [whose (?)] guidance men live. . . . his rays, making himself brighter than the sun's disk.[2] Burning . . . when the Nile is great. He filleth the two lands with nourishment . . . his setting. Men breathe in his breezes. He giveth to him who is < under > his guidance. . . . His [worshippers (?)] become possessors of pleasant things (?), those who rebel against him become without . . . his foes. His strength fighteth for him. His terror . . . are established and praise his beauty . . . praise is given to him. His enemies are under . . ." Here the text breaks off. It should be noted that the restoration marked (1), which I owe to the kindness of Professor Sethe, presupposes some corruptions in the second line. The entire titulary is that borne *e.g.* by the vizier of Thutmosis III, Rekhmere. The phrase marked (2), strange as it may seem in a hymn to the sun-god, seems to be the only translation possible.

The *verso* contains part of a magical book, and is interesting for its similarity to a better preserved text in Turin (*Pleyte-Rossi* 120-1). Superstition regards the world as haunted by a multitude of malign influences ever ready to pounce down upon and overmaster the unwary. The nature of the danger at hand being unknown, Magic has to provide against all contingencies by an explicitness of language comparable only to that of Law. The charm before us is intended to safeguard him who uses it against death; it is not sufficient however to refer to death in general, but each particular manner of death that may befall a man has to be separately specified. After an incomprehensible title the text appears to contain an invocation to "[all] enemies [male and female] . . . who might bend over < N the son of M > to do all things [bad and evil against him]. In the fourth line there is a reference to the "pestilences of the year" elsewhere connected with the goddess Sekhmet, and then comes the list of special kinds of death against which the charm affords protection. Among them we find "death by his urine," "death by thirst," "by the meat of cattle," "by entering in from without," "by arrows," "by falling," and "by beer." The continuation is lost, but probably consisted of threats directed against these evil influences.

CHAPTER X

THE SAITE AND LATER PERIODS.

79. At nearly a mile south of the great pyramid at Gizeh, on the southward slope of the hill, I saw a great quantity of stone chips. Large spaces which we cleared only showed rubble-core masonry, until the chambers were struck further up the hill. Gradually the large funeral chapel of Thary was uncovered, of which the plan is given in Pl. XXXVII. The walls, now destroyed, are marked in dotted outline. Of the north chamber, the roof still remains; the east, mid, and west chambers are unroofed, but complete to the full height of the walls; the south hall has only the lower part of the walls left, at the inner end. The north chamber was the first found, and on reporting it to Prof. Maspero in Upper Egypt, he ordered it to be removed to the Museum; but as the work went on, so much more was found, that it seemed needful to settle on the spot whether any of it was to be packed for export. As it was supposed that if the perfect east chamber was kept in Cairo, the broken and less perfect walls would be allowed to leave Egypt, I only copied the east chamber entirely, and left the rest to be completely done after removal. Mr. and Mrs. Firth copied the figures and some of the inscriptions, but the whole needed me to give several days to finish it completely. To stay on at Gizeh was impossible to me, as I had to organize the work of a hundred men at Rifeh, and could not keep them idle. At the close of the season Prof. Maspero decided to leave the entire building on the ground and rebury it. As I could not then stop to copy more, I have had to complete the copies as far as I can by photographs; and I have to thank Mr. Quibell for taking eight views which were of much help, combined with the fifteen that I had already taken. It is needful to state exactly what are the sources for the plates here published: Mr. and Mrs. Firth's parts are named F, and my own P. Plates XXXIII—V, all figures, F; all inscriptions facsimile, P. XXXVI, figures, F: inscription P written from rough copy, not facsimile, P. XXXVI B, north wall, F; east wall, and south wall, all F, except eight columns before Osiris, from a photograph, P. XXXVI C all F. XXXVI D all F. XXXVI E all F. XXXVI F all F, except east wall, upper half of four columns; south wall, upper half of four columns; and mid of right-hand columns, which were drawn thinner, of the actual size of the signs, P. XXXVI G, all figures, F; all inscriptions from photographs, P. All of the joining and ruling in of dividing lines was done in England, P.

The persons named in the tomb are (1) Thary, chief of the house of provisions, or commissary-general; (2) his first wife Ta-remthetu-en-Bastet, and (3) his son by her, Psemthek; (4) his second wife Ta-du-hor, and (5) his son by her, Gem-ef-ast-sep ("He seeks the chosen place"). The parentage of Thary was (6) his father Gem-ef-ast-kep ("He seeks the hidden place"), and (7) his mother Ta-du-hor; (8) his father's father Thary, devoted to Neit of Sais, whose (9) mother was Ta-sheb-en-neit. By the type of the names the tomb is early in the XXVIth dynasty. The family seem to have belonged to Sais at first, and then Thary added a great devotion to Sebek and Horus of the Fayum, probably from owning estates of his mother or first wife. His younger son continued the Saite connection.

In the plates there is one continuous band of inscription round the top of the east chamber in XXXIII—XXXVI. Titles and filiations are clear enough in these plates, and the demand to the guardians of each of the seven gates that Thary should enter. In XXXVI A are shown parts of the south hall, delicately carved with harpers and singers copied from some tomb of the Vth dynasty, quite different in style to the usual coarse work of the rest. In XXXVI B is the top of the wall already given in XXXVI; and the scenes of the east wall, east side of door and east jamb of door, of the north chamber. The back of the north chamber is in Pl. XXXVI C. It has the winged globe over the group of gods, short titles of the gods, and a pattern of tied lotus flowers painted underneath. On the same plate is the pair of figures of Thary and wife which are at the end of the long hall, and before which were doubtless figures of the family servants and offerers. The west chamber begins in Pl. XXXVI D. The band of inscription of larger size runs round the whole, in plates D, E, F. The walls are occupied with fifteen gates of Hades, with their guardians. The two curved wall-heads show the embalming of the mummy by Anubis, Isis and Nebhat, and the sisters protecting it afterwards. Pl. XXXVI G contains four narrow scenes. The reveals of the door of the west chamber seem to have borne figures of Thary and his wife Ta-du-hor. The north one is destroyed, but the south one shows "his wife Ta-hor"; and this would be parallel to the east chamber bearing the elder

Thary and his wife Ta-sheb-en-neit. In the mid hall the east and west sides are destroyed in the north part, but in the south part are the two walls divided in three registers, with the weighing of the soul, the hippopotamus, adoration of Seb and of Apis, offerings to the bark of Sokar, and adorations to Osiris and Isis. The part of the south wall which remains has two figures of Thary. The faces of the door-posts bear single bands of the titles and name of Thary. The only parts not copied are the north end of the south wall, and north side of the mid hall, which contain columns of inscriptions of names and titles.

80. The later burials at Gizeh yielded very little that was worth note, although a large number of tombs were opened, and we collected about 1,400 skulls of about 600—300 B.C., which are now at University College, London, for study in Prof. Karl Pearson's department. Four small glazed vases were found, probably Persian or Ptolemaic, and an ebony spoon handle ending in a duck's head, with a monkey seated upon it. Many amulets were scattered about, but groups were rare, and the best set is in Pl. XXXI, probably of the Persian period. Many triple coffins were found, mostly much decayed and broken. The best of them are given in Pls. XXXI, XXXI A, XXXI B, XXXVII A. In these are (1) the box coffin with corner posts only inscribed in one line down the top; (2) the inner box coffin with cornice, of which top and side views are given; (3) the body coffin. The inscriptions are copies made without discretion, the name of the deceased never being included. An interesting part of the formula on XXXI A and B is the burial being said to be "in the desert of Heliopolis," showing (as Prof. Maspero pointed out) that Gizeh was included in the Heliopolite nome. On XXXI A the personal name has been written on each of the three cases with black ink, and the copies are given on Pl. XXXVIII B. They record Amen-rekh-su, daughter of Zedher.

Two sets of limestone canopic jars were found in one tomb, Pls. XXXI A, B. One set stood in a row along the side of a chamber, in the order Hapy, Kebhsenuf, Duamutef, Amset. The other set had the first two on the south side, and then the second two on the north, in the same order. The pit was just to the north of the Neteren tomb on the top of the hill.

Among the shabtis found were very few of any consequence; most were uninscribed. The best was one of pea-green stoneware for Ba-hotep-ur; see Pl. XXXVII A.

To the south, in the plain, a crypt chapel was found of Roman age, with painted patterns on the limestone walls; see Pl. XXXVII A. There had been dwarf columns at the foot of the stair leading down to it, and a brick vaulted roof.

In the cemetery some tombs full of animals' skeletons were found. All the skulls in good state were preserved, and sent to the British Museum (Natural History). Mr. Oldfield Thomas has kindly given the following report upon them: "The skulls form a wonderfully fine set, which will no doubt prove of great value when some one arises with time and taste to work out such things in detail. I never saw so fine a series before. There are 192 cats' skulls, mostly *Felis ocreata*, but no doubt some are *F. chaus*. They are, however, a wonderfully varying lot, and would require much work for every one to be certainly and exactly determined. One might believe that the Ancient Egyptians had as many different kinds as we have now. Also 7 mongoose skulls (*Mungos ichneumon*), 3 wild-dog (*Canis lupaster*), and 1 fox (*Vulpes famelica*)."

81. Scattered in the cemetery at Gizeh were three demotic inscriptions, given on Pl. XXXVII A. The first and second are in Manchester, the third in Cairo. Sir Herbert Thompson has kindly translated them as follows:

1. *Wḥ-mw pr Wsr nb ko* (or *kn*) *p.te.Wsr s p.te.Hr.sm.to.* "The choachytes of the house of Osiris, lord of Kes (?), Pete-wsir (Petosiris), son of Pete-Hor-sam-to (Petearsemtheus)."

2. *Wḥ-mw ʿnkh-ḥp | mwt-f* (?) *t-trsh ḥnʿ ʿnkh-hp s p-te* (?) *-ḥp | hnʿ Ḥr . . . s Ḥr-p-rʿ* (?). "The choachytes Ankh-apis, his mother (?) (being) Tetersh (?), together with Ankh-apis, son of Pete-apis (?), and Horus, son of *Hor-p-ra* (?) (Harprês)."

3. *Wḥ-mw n pr-Wsr-nb-rst | pʾ-to s p-te-Wsr | wḥ-mw pr skh . . . s p-te-Wsr | s-ḥmt* (?) *Wḥ-mw tʾ-Mn tʾ-khnt* (?)*-ḥtp* (?). "The choachytes of the house of Osiris, lord of Rustau, Pato (Patous), son of Pete-wsir (Petosiris), the choachytes P-sekh . . . . . son of Pete-wsir (Petosrisis), the female (?) choachytes Ta-min (Taminis), daughter of Khent-hotep (?)."

From the absence of any funeral formula, these can hardly be gravestones; and as all record the names of choachytes and of partnerships of choachytes, it seems that these are the marks for the districts of the cemetery where certain firms of undertakers had the right of burying.

82. At Rifeh some cartonnages made up of papyri were found. I damped, opened, and cleaned them;

and then the Greek were submitted to Drs. Mahaffy and Smyly, and the demotic to Sir Herbert Thompson. On the latter a long report will be found in the next chapter. The Greek papyri are thus reported on by Dr. Smyly. "Among the most interesting are (1) Part of a copy of a letter explaining apparent oversights in a survey of land and crops in the neighbourhood of Lycopolis; due partly to a disturbance called *η Χαουνωφριος ταραχη*, in which most of the people were destroyed, and the land went out of cultivation, followed by a direction (very imperfectly preserved) to the officials as to the proper course to pursue.

"(2) A fragmentary petition from Petephois (Pedu-upuat), a taricheutes, which refers to the 34th year (of Philometor or Euergetes II).

"(3) Part of an oath, dated in the 27th year of Euergetes II. This date mentions both the Macedonian and Egyptian months, and is in accordance with the earlier identification of the two calendars: it is the latest date upon this system which has been discovered.

"(4) Fragments of a petition which refers to the Lycopolite nome, Lycopolis and a village called *Αραβων κωμη*.

"There are also numerous fragments of accounts, public and private; but none of them is well preserved or of much interest. I should, on palaeographic grounds, assign all these papyri to the middle of the 2nd century B.C."

83. The Coptic monasteries of Balyzeh and Ganadleh occupied much of the work of the season. A large part of the ruins at Balyzeh were completely turned over, but at Ganadleh only a short sampling was made, and enough remains there for many weeks of work. On Pl. XXXVII B are first some legs of Roman furniture from chairs and couches that were broken up and buried in the entrances to tombs at Rifeh. Next is a stone door-jamb with fret pattern, and a line of foliage scroll down the bevelled edge. Below is the upper part of a tombstone, with a large cross and border; under that a tombstone of Moses, who died on the 7th of Thoth, in the 4th indiction. Beside that are parts of two tombstones, with architectural design of an arch upon pillars. All of these are from Rifeh, a small cemetery lying south of that of the XVIIIth dynasty.

Down the outer edge of the plate are four stones from Balyzeh, in a curious geometrical style of figure, without any inscriptions.

In Pl. XXXVIII, fig. 1, is a brass lamp, which is perfectly fresh, as if just made; yet it was found in a linen bag crumbling with age, and as all dateable objects there are of the eighth century, this is probably as old. 2 is a small capital, of native Coptic work, while 3 is of purely late Roman style. 4 is part of a stone screen slab. 5 is a piece of cornice of late Greek style, like the early Christian work of South Italy and Sicily. 6 is of the same family, but somewhat degraded. 7 are pieces of a large cornice, brightly painted with red, yellow, and purple; the four blocks found are lettered on the back to show their order in building. The large cross stone 8 has much the character of manuscript decoration. This and the three following were found in the ruins of the church, and seem to have been memorial stones, perhaps of the builders of different parts, as they are neither funereal nor refer to the dead. The architectural design of 10 is an interesting motive, different in style from any others here. 12 is a thick, heavy, steel knife with flat end. It is engraved with a cross and four doves on one side, and four crosses in an arabesque on the other. The handle is of wood, with a very deep ferrule at each end, and ornamental cross-headed nails set in the butt.

The views in Pl. XXXVIII A show the picturesque position of the Deir. The plateau from which the distant view is taken is about a hundred feet over the Nile valley. A deep ravine runs up at the left hand, and old quarries were cut running through the ridge of hill and opening into the ravine. In these quarries the Copts took refuge; and then built out a town of brick in front during later times. This town, begun about 650 A.D., was deserted by about 800 A.D. Four silver dirhems found in different parts bear dates A.H. 100 of Omar, 133 of Es Saffah, 142 of El Mansur, and 192 of Er Rashid, or of 719, 751, 769, and 808 A.D. The manuscripts show the same age, as Mr. Crum finds the names of Abd el Aziz ibn Merwan 685 A.D., Qurrah ibn Sharyk of 710 A.D., 'Ubaydallah ibn el Habhab 724 A.D., and Al Qasym ibn 'Ubaydallah of 730 A.D. And there are no manuscripts of which the writing would suggest later dates. Hence the whole history of the place seems limited to little over a century and a half after the Arab conquest. This small range of date makes all the sculpture here of value for comparative dating.

The manuscripts found here are described by Mr. Crum in Chapter XII; a leaf of the finest writing, of the IXth chapter of the Epistle to the Hebrews, is given on the plate. The underlinings are in red ink, and the parchment is remarkably thin and fine.

A leather case was found, containing five large needles, two nails, two staples, and a knife, which is inscribed as monastic property of Saint Apollo, "Ap-apollo." The details of these needles can be better seen in the drawings on the next plate.

On Pl. XXXVIII A are also three views. At Zowyeh, between Rifeh and Balyzeh (see Pl. VIII), there is a large four-square fortified Coptic village, which I have called Deir Zowyeh for distinction. The photograph shows the ornamental brickwork round the upper part of the wall. The ground to the west is deeply covered with late Roman pot-sherds; so it is clear that this is an early Christian settlement. It was probably a branch from this that built the Coptic houses high up in the valley mouth, by the VIth dynasty cemetery.

On the map will be seen a hut marked on the crest of the hill. This is photographed on the plate. It is on the highest point, and yet the door is turned away from the valley, so that it does not command a look-out view. The age is perhaps the same as that of several cleared roads near it, one of which is on the plate at the side of the hut. These roads lead to nowhere. They cannot have been parts of a long track, and their purpose and age are quite unknown. Possibly there was a prehistoric settlement of mat huts on the hill top. Certainly, as no potsherds are found there, we can hardly date the works to Roman or historic times.

CHAPTER XI

THE DEMOTIC PAPYRI

By Sir Herbert Thompson

84. The demotic papyri consist of about eighty fragments, all derived from mummy cartonnages found at Rifeh. Of these nine are probably of a literary nature, seven of them forming part originally of one document; they yield no consecutive meaning, but from the words that occur in them most likely they formed part of an historical romance. The remaining papyri are all of a legal or business nature. From their character it seems likely that most of them are derived from the archives of some temple. The longest document of all (E 1) is probably a list of dependents on a temple. The next in point of size (B 2) is a conveyance of land by a body of men, probably priests. There is a contract to embalm and perform liturgies (B 3), and a fragment of a temple regulation as to vestments (C D *2b*). A considerable number of papyri relate to the rental or taxation of land, the charge on it being expressed in artabas of wheat (A 1–5, B 10*c*, E 11, 13, F 1). One of the most interesting is a list of holders of crown land with the amount of their rents (E 3).

As far as one can tell, the papyri are all of local origin, except the literary fragments, as to which nothing can be said. The name of Shas-hotep (of which Rifeh was the necropolis) occurs in B 2, E 3, and E 8, and local god Khnum furnishes an element to a majority of the names. On the other hand, the neighbouring city of Siut is not mentioned, nor its god Upuat.

The only piece fully dated is the conveyance (B 2) of the 28th year of Philometor (153 B.C.). But as another fragment in the same group is certainly of the same reign, while two more refer to the 28th year and one other to the 26th year, there is little doubt that the "B" group all date from about the middle of the 2nd cent. B.C. In E, the next most important group, we have references to the years 27, 28, 33, and 35, which point to the same time, and this is confirmed by the fact that the names of two persons in E 6 and E 7 are found also in B 1. In fact there is no reason for removing any of the fragments from the latter half of the reign of Philometor or a little later.

Perhaps the most striking fact in these papyri which are written in the native language is the prevalence of Greek names; and moreover genuine Greek names, such as Lycophron, Andronicus, Aristodemus, etc., rather than names of the type of Ammonius, Apollonius, Hermias, etc., which abounded in Egypt, and always raise a suspicion that they hide an Egyptian originally named after Amon, Horus, or Thoth. The document E 3 also points to the settlement of a considerable body of cleruchs at Shas-hotep.

85. A 1–5. Small fragments of a rental register (?), in which parcels of land, expressed in aruras, are placed side by side with amounts of corn expressed in artabas. The ratio is not a consistent one, varying from about 3 to 7 artabas per arura.

86. B 1. Consists of 2 whole columns and fragments of two others. It is a register of names, mostly Greek, with sums of money attached, frequently with the addition of *n-tṭ Pte-ʾS.t* "from (?) Peteesis," implying payment through some official (?). Of 3 amounts it is stated that Senesis (a woman) paid them in; of 3 others that Aias (son of) Senesis paid

them in. It is probably a banker's account. One of the names, Dositheos, son of Nikaios, is also found in a similar account E 6; but the handwritings of the 2 MSS. are not the same. Another name, *wyrhn* son of Petechous, occurs also in a similar account E 7. (*wyrhn* represents a foreign name; possibly an eccentric spelling of Herôn.)

B 2. recto. Fragments of a conveyance of real property of which the two contracts, viz. (A) agreement for sale, and (B) the cession are on the same papyrus. They are dated Epiphi 10 in the 28th year of Philometor (Aug. 5, 153 B.C.). The protocol enumerates the priesthoods both of Alexandria and Ptolemais, but gives no priests' names; in one or two particulars it does not follow the normal form (see translation and notes). The property conveyed consists of some waste-land (ψιλὸς τόπος), qualified as *bk* (meaning doubtful), near the necropolis of Shashotep (Rîfeh). The vendors are numerous, and were probably members of a corporation connected with the cult of the gods Euergetai, Philopatores, Epiphaneis, and Philometores (prob. a local dynastic cult). Nine of them are indicated, though the names of two are missing, viz:

1, 2. Setyrbon and his brother . . . . . , sons of Harmonthes and Shmety.

3, 4, 5. . . . . Khnum, ... , and Petekhnum, 3 sons of Menapis and Senapis.

6. Khnum, son of Psen-p-Khroou and Tabekis.

7. Thoth, son of Setyrbon and Shmety.

8. Khnumortais, son of Psen-p-Khroou and Triphis.

9. Harpaesis, son of Pete-Khnum and T . . . . . .

The name of the vendee a (single male person) is lost.

B 2. verso. Fragments of a banker's (?) account. Fragments of 5 columns, one headed "year 28," consisting of names and sums of money, several preceded by what seem to be technical terms of banking, *a te* ("paid in"), *a 'n* ("taken out" (?)), *ššt* (?) ("delayed payment" or sim. *cf.* Griffith, Rylands' pap. pp. 165, 292).

B 3. Fragment of which probably only about half lines remain. Apparently part of a contract to embalm and perform liturgies for a deceased person —dated 16 Mesore of the 28th year of the reigning sovereigns (no doubt Philometor and Cleopatra II), see translation.

B 4. Various fragments relating to land measurement, set out in a form more or less similar to the Greek documents (B.M. no. 267 Kenyon, Gk. pap. II, 129; pap. Tebt. no. 87).

They are very much abbreviated, and the details beyond the figures do not admit of decipherment at present.

B 5. A list of landholders—all male names and mostly foreign—followed by the amount of land in aruras held by each, and the rent in artabas of corn. In two instances col. *a*. 7, 9 we have the rent also given, thus: "aruras 20 artabas 6 = artabas 120" and "aruras 5 artabas $2\frac{1}{2}$ = artabas $12\frac{1}{2}$," which shows that it is a question of either a rent or a tax on land; but usually only the amount of land is given—they are all small lots varying from $1\frac{3}{8}$ arura to $25\frac{5}{8}$ aruras generally with a fraction—followed by the total of artabas payable, and the rent works out at a very variable amount per arura, from $1\frac{1}{5}$ art. to $8\frac{2}{3}$. If it were a tax, it would be much more likely to be uniform; hence it is probably rent calculated in each instance in relation to the quality of the ground, etc.

B 7. A fragment of an account, which is obscure and tantalising. It is concerned with ibises, hawks, and other animals (?), all determined with the divine determinative, on account of which payments in fluid measure (loḳ = κεραμια) are made to certain persons. The other animals (?) named are *hte* (? ϩⲟⲉⲓⲧⲉ, hyaena, a feminine word; it might be read *hbe*, but is written differently from *hb* "ibis" which is also masculine), and an incomplete word which suggests *ιιn* "ape" or *ιḥm* "eagle." A suggestive circumstance in connection with the divine (?) ibises is that the name *P-wr-ty* occurs 3 times. It means "Great of Five," and was the title of the high priest of Thoth at Hermopolis. On the other hand, it was a not uncommon proper name (= Gk. πορτις), and is found as such in these papyri, viz. B 2 verso and B 5, as well as here.

See translation.

B 8*a*. Fragment of protocol of contract of the time of Philometor.

B 9. Small fragments containing (*a*) a reckoning of artabas, (γ) prob. a fragment of a contract, (δ) a fragment dealing with land measurement, (ε) a list of names, all Egyptian.

B 10. Similar fragments.

B 11. recto and verso. Accounts of payments of corn, paid on stated days of the month to individuals or for certain purposes. The "fullers" are named and (3 times) the "temple-service" (? ⲟⲩⲱϣϣⲧ "worship"), the "year 26" is mentioned.

87. C, D, 1 *a*. Small fragment of a contract (?) mentioning the "treasury of the temple" and "the priests of the five orders."

1 *b* mentions also the "five orders" and the "gods Adelphoi, Euergetai, and Philopatores."

1 *c* mentions the "business of the priests," the "gods Philopatores," "gods Epiphaneis," and includes the phrase "until the year 26."

1 *d* is clearly of the same nature.

C, D, 2 *b*. Fragment of a document connected with temple-vestments (see translation).

C, D, 3–12. Fragments, some uncertain, the rest unimportant, lists of names, etc.

88. E. 1 is the largest papyrus containing 19 columns, of which only two are complete. These two (*m*, *n*) contain respectively 29 and 30 lines.

The papyrus consists of lists of names, male and female, nearly equally divided, the males slightly preponderating. The names are nearly all Egyptian. The male names are given usually with filiation, "N, son of N," but without description or profession except E 1, "the first scribe Psenkhnoumis, son of Pete-êsis." The filiation is frequently replaced by the words "his brother," "elder brother," or "son," *i.e.* of the last foregoing male name, once by "his son-in-law" (*p* 24). The female names are without filiation, but always described as *tef rm.t*, "his wife" (*i.e.* of the preceding male name), except occasionally when "his wife" is replaced by "his mother" or "his daughter"; *rm.t* lit. "woman" here replaces the more usual *ḥm.t* or *s-ḥm.t* as in I Kh. 6/20, Spiegelb. Demot. Inschr. (Cairo Cat.) 31108, Ryl. pap. xvii, 5. Only thrice do two female names follow each other: in *b* 11, 12 and *q*, 28, 29 the first is "his wife" and the second is "his mother"; but in *m* 16, 17 we have two consecutive female names, each "his wife." In four other instances (*c* 5, *f* 19, *l* 22, *t* 19) we have a second female name described as "F the wife of M."

The names are divided into groups of irregular size, which are summed up by a line in this form, "individuals *x*, of whom males *y*." The highest numbers are "ind. 48 of whom males 25," and the lowest "ind. 3 of whom male 1." Each group is headed by a word, which, if I could translate them all, would probably go far to determine the nature of the document; but several of them are very difficult. However, those that are recognisable seem to indicate that the division is one of occupations; thus *b* 25 is *mte* probably from its determinative of a foreigner **ⲙⲁⲧⲟⲓ**, "soldier"; *d* 16 is *rm ef'r ḥbs*, "a man who who makes clothes"; *f* 6 is the "man of Khnum," perhaps a temple slave; *f* 28 is "the workman (?) of the temple of Khnum, the great God"; *k* 19 is the carrier of milk-vessels; *m* 1 "the fuller"; m 7 *ḫry*, some occupation connected with clothing; *n* 1 is *qse*, "embalmer": *o* 17 is ḥ'k, "barber."

Hence we shall be justified in assuming that this is probably a list of persons connected with the temple of Khnum, which must have existed at Shashotep, as he was the local god. It is curious that the occupation is always denoted by a substantive in the singular, "fuller," "barber," etc., though followed by a list of names. Further, in a division by occupations one would not have expected the names of the female relations to be included; and yet it cannot be a census, as the sons and daughters mentioned are very few in number, and in the case of a son his name is usually followed by that of his wife, showing that he is adult. Family relationship, however, is the basis of the enumeration within each professional group, and suggests that the occupations were usually hereditary.

E 2. A list of male names.

E 3. This papyrus seems to be an account of the returns—rent in kind—made by land which, to judge by the distribution of it, must have been γῆ βασιλική. It is distributed among horsemen (= ἱππεῖς), foot-soldiers (= πεζοί), and sailors (= ναυκληρομάχιμοι?), though I am not sure of the reading of the last word; also among groups of men described as the "men of X," X being in every case but one a man bearing a Greek name. These groups correspond doubtless to the military corps described in the Greek papyri as "οἱ διὰ X." In two instances (col. *a*. 19, col. *b*. 2) we have the men of a locality. Portions of the land are described as exempt from rent. The rest pays on an average about 5½ artabas per arura.

The allotments were made "from the year 1 of the king's father" and "up to the year 16 of the king's father." If the document dates, as presumably it does, from the reign of Philometor, those years would refer to Epiphanes, during whose reign there were prolonged disturbances in the south of Egypt. In the 1st year of Epiphanes troops were sent southwards from Thebes to deal with the rebels, but the revolt was not finally quelled till 185 B.C., the 21st year of Epiphanes. Hence there was ample occasion for the creation of military colonies at Shashotep and other towns in Middle Egypt during the years when Thebes itself and most of the south country were in the hands of the rebels.

E 4. Fragments of six columns containing lists of male names only, divided into small groups by a summation at intervals.

E 5. A similar fragment.

E 6 *a*. Fragments of two columns, containing a list of names, both male and female, about half being Greek, followed by the word *ꜣsw* and a figure. *ꜣsw* is presumably ⲁⲥⲟⲩ, "price," "payment," though it is usually spelt differently in this sense. Here it may mean perhaps "cash payment." It is sometimes replaced by *'p*, "reckoning, account," and once by *šše* (?), "delayed payment" (? *cf.* note on B 2 verso). Thus the papyrus is probably part of a banker's ledger with entries of payment into the bank, or else of a tax-collector's ledger.

There is also Greek writing on both recto and verso, which may refer to similar accounts.

E 6 *b* is an account of a similar nature, and may have formed part of the same document as the foregoing. The handwritings are probably the same.

E 7. A similar fragment, bearing at the end the date 22 Thoth of the year 35; 147 B.C. if Philometor, 136 B.C. if Euergetes II.

E 8. A list of male names, each followed by the fraction ½. The heading very faint, except the place-name Shashotep and the proper name Peteesis, and the date "year 27."

E 9. Three small fragments with proper names and sums of money. One (*c*) contains the date "year 33."

E 10. Parts of two columns containing names (all Greek) and large sums of money.

E 11. Probably fragment of a rental register.

E 12. Contents uncertain; dated 18 Mechir of 28th year.

E 13. Fragment of rental or land-tax register.

E 15. Fragment of private account, probably; miscellaneous items, including a "petition to Thoth (*ꜥš mbḥ Tḥwt*) 5″ [*tbn* ?]), and in the next line "wheat ½ 5 *tbn* 5 *kite*," which, if ½ = ½ artaba, would work out at 220 drachmas the artaba. According to Grenfell, pap. i, p. 36, 49, the price of an artaba in the 2nd cent. B.C. was usually 250—300 dr.

89. F 1. Part of a rental or land-tax register, the ratio of corn to land working out at 7 to 8 artabas per arura. Nearly all the names are foreign.

3. List of male names, occasionally with relationship, "his brother," etc., divided into groups of from one to about twelve, with summation.

5 *a–c*. Three fragments of a contract dated Pauni 14 (?) in "the 23rd year."

5 *d*. A list of names, all male.

6 *d*. Probably fragment of a letter.

G 1. Fragment of business letter, or report, addressed in the 2nd pers. plur. and referring to priests, various gods, sums of money, and pledges.

H 1–5. Five fragments, all in the same handwriting; perhaps part of an historical romance, to judge from the scraps of translation herewith.

H 6–7 are probably also fragments of a literary work of a similar nature.

H 8. Fragment of a legal document, signed by four parties (or witnesses), and mentioning "from the year 8."

K 1. Fragment of a letter or report (?) couched in the 1st pers. plur.

K 2. Three small fragments in the same handwriting as H 1–5, and perhaps part of the same MS.

90. The following is a tabular statement of the material:

No.	Date.	
	Headpiece A.	
1	—	} 1–5 rental register.
2	—	
3	—	
4	—	
5	—	
6	—	uncertain.
	Headpiece B.	
1	—	Banker's account.
2 recto	28 Philometor	Conveyance of waste land at Shashotep.
2 verso	year 28	Banker's account (?).
3	year 28	contract to embalm, etc.
4	—	land measurement.
5	—	rental register.
6	—	list of names and some figures.
7	—	account relating to ibises.
8 *a*	*temp.* Philometor	fragment of protocol.
8 *b*	—	uncertain.
9	—	fragments.
10	—	*a b*, fragments with fractions of aruras. *c*, rental register.
11 recto	—	temple (?) accounts.
11 verso	"year 26"	ditto
12	—	two small fragments of contracts.
	Headpiece C, D.	
1	"to year 26"	several fragments of contracts.
2 *a*	—	uncertain.

No.	Date.	
2 *b*	—	fragment of temple regulation as to vestments.
3–12	—	fragments; lists of names or amounts, some uncertain.
	Headpiece E.	
1	—	list of persons attached to temple of Khnum (?).
2	—	list of names.
3	various years	list of cleruchs and allotments.
4	—	list of male names.
5	—	ditto.
6 *a b*	—	Banker's accounts.
7	year 35	ditto.
8	year 27	list of names.
9	year 33 (*c*)	list of names and sums.
10	—	Banker's account (?).
11	—	Rental register (?).
12	year 28	uncertain.
13	—	Rental or land-tax register.
14	—	uncertain.
15	—	private account.
16	—	accounts.
17	—	list of names.
	Headpiece F.	
1	—	Rental or land-tax register.
2	—	list of male names.
3	—	ditto.
4	—	uncertain.
5 *a b c*	23rd year	fragments of contract.
5 *d*	—	list of male names.
6 *d*	—	fragment of a letter (?).
6 *b c*	—	accounts.
	Headpiece G.	
1	—	business report (?).
2	—	small fragment with numbers—nature uncertain.
3	—	small fragments — chiefly names.
4	—	fragments with numbers.
	Headpiece H.	
1–5	—	fragments of historical romance (?).
6, 7	—	literary work (?).
8	"from year 8"	legal document, with 4 signatures.
9, 10	—	uncertain fragments.
	Headpiece K.	
1	—	fragment of report (?).
2	—	small fragments—probably belonging to H 1–5.
3	—	small fragments—probably belonging to H 1–5.

91. In the following translations of the more important pieces round brackets contain explanations, and square brackets contain restorations of missing text.

Papyrus B. 2 begins with (A) Agreement for sale:

(l. 1) "Year 28, Epiphi 10 of King (1) . . . . . beauty (2) (εὐχάριστος), there being the priest of Alexander, the gods Adelphoi, the gods Euergetai, the gods Philopatores, the gods [Epiphaneis], the gods [Philometores and the bearer of the trophy] of victory before Berenice [Euergetis] (l. 2) the bearer of the golden basket before Arsinoe . . . . of P-sy (Ptolemais) (3) which is in the district of Thebes, the priest of Ptolemy the [Soter], the priest of King Ptolemy Philometor, the priest of Ptolemy Philopator, the priest of Ptolemy Euergetes, the priest of Ptolemy (*sic*) (l. 3) the priest of Ptolemy Philadelphus, the priest of Ptolemy . . . . [Arsinoe] Philadelphus, the priestess of [Cleopatra the] goddess Epiphanes Eucharistos, the bearer of the golden basket before Arsinoe Philadelphus, Say the . . . . . of the gods Euergetai the gods (l. 4) Philopatores, the gods Epiphaneis, the gods Philometores . . . . two together, their mother being Shmety, ... -Khnum, son of Menapis (4) . . . . . son of Menapis, Pete-Khnum, son of Menapis, three together, their mother being Senapis, Khnum son of Psen-p-Khroou, his mother being

(1) *cf.* l. 1 of the Cession (B). The king's title "Pt. son of Pt. and Cleop. Epiphaneis" is unusual at this date. It is the usual style of demotic contracts from year 6 to 19 of the reign (Berl. 3112, 3141, Louvre rev. ég. ii 93, Rylands xv); but in year 20 and later the style is always, except here, "Pt. and Cleop. his sister, children of Pt. and Cleop. *ἐπιφανεῖς*" (B.M. 1201–2, Leid. 378, Revill. N. Chr. 113, Louvre 2416–7, Berl. 3097, Strassb. 21, Rylands xvi).

(2) *cf.* l. 3 *nt 'r mt t-nfr.t* = *εὐχάριστος*, a third and apparently new demotic version of this title; the first occurs in Rosetta l. 3 and the second in Berl. 3070, 3097, 3111, 3141, Strassb. 21, Ryl. xv.

(3) The Ptolemais priesthoods are always irregular in their order except that Soter the founder comes first and the reigning king next.

(4) *cf.* Liebl. 1259, Petrie, *Abydos* 1, 39, 49, lxxv, Hapimen "Apis endures."

Tabekis, (l. 5) Thoth (son of?) Setyrbon, his mother being Shmety, Khnum . . . .
. . . .
thou hast given, our heart is satisfied with, the silver, price of the hired (?) (1) waste-land . . . . . . (l. 6) waste-lands again which are opposite the treasury built (of stone) in . . . . [the necropo]lis of Shas-[hotep] . . . . which is in the possession of his children, on the West the remainder of thy waste-land . . . . 2, on the North-west . . . . (l. 7) . . . . . we give thee the aforesaid hired (?) waste-land . . . [by this writing] for silver, [we have] received [its price in silver without remainder] our heart is satisfied with . . . . [no man] on earth [shall be able to] possess it except thee at any [time?]; the man who shall come [against thee?] to take it . . . . (l. 8) in our name, the name of father, mother, brother, sister, (or) any man on earth—myself (*sic* sc. ourselves) likewise—we will remove him [from thee] . . . .
thou hast control of it in our name; the oath, the causing to stand (ἐπίδειξις) that shall be made against thee [in the court of] (l. 9) justice on account of the legal right and writing aforesaid thou art (entitled) against us to cause us to do it, we will do it for thee. Wrote . . . . . .

(B) Cession:

(l. 1) "Year 28 Epiphi 10 [of King] Ptolemy son of Ptolemy . . . .
. . . .
the bearer of the trophy of victory before Berenice Euergetis, (l. 2) the bearer of the golden basket before Arsinoe Philadelphus, the priestess . . . .
. . . . Ptolemy Euergetes, the priest of Ptolemy (l. 3) Philadelphus, the priest of Ptolemy Epiphanes, the priest of Ptolemy . . . .
. . . .
the gods Euergetai, the gods Philopatores, (l. 4) the gods Epiphaneis, the gods Philometores, Setyrbon son of Harmonthes . . . .
. . . .
son of Setyrbon (l. 5) his mother being Shmety Khnum son of Psen-p-Khroou his mother being Triphis, Harpaesis son of Pete-Khnum his mother being T . . . .
. . . .
(l. 6) hired (?) waste-land which is among our waste-lands towards the necropolis of Shas-hotep which . . . . writing for silver . . . .
(l. 7) writing of divestment against (?) them, year 28, Epiphi 10 of King Ptolemy living for ever . . . .
. . . .
(l. 8) aforesaid, thou makest (?) against us the legal right (and) the writing for silver . . . .
. . . .

92. The papyrus B. 3 is a contract for embalming. ". . . . . I will bind him, anoint him, embalm him . . . . It is thine, thy . . . . which are in thy treasuries (*pr. ḥt. w*=ταμιεῖα), we have received . . . . .
. . . . . 5 talents, its half . . . talents, 5 talents again at 24 copper obols to the tetradrachm . . . . thou hast possession of them and they . . . . the penalty (for?) anything and everything on earth . . . .
every . . . . on earth . . . . [the seat] which is in the middle of our district (?), the two . . . . aforesaid . . . .
portion of the men . . . . . to our treasuries, they giving burial, they pledging (?) the middle of the three seats . . . . us, and they (?) shall confirm it, he . . . . he praying ten times a month . . . . and I will give a further ten talents [its half] 5 talents, making 10 talents at 24 copper obols to the tetradrachm . . . . the sacrifices and libations of the kings . . .
. . . . as aforesaid, I am (entitled) against thee in the legal right, the writing (?) . . . . . . year 28 Mesore 16 of the kings who live for ever . . . . .

Note.—For payment of a fine to "royal libations and sacrifices," *cf.* Vatican contract for sale of wheat, Revill. rev. ég. iii 26 and pl. 6, the "pension alimentaire" of Revillout rev. ég. iii 137, and Griffith Rylands xvii and note p. 144 *ib.* The fine is paid to the στεφανος (?) in Spiegelberg, Reinach 6/20 and p. 209.

93. An account in B 7 relates to ibises, hawks, and other animals.

B 7, col. *a*.

1.	ibis 1	makes lok (κεράμιον)	1
2.	ibis 1		=1

(1) *bk*—the word means "servant" (ⲃⲱⲕ)—then "wages" or "rent" (ⲃⲉⲕⲉ); but the meaning here is doubtful. In Spiegelb. Demot. Inschr. (Cairo Cat.) 30641 it seems to mean "rent" of an island; in Rylands xii *zy.t bk.t* = "supporting (?) wall." Possibly *bk* here is a substantive and means "usufruct." But contra in all other respects the conveyance seems to be an out-and-out sale.

3. brought . . . . from Portis . . . .
4. ibis 1 = 1
5. day 21, from (?) Portis to (?) Lycophron
6. one *hte* which they brought on the mountain ½
7. . . . hawk 1 ½
8. one *hte* hawk . . . . . ½

Col. *b*.

1. . . . day 29 from (?) *P-šn-Blḥm* (ψενβλεμμυς) ibis 1 = 1
2. . . . . ibis 1 = 1
3. for month of Thoth (?) lok 6½
4. Paopi from (?) Portis . . . . Archelaos (?)
5. took *τιn* (?? *ιḥm*?) 4 = lok 2¼
6. day 21 (?) Harpaesis the younger . . . .
7. brought a shepherd Petcesis the shepherd
8. one *hte* = lok ½
9. day 25 from (?) Anup-p-rί (?)
10. one *hte* hawk ¼
11. day 29 one ibis = lok
12. Pa-tbekis the shepherd
13. for Paopi lok 4¼

Col. *c*.

1. Athyr . . . .
2. . . . . .
3. the treasury of L . . . .

Part of a protocol in B 8 *a* runs thus:

1. . . . . Ptolemy and Cleopatra the gods ἐπιφανεῖς, the priest of A[lexander . . . .
2. . . . . . . Arsinoe Philadelphus, the priestess of Arsinoe Philopator . . . .
3. . . [Ptolemy Philo]pator, the priest of Ptolemy the god ἐπιφανης, the priestess . . . .
4. . . . . the god (?) Euergetes Pa (?)-ns . . . . . .

The papyrus CD 2 *b* contained regulations about vestments.

1. . . . "the service which is concerned with (?) it . . .
2. . . . "if there is a carrying . . . .
3. . . . "house of vestments (*mnḥ*)
4. . . . . .
5. . . . service which is appointed (ⲡⲱϣⲛ ?) to them
6. . . . according to (?) the list of vestments (*ḥbs*) . . . which are . . .

94. The papyrus E 3 is a list of cleruchs and allotments.

Col. *a*.

N.B.—(fr.) after a number means that a small fraction less than ½ or ¼ follows it.

1. . . . . . . = 112½ (fr.) artabas . . . . 5 aruras 22½ (fr.) artabas
2. . . . .
3. . . . . 160 artabas
4. . . . . 1046 (fr.) aruras = 5736 (fr.) artabas
5. . . . . = 320 artabas
6. . . . . = 6056 (fr.) artabas (?)
7. . . . .
8. . . . . = 829 (fr.) artabas
9. . . . . from the year 25 the . . . . and the families of the horsemen
10. . . . 58 325 (fr.) artabas (?)
11. . . . 1156½ ¼ [aruras] = 6381 (fr.) artabas (?)
12. . . . 1¼ arura 8½ ¼ artabas (?)
13. the foot soldiers up to year 16 of the king's father, who are exempt from rent
14. the company (?) of Aristodemus 35 aruras
15. from year 1 of the king's father their single (?) . . . . which is exempt from rent 169¼ (fr.) aruras
16. . . . 5 aruras
17. the men to whom the king has made . . . . 505 (fr.) aruras = 2639 (fr.) artabas
18. . . . 100 aruras 533 (fr.) aruras (?)
19. the men of the town (ϯⲙⲉ) of Memphis . . . . = 272 (fr.) artabas
20. the men of Thrasycles . . . . .

Col. *b*.

1. the men of Hermias 10 aruras 60 artabas
2. to the men of Qqe (?) (place-name) 25 aruras 121 artabas
3. the men of Gymnus who are inscribed . . . . 15 aruras 70 artabas
4. the men who have been among . . . the sailors (?) of Shashotep.
5. 13 aruras 86¼ (fr.) artabas (?).
6. the foot soldiers up to year 16 who are exempt from rent 35 aruras.
7. and from year 1 who are exempt from rent 169¼ aruras.
8. (those) who have a rent written against them 640 (fr.) aruras = 3367¼ artabas
9. . . . . . . 106 aruras 589 (fr.) artabas (?)
10. to the foot soldiers 844¼ (fr.) aruras
11. and those which were given them from the year 22

12. the foot soldiers . . . . 124 aruras 962 (fr.) artabas
13. . . . 40 aruras = 213¼ (?) artabas (?)
14. the men of Totoes 113½ (fr.) aruras = 676 artabas
15. the men of Pete . . . 35 (fr.) aruras = 209 artabas
16. the sailors (?) to whom was given the portion from year 1 17 (fr.) aruras 82 (fr.) artabas
17. and those which were given them from year 12 36 (fr.) aruras 133 (?) (fr.) artabas.
18. and those which were given them from year 25 6 aruras 27½ artabas
19. . . . . the topogrammateus Ql. . . . 24¼ aruras 150 (fr.) artabas
20. to the foot soldiers up to the year 16 who are exempt from rent 35 aruras
21. and from year 1 who are exempt from rent 169¼ aruras.
22. (those) who have a rent written against them 657¼ (fr.) aruras = 3 (?) . . . artabas
23. and from year 12 (?) 359 (fr.) aruras . . .

(We may note that this surviving piece of the register accounts for 8½ square miles of land, so that there must have been altogether a great amount of foreign ownership about Rifeh, though not necessarily a foreign population of cultivators.—W. M. F. P.)

Notes.

col. a, l. 9, "horsemen," *ἱππεῖς rm-w ḥtr*, *cf.* Spiegelberg, pap. Reinach, p. 193 n. 1a; "families of the horsemen" *cf.* *ἱππέων μισθοφόρων υἱοὶ*, pap. Reinach, No. 31, p. 127.

l. 13, "king's father." For frequent references to the "king's father" see Index ii to pap. Tebtunis, p. 606.

"rent," *šm* (?) *cf.* Spiegelberg's pap. Reinach, p. 181–3 and 240 and Rec., etc., 28/196. The equivalent *šm* (?) = *ἐκφοριον* is proved by a bilingual ostracon in the possession of J. G. Milne, Esq.

l. 14, "company," *stne*, *cf.* Spiegelberg A Z, 42/55.

l. 19, "town," *tme* = ϯⲙⲉ, which may be in either town or village. Perhaps rather the latter, implying a local village of the same name as the City of Memphis, such as we find in the Fayum (Wessely, *Top. Fay.* p. 105).

col. b, l. 3, *Gymnus* is of course a Greek name ending in -*os*. Possibly it is *Tymnus*.

l. 4. "sailors" (?) *ḫn-w* (?), reading doubtful—occurs also in l. 16 and again in one of the headings of pap. E 1. I take it to be the same group as in Ros. 10 (*οἱ εἰς τὴν ναυτείαν* (and IKham. 3/28. *cf.* the *ναυκληρομαχιμοι* of Tebt. 5/46. "Shashotep" *i.e.* Rîfeh.

l. 11. "year 22" may be "year 12."

l. 16. "portion." This word (*tᵒ*) which ordinarily means "share, part, portion" (*μέρος* in Ros. 10) has in one passage of Ros. l. 9 the technical meaning *ἀπόμοιρα*: here I presume it = *κλῆρος*.

l. 9. "topogrammateus" *sḫ-mt* *cf.* Spiegelberg A Z 42/56.

95. A fragment apparently of an historical romance is in papyrus H 1–5.

1. (beginnings of lines only):

"king . . .
". . . . king . . . .
"I arrived at Thebes (?), mounted (?) . . . .
"the god great (?) . . .
"I said 'Peace,' I have not . . . .
"the dream . . . . .
"I was . . . . .

2. (middle of lines)

". . . . . he has not (?) told me
". . . . produce from the month (?)
. . . . .
. . . . .
. . . . general (*mr mšᶜ*) . . .
. . . . temple of Osiris . . .
. . . .
. . . scribe (?) of the house of life of the king . . .
. . . .
. . . . . house of life of the king (?) . . .
. . . with them
. . . . I have not delayed . . . .
. . . . happen

3. (ditto)

". . the . . . . of Syene (?) make the greetings (ⲥⲙⲏ), the adoration (ⲟⲩⲱϣⲧ) . . .
. . . I . . . before the king . . . .
I have not delayed the day (?) of diminution (ⲥⲟⲃⲕ).
. . . . sacrifice (and) libation before . . .
. . . . ever . . . . . I went on board . . .
. . . . the chief of the army (*p ḥry mšᶜ*) Hor (son of ?) Petemont (?) the chief of the army . . .
. . . . greetings, the adoration of the king and the army of the king . . . .
. . . . I know him . . . .
. . . . the army of the city (?) . . .
. . . . the army of the king . . .
. . . . I have not delayed

4. ditto.

". . . . king . . .
". . . . the land of Ethiopia . . .
. . . . . the land of Ethiopia
. . . . on board
. . . .

5. (beginnings of lines only)

"I reached a . . . my heart
". . . them, I bring (?) them . . .
"I . . . I . . .
". . . . . . .
". . . . . . .
"say, Let them bring . . .
. . . .
. . . Si-Tum, if

CHAPTER XII

THE COPTIC MANUSCRIPTS

By W. E. Crum.

96. Excavations on the site of a monastery have naturally produced a harvest of Coptic manuscripts. The crop is of the usual miscellaneous sort, in more than the usually dilapidated condition. To make a satisfactory separation of wheat from chaff, among hundreds of disconnected parchment and papyrus fragments, would require far more study than it has as yet been possible to give. What can here be said therefore is offered merely as a preliminary description.

First, as to the name of the monastery, around the ruins of which the MSS. were scattered. Over a dozen of the private documents mention "the monastery of Saint (*ἅγιος*) Apollo"—its *προεστώς* is the author of deeds, as a corporation (*δίκαιον*) it is a party in contracts, writers of letters describe themselves as resident in it. Thus we may assume that the present Dêr Balyzeh represents the ancient monastery of St. Apollo. In several instances its situation is defined as "in the nome (*νομός*) of the city (*πόλις*) of Sbeht." Now this city, which, on the strength of the equation Sbeht = *'Απολλωνείας*, was identified by W. Max Müller with Edfu (*Rec. Trav.* xxi. 199), had been shown by Amélineau to be rather the name of a "Lower Apollinopolis" (*Géogr.* 463. On the sites of two towns named Apollinopolis the Less, see Wilcken in *Arch. f. Pap.* iv. 163). Sbeht then must be sought a good deal farther north, and we may doubtless find it in the modern Kôm Esfaht, only 8 miles south of Balyzeh.

Who this Apollo was we do not know: whether the founder of the great monastery at Bawît, 50 miles farther north, or some namesake (see *Aeg. Zeits.* xl. 60). A limestone stele from Balyzeh invokes the Trinity, archangels, etc., and "our fathers, the superior, Apa Apollo, Anoup, Pegôsh and his brethren," thus recalling the Bawît triad Apollo, Phib, Anoup. The martyr Pegôsh in Zoega 23 is from Terbe, perhaps Rifeh; see below.

97. The manuscripts are clearly the *débris* of the monastic library and charter room: there are but few private documents which might not have been preserved in the latter. Almost all relate, more or less immediately, to the business or officials of the monastery.

Literature is represented, in the first place, by a considerable number of biblical MSS., mostly on parchment, one or two of which may well be of the 5th, and the remainder of the 6th or 7th centuries. From the Old Testament, we have fragments of Genesis, Deut., 1 and 2 Sam., 1 and 2 Kg., Psalms; from the New, of Matt., Lu., Joh., 1 Cor., Phil., Col., 1 and 2 Tim., Tit., Heb., Ja., 1 Joh., Rev.; these latter being in time to be used by Mr. Horner in his forthcoming edition. Besides these, all of which are of course in the Sa'idic dialect, there is a small fragment of Phil. in Middle Egyptian, as well as a minute scrap, of about the 6th century, from Exodus iv, in Greek. For the most part, the passages legible are of such small dimensions as to be of little critical value. Best preserved are parts of Heb. vi—x and Colossians. One MS., when complete, had a page of over 31 × 22 cm.; one (the only fragment as yet from Dêr Ganadleh) of only 7 × 6 cm.

Next to the canonical Scriptures, we may name two leaves from apocryphal works, among the most interesting in the collection. The first (6th or 7th cent.) shows Christ addressing the angels: "Lo, then, my (?) holy angels, I have chosen you and have revealed unto you all my mysteries, from the beginning of creation (*κτίσις*) until now. So have ye known, by that which I revealed unto you, that it was pride did cast the devil forth from his first estate (*ἀρχή*), and he was cast forth into outer darkness by reason of his pride. So have ye seen that pride is the mother of all sin (1 Tim. iii. 6). He that humbleth not himself among you, the same is a devil."

The other, of about the 6th century, I take to be from that pre-Irenaean Apocrypha of John, whereof C. Schmidt eleven years ago gave a preliminary description (*Sitz. Berl. Akad.* 1896, 841). The leaf is paged 41, 42: "' . . . reasonable (*λογικός*) power, ere it had been revealed. Its name was not this, but (*ἀλλά*) its name is Silence (*σιγή*). For (*ἐπειδή*) all they that are in the heavenly paradise (*παράδ.*) are all sealed with silence. Those then that shall partake thereof (*sc.* ? paradise) do become reasonable (λογ.), having known all things, and they seal the five (?) powers with silence. Behold, I have explained (ἑρμηνεύειν) unto thee, O John, concerning Adam and Paradise (παρ.) and the five trees, in a figure to be understood (σύμβολον, νοερός).' When I, John, had heard these things, I said, 'I have begun in a good beginning (ἄρχεσθαι, ἀρχή), to fulfil knowledge (γνῶσις) and hidden mystery (μυστ.) and figures (σύμβ.) of truth, I having been (thereunto) urged (προτρέπειν) by Thy love' (ἀγάπη). [*Here a dividing-line.*] 'I desire further to ask of Thee that Thou wouldest explain (ἑρμ.) unto me, if Thou wilt, concerning Cain and Abel, after what fashion (τύπος) did Cain slay Abel. And not this only, but (ἀλλά) . . . by Thy (MS. "our") word unto him 'Where is Abel, thy brother?' But Cain denied (ἀρνεῖσθαι), saying,'Am I the keeper[.'" This last word is *hourit*, not hitherto found in literary texts.

Beside these Gnostic works may be placed an obscure charm (φυλακτήριον), which is accompanied by a prayer for the "*papa* Papnoute, the man from the Oasis" (*Prm-ouahe*, presumably the Great Oasis). It has the unusual formula, "that God may reckon him with the sheep upon the right, both him and all the children of our father Adam."

98. There are remnants of several liturgical books; among them, a papyrus MS. in a fine hand (6th or 7th cent.), showing parts of the Intercession, Thanksgiving, and Creed, in Greek. The text is not exactly that of the published anaphoras. Another MS., of very small dimensions, contained prayers in Coptic for the monastery, its head and members, and the bishop. A third shows a passage from the Coptic St. Basil.

Church law is represented by parts of the Canons of St. Basil, whereof another MS. is preserved at Turin (*P. S. B. A.* xxvi. 57), and by the title—nothing more remains—of what may possibly have been the Rules of Pachomius (though as yet no independent Coptic text of these has come to light). "The ἐντολαί of our beloved, saintly father, Apa [4 *or* 5 *letters*] the man of God, which he received of God, to give unto his people, (when about to?) end (his life) in peace, according to the lot of all men, and to . . . , and to enter into his inheritance, the place where his treasure is, that he had gathered . . ."

Of Homilies or Epistles, I have distinguished about eight. One has the title: "A Sermon of the . . . and apostolic, Saint (ἅγ.) Athanasius, archbishop of Rakote, after that he had returned (?) from the first exile (ἐξοριστία) . . . , teaching men that they should repent and be saved from punishment (κόλασις)." The text begins: "If man that hath walked the earth shall die, what remembrance shall be left to man? . . ." This seems not to be among the known works of Athanasius. Another fragment quotes Ezekiel xliv 2 in a remarkable form: "This gate shall be closed; none shall enter in to it, except it be the . . . of the King of Glory; and He it is shall eat bread therein. . . ." This is referred to the Virgin, while the "interpretation" of the name "Jesus" is given as ζ. σου. (On the sibilation for initial I, see the usual spelling of Zesus, Sustus, Zenuarus, for Jesus, Justus, Jenuarus, on the Roman glass bowls. Garucci, *Vetri ornati di figure in oro*, xxiii, xxiv, xxxiv.—W. M. F. P.) Another homily treats of forgiveness to be obtained by fasting and repentance: sins are not, as the heretics hold, forgiven yearly.

It is observable that nothing of Shenoute's has come to light. There are several fragments of a 6th or 7th century MS. of the *Apophthegmata*, corresponding to Migne, *P.L.* lxxiii. 859 D, 860 A, while another leaf, seemingly of the same MS., mentions Cyril, Celestine, and Nestorius.

99. Among the *Acta* or narrative texts is a remarkable fragment relating to Antony and Athanasius (*c.* 7th cent.). A speech of the former, with a reference to Solomon's temple, ends: " . . . I go unto the Lord in peace" (ἡσυχία). "And when," it continues, "the saintly old man had thus spoken, the blessed Athanasius wept, because that he had not [*long gap*] the blessed Antonius, on the day (?) . . . he went to rest in peace (εἰρήνη). And his disciples (μαθ.) related unto us his life (βίος), and we wrote it in a book privily . . . ," after which lacuna, the text ends. This purports apparently to be an account, by one of Athanasius' followers, of the manner in which the *Vita Antonii* was composed. Next we may mention two leaves relating to Apa Hamoi. An anchorite of this name was the teacher of St. John Colobus (Zoega 117). This work was of some length, as these leaves are paged 141, 142, 245, 246. The first refers to a visit paid him by the angel Gabriel, the second to one from Michael, who says, "Arise and go into the city: I am with thee in every place where thou art." Two other leaves are from the story of Euphemia and the devil, in the Encomium on Michael by Eustathius of Trake (see Budge's Bohairic text, pp. 93, 94, 105, 106. In the Brit. Mus. and at Berlin are leaves from other copies of this popular

story). The fragment bearing the title of Pachomius' (?) Rules, mentioned above, happens to preserve also the subscription of the text which preceded them: "This is the *βίος* of our beloved, holy father, Apa Jacob, the anchorite, which he ended on the 25th day of Thoout." No such saint is commemorated in the Egyptian *Synaxarium*; and those in the Greek *Synaxarium* (Delehaye) on Jan. 28, Feb. 21, Oct. 10, are at any rate not Egyptians. Part of another story awaits identification. It tells how a certain saint (?) went to the public bath to wash and, entering the *θόλος*, permitted none to accompany him; "for it was 60 years since he had washed with water, neither had he suffered himself to behold his own nakedness." [*After a long lacuna*,] "he served him and poured water over him from a silver vessel, until he departed. And as the bishop walked forth, the man fell down and besought him, saying, 'My father, when I come to thee, I will show thee how . . .'" A minute fragment gives evidence perhaps of a Middle Egyptian Life of Paul the Simple; though the phrases do not occur in Jerome's Life. "But the blessed Apa Paul . . . while within his cave, thinking him to be a workman" (*τεχνίτης*). "He followed in the footsteps of the saint." The name preserved in another fragment shows it to be connected with the strange legend of Diocletian's Egyptian origin (Amélineau, *Actes*, 164, 165): "Saying [the devil *loq.*] 'My son, Agripitos (*cf.* Zoega 60), thou seest how that thy father hath appointed thee king. Do my will then in that wherein I bid thee, and thou shalt . . . this.' The king said, 'Everything that thou shalt say, thy son will (perform it).'" The phrases preceding this: "Next day he saw the horses in disorder," "instrument" (*ὄργανον*), "the king's daughter," point to the incident of young Diocletian's flute playing, which captivated the princess.

100. Part of a leaf preserves the only example, I believe, in Coptic of those preliminary reckonings, familiar in Byzantine chronicles. They most resemble those in Eutychius (Gelzer, *S. J. Africanus*, ii. 410), but are generally different or erroneous. The names legible are, Ptolemy Philopator, Soter, Alexander with 40 years, another with [2]9 years, "Cleopatra his daughter," another with 43½ years; then a summing up till the . . . year of Augustus. Then, "In the 28th year of Augustus, Our Lord Jesus Christ (was born)"; then another summing up, including the name of Tiberius.

Finally, some dilapidated fragments show the remnants of a curious series of aphorisms in Greek, which may be mentioned here, since, though based upon a pagan text, they have been adapted to Christian taste. The aphorisms were numbered, and each was followed by a *ἑρμηνεία*, or commentary. They are, Mr. Kenyon points out, closely related to Menander's *monosticha*. I give the following examples, with certain readings which he has kindly suggested. No. 15, *ουκ εστιν καιρος ποιησε αρτι· μη σπευδε πλουτιν· μη ταχυ πενης [γενῃ]*. The comment on No. 16 is short: *επι κινδυνον εστιν το κεφαλεον*. No. 20 (?) *μηδε . . . αγαν ευλαβηθῃς αλλα κατα[κρατος μα]χου . . . σεαυτον [μη] θορυβι μηδενος σε[διω]κοντος*. The words *τοις εκ θεου δηλουμενοις* and *ο αγγελος του θεου* are also discernible.

101. The number of documents whereof remnants are discernible is large; but I have only been able to take account of the more conspicuous. Besides those naming Apollo's monastery, some others preserve place-names. One has Patmow, Patsoote, and Panatemik (abbreviation). Two mention the hamlet of Tmoumêr, in the Antinoite nome, which itself is several times named. Further, Apotheke (perhaps), Sioout, the hill of Sioout, the pagarchy of Sioout, as well as the Greek forms Lycopolis, Hypsele, Cusa. Erêbe (perhaps also as Têrbe), for Rifeh, was already known. (*Ἐρέβη* in Greek; *v.* Canon ii. of Theophilus, Migne, *P.G.* lxv. 36.) "The nome (*toš*) of Busiris," which one would seek in the Delta, and "the village of Jkôw" (Aphroditopolis) also occur. An interesting name is "The Holy Rock" (*πέτρα*). Might this be connected with the rock, marked with Christ's footprints, in the legend of the Holy Family's sojourn at Kôs? The name is thus given in Paris MSS. Coptes 131^5. 102, 132^1. 42. For the legend, see the narrative of Timothy in *Brit. Mus. Or.* 604, and Abû Sâlih 75 *b*, 76 *a*. Perhaps this same "rock" appears in Zoega, 370.

102. Of the persons named, four are important, as being historically identifiable, occurring in Arab history as Muslims. 'Abd al 'Azîz ibn Marwân, governor in A.D. 685, is named in a protocol, the official mark or authorisation written across the top of each sheet of papyrus. Ḳurrah ibn Sharîk (*κορρα χ* [*sic*] *σζεριχ συμβουλος*), governor in 710, writes (through a secretary of course, and in Coptic), apparently to the clergy of St. Colluthus' church in Antinoe. 'Ubaid allah b. al-Ḥabḥâb, governor in 724, is named in a "protocol." There are parts of two letters from Al-Ḳâsim b. 'Ubaid allah, treasurer in 730, both having been subsequently covered with Coptic texts. Hence we may conclude that the

documents belong as a whole to the first half of the 8th century. (These officials are given in the *Student's History of Egypt, Middle Ages*, pp. 46–48, by Stanley Lane Poole. Note that this official mark, which doubtless showed a duty paid on the material, was imposed by the governor in 685 and 710, but later by the finance minister in 724 and 737, the latter being the monumental date for Qasym ibn 'Ubaydallah.—W. M. F. P.) 'Abd allah b. Ghazwân (*Abdella šn Gazouan*), amir of the pagarchy of Siut, was not otherwise known. A strange name for a Christian is Apa Amrou. Halê, as elsewhere, stands for 'Alî.

Various officials of the monastery are mentioned; most frequently the priest Ammonius, presumably either abbot or steward, since he represents the community in legal documents. The abbot is, as elsewhere, called "the great man" (*noġ nrôme*) or "our father." The title of ἡγούμενος occurs but once. *Προεστώς* is properly the prior, but the term seems to be applied (elsewhere, at any rate) to the abbot. We also meet with the archdeacon, chartularius, and administrator (διοικητής). The body of the brethren are termed "the great brethren," "great children," "the people of God."

103. Many of the documents relate to taxation. Often they are receipts, some for the annual ἀνδρισμός, or poll-tax; others, more vaguely, for the δημόσιον, twice defined as "the δημόσιον of the monastery." Now and then the needful sum had been advanced by one of the community, and we have the acknowledgement by the δίκαιον of the debt. The collecting is done by a βοηθός, who appears to be, at the same time, one of the clerics. A remarkable tax is the subject of three receipts: it is levied annually upon weavers or their work (δημόσιον *n tale štên*, δημ. [*n*]*psôhe*). On this see also Wilcken, *Gr. Ostraka*, i. 172, for such a tax in Roman times. It is recorded that the first conquerors required a contribution of linen of the Copts; Kremer, *Culturgesch.* i. 61, 62.

104. One of the most interesting documents, and almost alone in being practically complete, is the following marriage contract: "In the name of God, etc., I, Victor, son of Macarius, the priest, with his mother Tegroompe and John, his elder brother, in the monastery of St. Apollo, in the nome of the city Sbeht, do write to Sophia, daughter of Anthyria, of . . . , in the nome of the city Šôtep (Hypsele). [Greeting.] Since (ἐπειδή) God willeth that we should unite one with the other, in righteous wedlock (? γάμος), after the manner of every free man (ἐλεύθερος) and of every wise (*sabe*) woman; therefore have I given thee a half *solidus* and a *tremis* in gold, as bridal gift (*šap*); that thou mayest come and enter my house as a free woman (ἐλ.). And for my part, I (undertake) not to neglect (καταφρονεῖν) thee more than (παρά) as it were my own body (σῶμα). Neither shall I be able to put thee forth without a cause (αἰτία) having legal (νομός) ground. But (πλήν) should I wish to put thee forth, I will pay 6 *solidi* for the matter. And thou also art in like conditions. Shouldest thou wish to depart of thyself, thou shalt pay this fine (πρόστιμον). For thy security then, I have drawn up this deed (χάρτης). 23rd of Hathor, 11th Indiction. I, Victor, with my father and my mother and my brother, that did already write, we do assent (στοιχεῖν) to this deed." The word *šap* as a bridal gift is familiar in demotic (see Griffith's forthcoming Rylands *Catalogue*, 268, § 4, 8, transl p. 134), but is new in Coptic, so far as I know. In the phrase "that thou mayest come and enter my house," *Etrerei ehone ehoun epaêi*, either read *etrerei ehoun e-*, or "Come, as being related, to my house." Compare *hôn ehoun* in Jême deeds.

105. As in all such collections, a number of fragments are from lists or monastic accounts; among them the largest pieces we have (one over 45 × 32 cm.). Plenty of small additions to our knowledge may be gathered from them, more indeed than can well be set out here. One account is termed indifferently κοντάκιον and τομάριον. This large leaf is a record of various payments made: among them, "the wages of the workmen (τεχνίτης) at *or* in the sea" (θάλ.), whatever that may mean; and repeatedly "the expenses (δαπάνη) of the faithful" (*al moumenin*; presumably the charge imposed in the early Moslem period upon the Christians). Further, there is "the tax-contribution (διάγραφον) of the monks." Each item is paid through a representative, among whom occur the names Achillites (Ἀχιλλείδης, probably the origin of the Copto-Arabic Archellites), Diomedes, Lampon (Λάμπων). Another fragment is from a wine account, headed, "The following is the expenditure in wine for the service (διακονία) of the monastery." Among the entries are: 3 jars (κνίδιον) for "the great man's table," 4 for "our table," 36 for the church, 16 for the ship's carpenters (καλαφάτης), 65 for "the festival of our father."

106. A word may be said in conclusion as to the dialect which these texts exemplify. It is, on the whole, a pure Sa'idic, and being located farther south,

is even less tainted by Middle Egyptian forms than that spoken at Ashmunain. Yet, on the other hand, it shows none of the peculiarities of the almost contemporary documents from Thebes (Jême). The 2nd plur. prefix *petne-*, so characteristic of Ashmunain texts, appears very rarely; once too *hijô-*, *ejô-* for *hijn-*, *ejn-*. The form *ntbe* = *etbe*, peculiar apparently to the neighbouring Jkôw papyri, is found once. One phonetic feature of our texts is, however, remarkable. There appears to be already undeniable confusion in the sounds of *janja* and *ġima*: we find *noġ-* for *noj-*, *ġpo-* for *jpo-*, *ġiġ* for *ġij*; also *jôšt* for *ġôšt*. This is certainly not yet observable in the Theban texts of the 8th century, still less in those of the 7th and 8th from Ashmunain; but traces of it may perhaps be discovered in the Jkôw papyri of the same period.

The relatively very small proportion of Arabic texts in the collection is noticeable. Presumably the neighbourhood had as yet been little affected by the conquerors.

Besides the manuscripts here described, the two monasteries have afforded a set of memorial tablets, reproduced in this volume (Pls. XXXIX, XL), and one of which has been already referred to. They are interesting for the names they show. The circular stele invokes five personages, presumably deceased monastic worthies, on behalf of a certain Apa Victor, who came from "the *castrum* of Apa Victor," an unknown village. The first stele on Pl. XL commemorates a woman from Hagé (Zoega, p. 366); the second, with the above invocations increased by two, records the death of a man from Sip, an obscure place, once mentioned elsewhere (Amélineau, *Géogr.* 466).

Museums containing the Objects shown in the Plates

The objects in the plates are now in public museums, which are designated by the following letters in the list below: Bd. Bordighera, Bo. Boston U.S.A., Br. Brussels, Bt. Bristol, C.e. Cambridge Ethnology, C.f. Cambridge Fitzwilliam, E. Edinburgh, H. Hitchin, K. South Kensington, L. Liverpool, Mc. Macclesfield, M. Manchester, Mh. Munich, N. New York, O. Oxford Ashmolean, P. Philadelphia, R. Rochdale, S. Southampton, U. University College, London, Y. York.

Plate II Small vases, M.

III Flint armlets, Br. P. Hawk bracelet, U. Palettes, Cairo, M. Small vases, M. Ivory cylinder vase, Br.

III A Adze, Br. Flint polished, Cairo. Sealing, M. Flint inscribed, U.

IV Marbles, Bd. Bo. Br. Bt. Cairo, C.f. M. Mh. N. O. P. R. U. Toilet objects, M. Flint knives, Br. Gazelle heads, Cairo, K.

V Listed in previous plates.

V A–D, VI B–E Stone vases, Br. Bt. E. L. M. Mh. (many not yet joined and distributed).

V E Stucco, M. P. Sealings of Neteren, Br. M.

VI E Lump of copper tools from T, M.

VII A Nofer-her-ne-ptah, M. Akhetab, C.f. Per-ne-ankh, P. Erdu-ne-ptah, Cairo, L.

VII B Res-he-nofer, M. Head, K. Table, P.

VII D Altar of Nezem, M. Model tools, Br. M. Mh.

VII E Porphyry vases 34, 36, M. Alabaster vases, Bo. Bt. K. Mh. N. R. Y.

VII F Pottery, VIth dynasty, O. R. U.

IX Kheti coffin, P.

X Khnumu, N.

X A–E Whole tomb, M.

X F Baskets, Brit.Mus. Bt. Pot figure, U.

XI Khnumu-hotep, E.

XI A Pottery bowl, K.

XII Ivory wand, P. Apes, Mh. Copper edge in stick, Cairo. Perfect dagger, Bo. Axe and handle, L. Dagger blade, M. P. Axes, M. P.

XIII E 1, 2, U.

XIII F–H, M.

Soul-houses:

Boston 10, 13, 29, 31, 66, 67, 93, 114, 133, 155, 156, tray.

Bristol 44, 60, 78, 130, 142, 149, 153, 2 trays.

Brussels 12, 52, 68, 3 others, tray.

Cairo 102, 129.

Cambridge, Ethnol. 55 and 1 other; Fitzwilliam 2, 79, 87.

Edinburgh 43, 73, 118, 121, 128, and 3 others.

Hitchin 34, 152, tray and pieces.

Liverpool 5, 96, 104, 150, and 2 others.

Macclesfield 37, 98, 136, 1 other.

Manchester (the type set) 6, 35, 38, 41, 58, 59, 69, 74, 77, 80, 97, 101, 106, 116, 120, 126, 132, 151, door Pl. XXII, Pl. XX under 46, tray and 2 others.

Munich 14, 20, 40, 115, 135, 148.

New York 22, 70, 71, 86, 103 and pieces.

Oxford 4, 16, 18, 25, 56, 119, 2 others.
Philadelphia 3, 30, 65, 89, 147, 1 other, tray.
Rochdale 10, 19, 33, 123, tray.
Southampton 15, 3 others, 2 trays.
York 17, 50, 154, tray.
(As the numbers were difficult to read, and I had no opportunity of checking them myself, some have escaped notice, and are listed as "others.")
XXIII 1, U. 19, L.
XXIV Box, C.f.
XXVII Coffin head, K. Group 20 and 223, O. Pasar, M. Camel, M. Wand, Cairo.
XXVII B Duck's-head stool legs, M. Stool, K. Arm wand, Hathor, M. Lion and dish, Mh. Alabaster canopics, P. Hathor head, Cairo. Girl, Br.
XXVII N Haremakht, Bo. Remthet-bast-nesat, Br. Hutha, Bt.
XXXI Not distributed, nor the following coffins.
XXXI A Canopics, E.
XXXI B Canopics, P.
XXXVII A Two demotic, M. Largest demotic, Cairo. Rest not distributed. The remainder have not been distributed, as they await exhibition next year.

ADDENDUM TO "HYKSOS AND ISRAELITE CITIES"

In Pl. XLVIII of the double volume are shown two inscriptions, which were supposed to be in an early Greek alphabet, see pp. 60, 61. Since Mr. Duncan's chapter was written I have noticed that the inscriptions are in the Tifinar character, as used among the Tuareg of Algeria at present. They are, perhaps, the oldest examples of that alphabet, as the stones were much weathered and worn when reused for the roofs of graves of about the 3rd cent. A.D. The inscriptions are to be read with the hinge of the plate upward, from right to left. The alphabet may be found in *Essai de Grammaire de la Langue Tamachek*, by A. Hanoteau, 1860, pp. 3, 4. The two inscriptions read

TH, M?, Y, TH, N, SH, R, Y, J
TH, M, N, Y, M, SH, Y, RT?, Y, J

It seems that there is no filiation stated, as there are no pairs of letters the same in the middle of the lines. And as the beginning of the lines (at the right hand) is the same, it is probably a formula or title. The one sign not directly identified is the third in the second line, the swastika. As the first two letters are the same, it may be that this third is a variant of that in the upper line. R has two forms, a square and a circle: in the upper there seems some ligature intended by the short projecting stroke. In the lower it seems most likely that the swastika is a combination of the square R and cross T, as the cross T is usually combined with preceding letters.

Thus the first three letters read *Jyr* and *Jyrt*. This T affix to a verb conveys the sense of becoming, or passing into a condition (*Hanoteau*, pp. 66, 75). *Jyr* or *Gir* seems to be the Kabayl *Geri*, "rests," or "remains"; and *Jyrt* would be "he has come to rest," or "to remain." This is equivalent to *hic iacet*; and we may well compare the kindred senses of both the Kabayl and the Latin,—*Iger*, "was cast," or "he flung," and *iacio*, "to cast," or "hurl." This seems, therefore, to be a fit opening to a funeral inscription.

The personal name should follow on this; and in the second line we have *Yshmyn*, which seems obviously = Ishmael, with the special Egyptian change of *l* to *n*, Ismayn, as now used in Egypt. The upper inscription has *Shnthy*, which I do not recognise as a name.

The last two letters may be the same in both lines, the upper being partly weathered away. The lower clearly reads *Mth*. This is obviously the root, common to Kabayl and Arabic;—*muth*, "died," Kabayl; *mat*, "dead," Arab.

We seem, then, to have here Libyan inscriptions put up over Arab people, on the east side of the Delta. The meaning of the inscriptions, "Here lies Ismayn dead," "Here lies Shenthy dead," is likely enough for such stones in such a region. The strange thing is finding the Libyan alphabet on the wrong side of the Delta, and of that there can be no question.

W. M. F. P.

INDEX

PANELLED BRICKWORK, WEST SIDE, LOOKING S.

ROW OF GRAVES, WEST SIDE, LOOKING S.

PIER IN CORNER OF LARGE CHAMBER.

VASES IN BASKET, GRAVE V. 15.

FLINT ARMLETS. GRAVE 23.

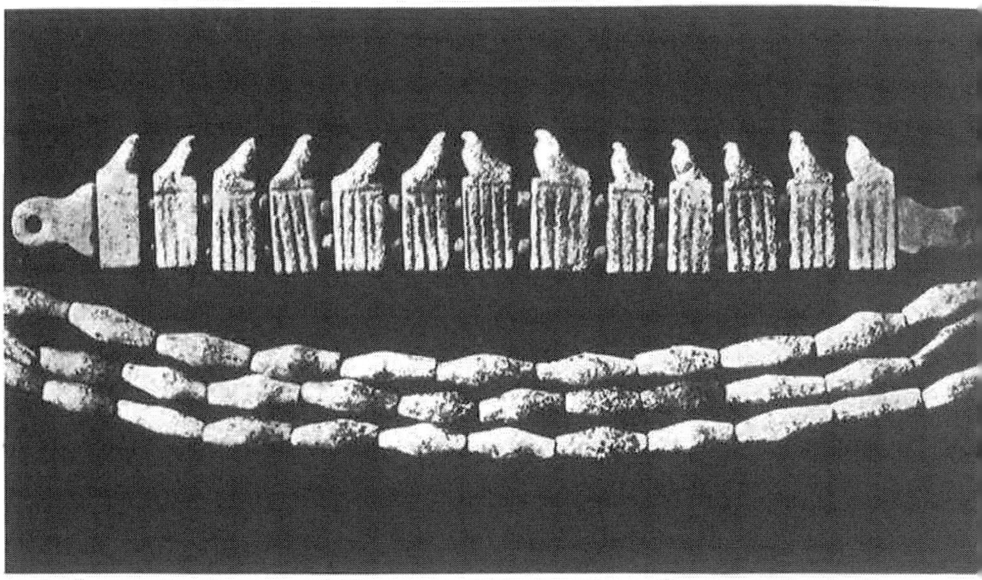

BLUE GLAZED POTTERY BRACELET AND NECKLACE.

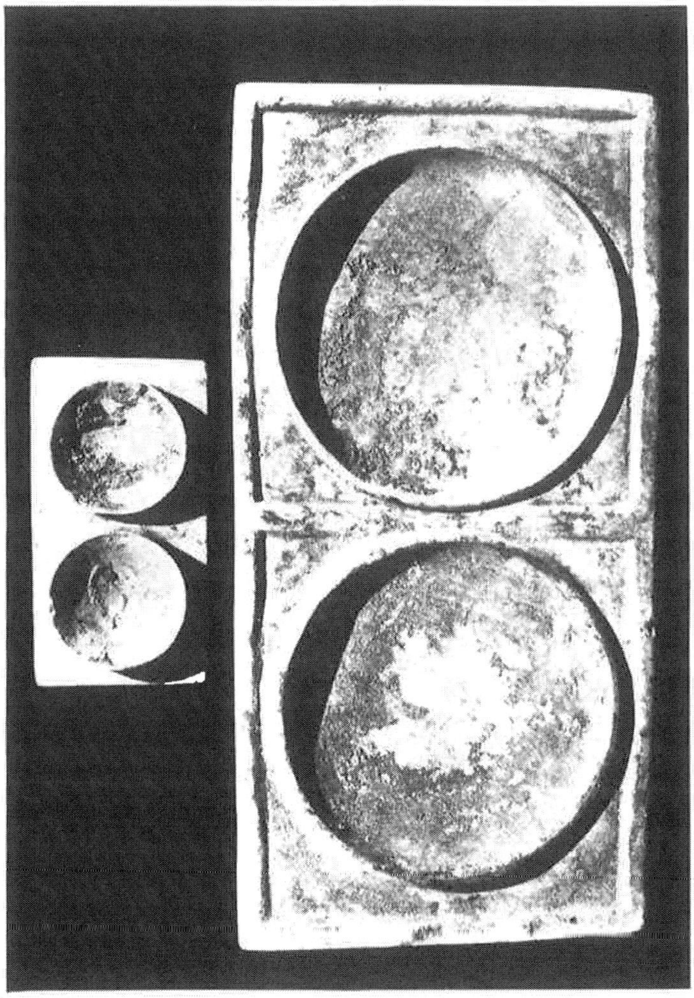

SLATE PALETTES. GRAVE 56.

VASES OF SERPENTINE, CRYSTAL, LAZULI, &c.

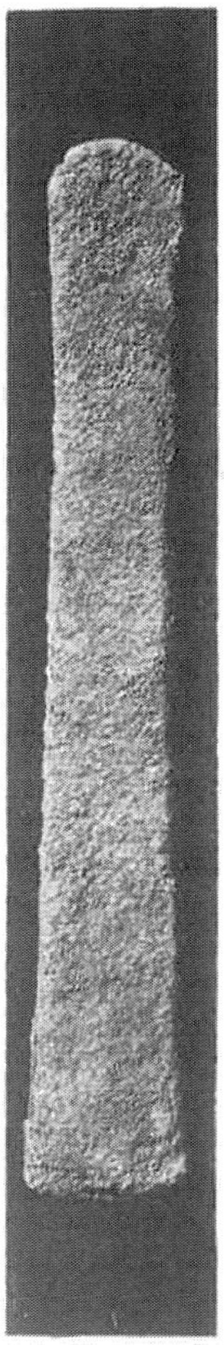

COPPER ADZE GRAVE V.13.

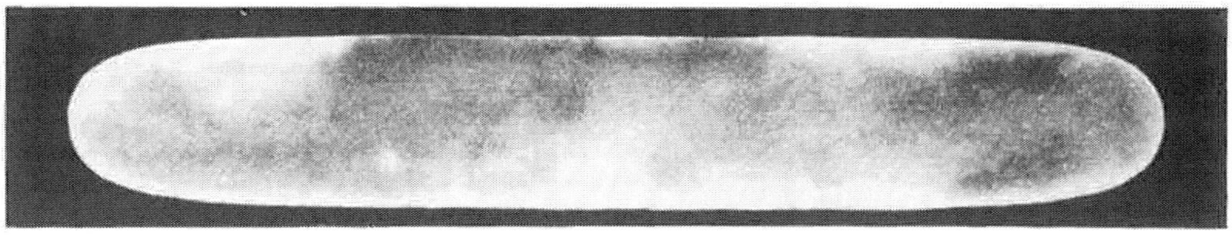

POLISHED FLINT. IIIrd DYNASTY MASTABA T.

STONE PLATFORM EAST OF MASTABA T.

SEALING OF KING ZET.

NUMBERS ON FLINT. GRAVE V. 56.

VIEW OF GRAVE V. 38.

VIEW OF GRAVE 39.

1:1 QUARTZ PLAYING MARBLES, T. III DYNASTY.

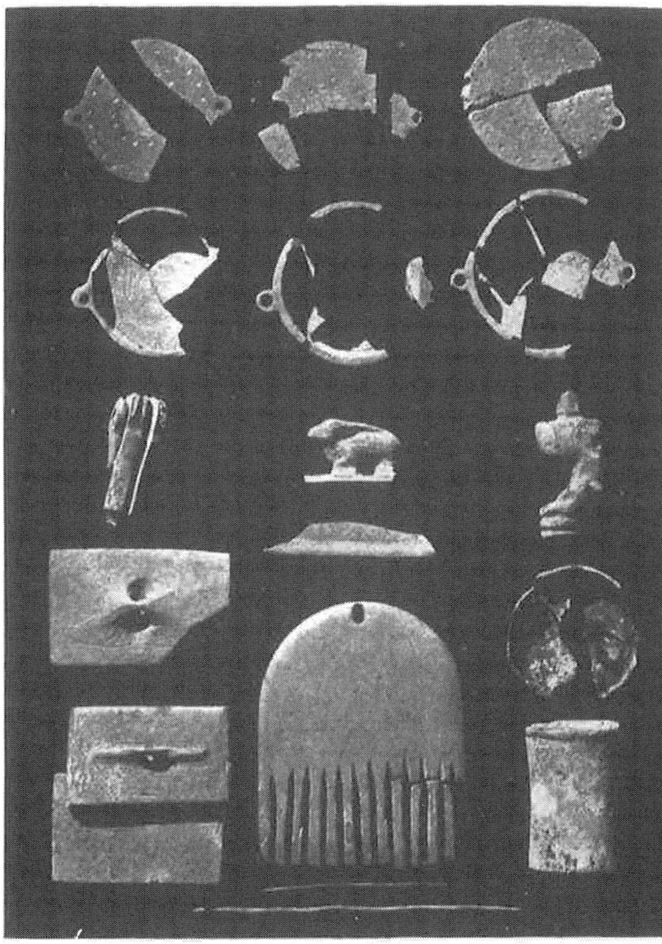

1:1 IVORY AND GOLD TOILET OBJECTS, V. I DYNASTY.

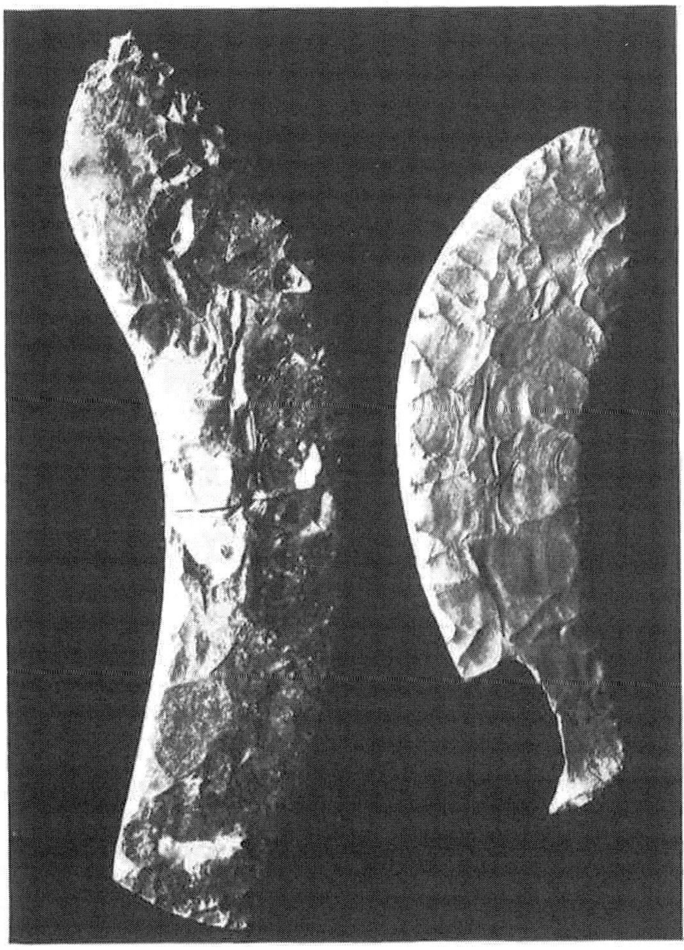

2:5 FLINT KNIVES, V. I DYNASTY.

7:8 IVORY WANDS, GLAZED DISC, V. I DYNASTY.

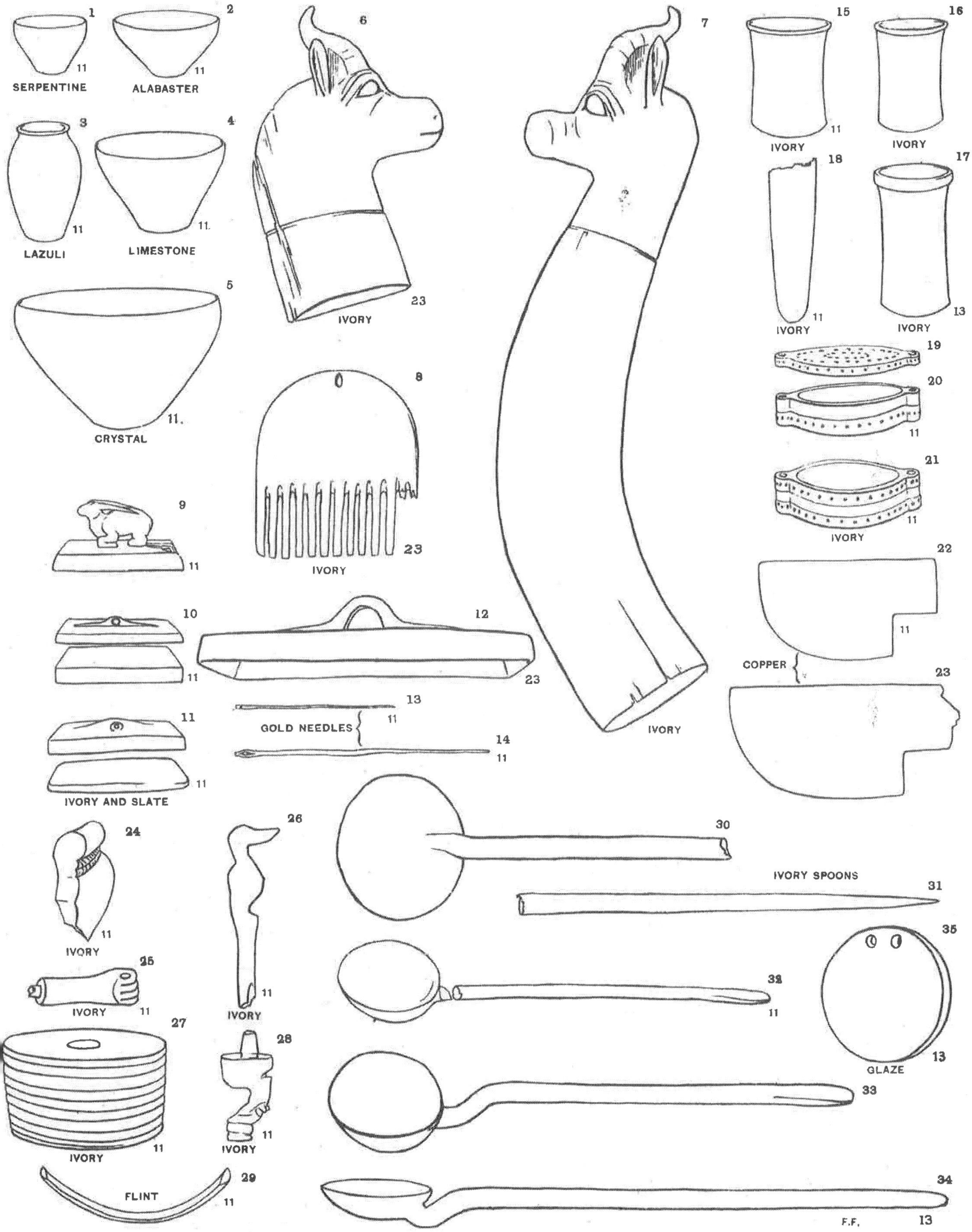
1
11
SERPENTINE
2
11
ALABASTER
3
11
LAZULI
4
11.
LIMESTONE
5
11.
CRYSTAL
6
23
IVORY
7
IVORY
8
23
IVORY
9
11
10
11
12
23
11
11
11
IVORY AND SLATE
13
GOLD NEEDLES
11
14
11
15
11
IVORY
16
IVORY
18
11
IVORY
17
13
IVORY
19
20
11
21
11
IVORY
22
11
COPPER
23
24
11
IVORY
25
IVORY
11
26
11
IVORY
27
IVORY
11
28
11
IVORY
29
FLINT
11
30
IVORY SPOONS
31
32
11
33
34
13
35
GLAZE
13
F.F.

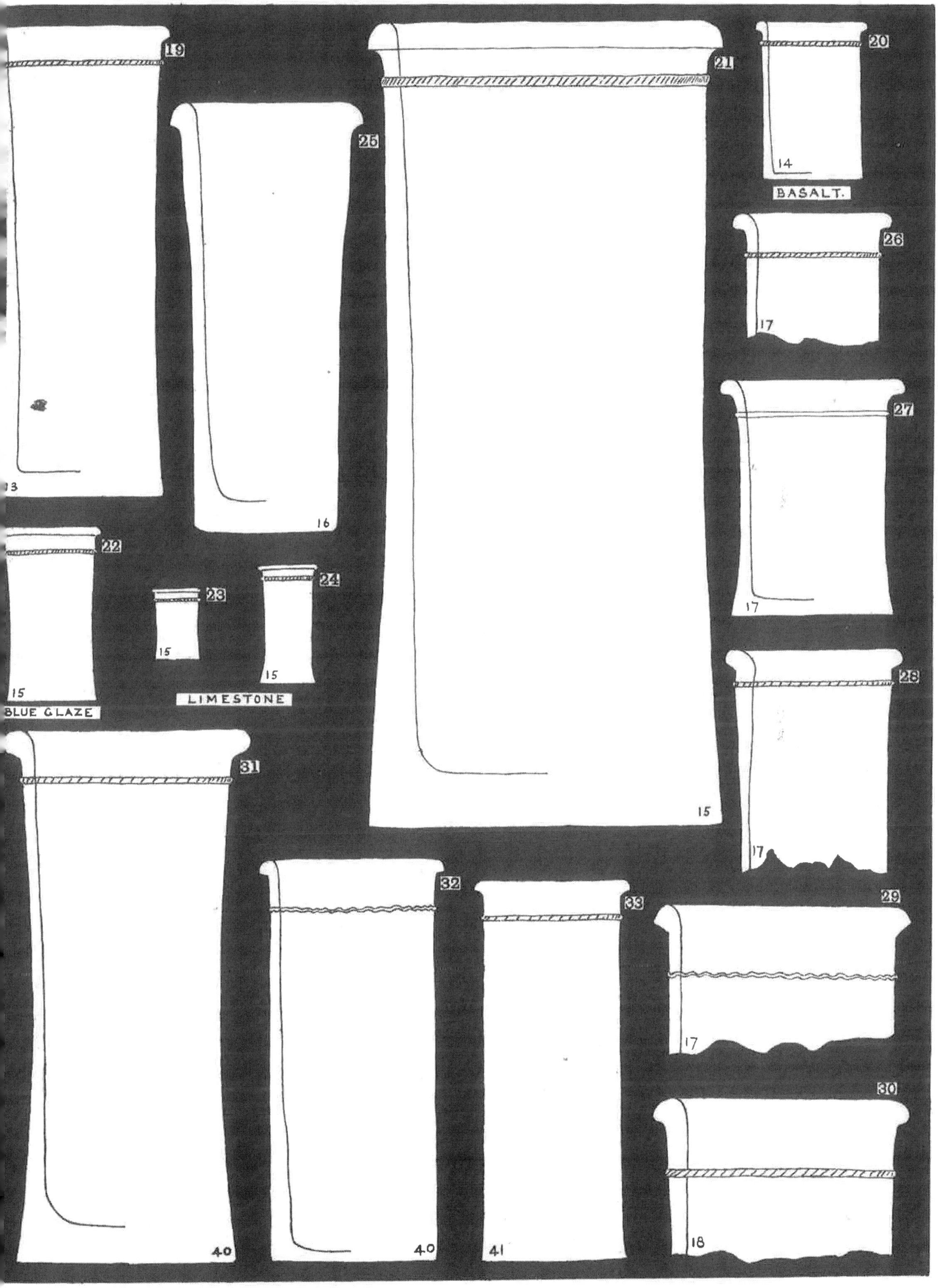
19
13
25
16
21
15
20
14
BASALT.
26
17
27
17
28
17
22
15
BLUE GLAZE
23
15
24
15
LIMESTONE
31
40
32
40
33
41
29
17
30
18

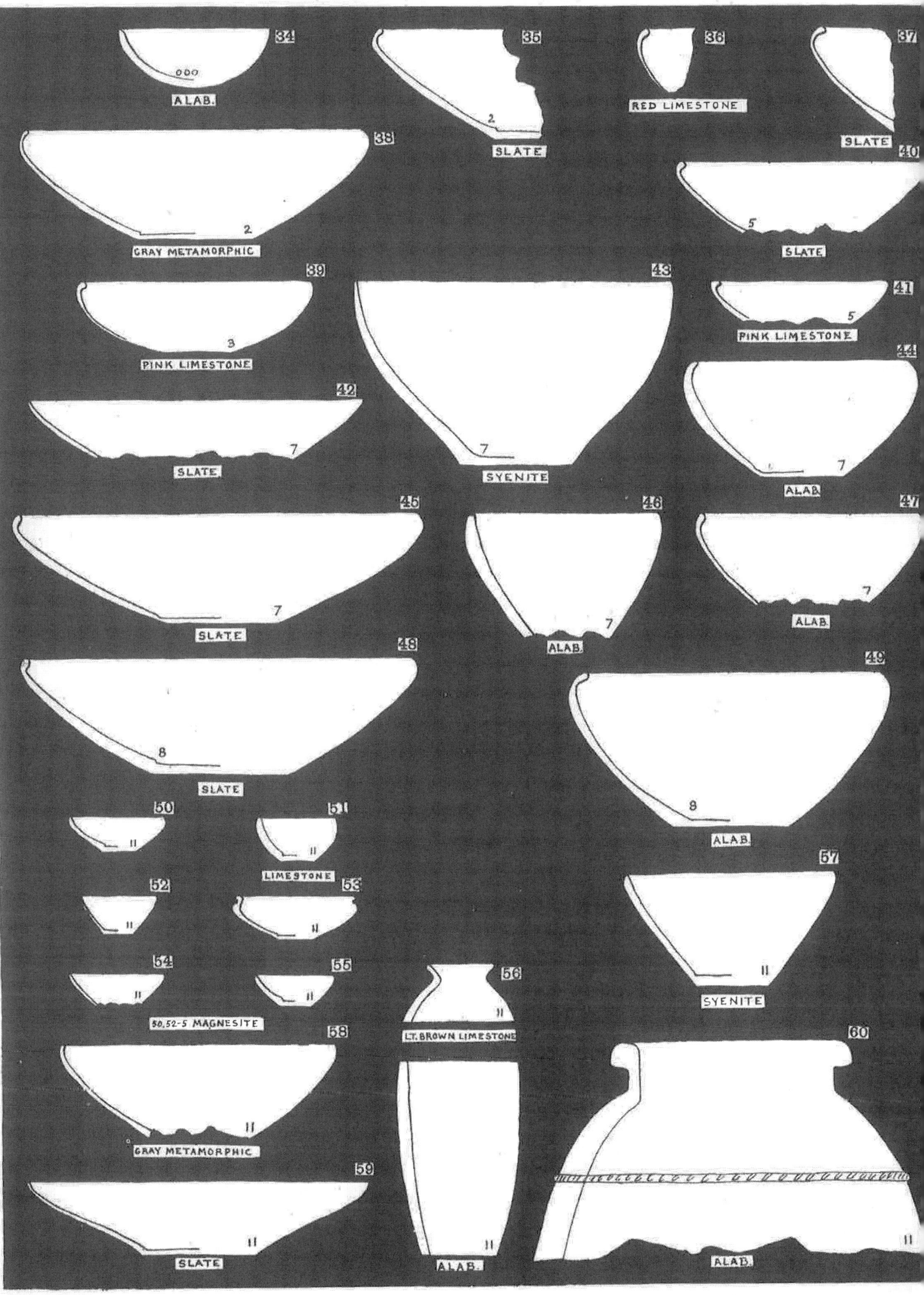
34
ALAB.
35
SLATE
36
RED LIMESTONE
37
SLATE
38
GRAY METAMORPHIC
40
SLATE
39
PINK LIMESTONE
43
SYENITE
41
PINK LIMESTONE
44
ALAB.
42
SLATE
45
SLATE
46
ALAB.
47
ALAB.
48
SLATE
49
ALAB.
50
51
LIMESTONE
52
53
54
55
50,52-5 MAGNESITE
56
LT. BROWN LIMESTONE
57
SYENITE
58
GRAY METAMORPHIC
59
SLATE
ALAB.
60
ALAB.

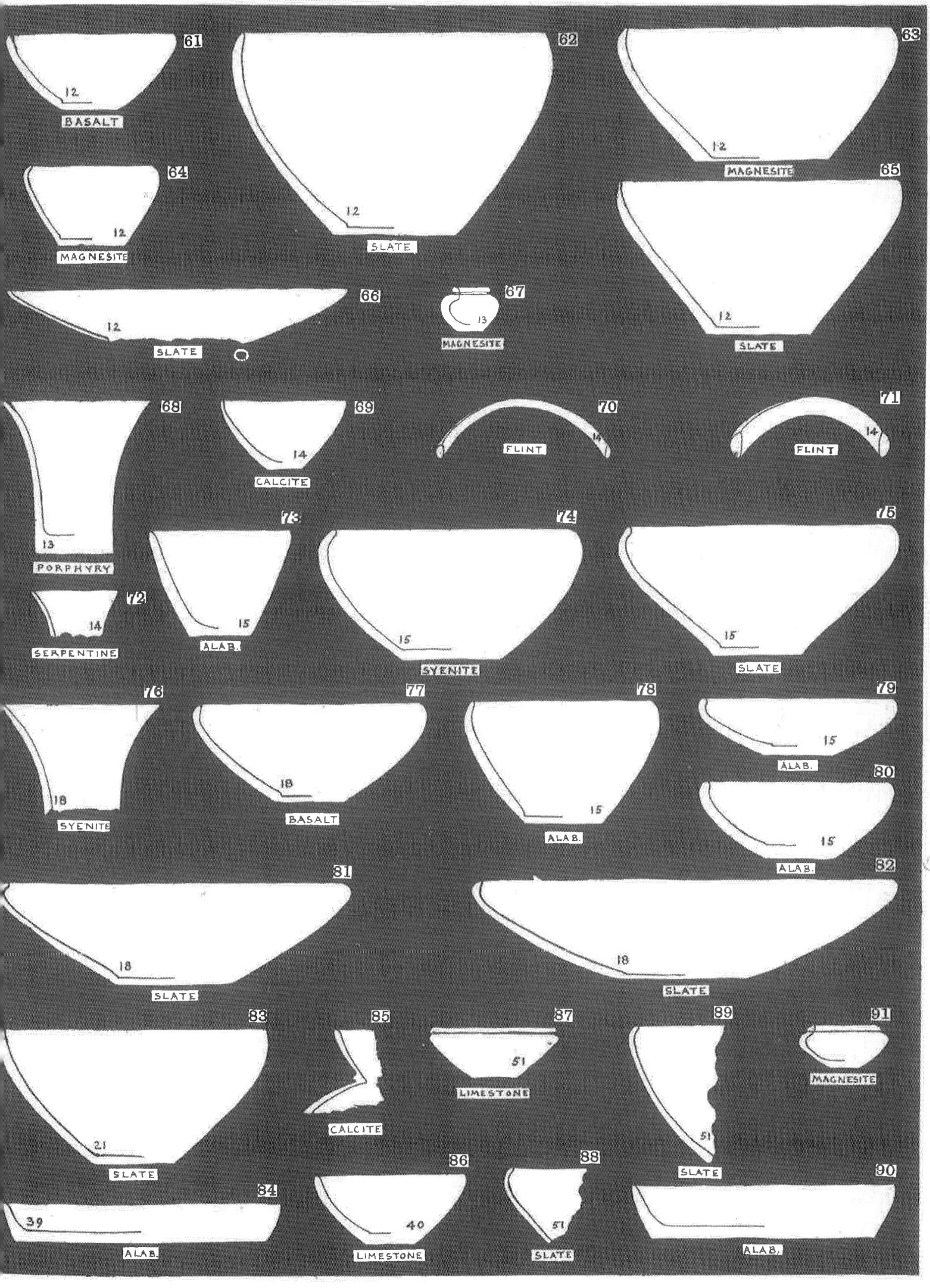
61
12
BASALT
62
12
SLATE
63
12
MAGNESITE
64
12
MAGNESITE
65
12
SLATE
66
12
SLATE
67
13
MAGNESITE
68
13
PORPHYRY
69
14
CALCITE
70
14
FLINT
71
14
FLINT
72
14
SERPENTINE
73
15
ALAB.
74
15
SYENITE
75
15
SLATE
76
18
SYENITE
77
18
BASALT
78
15
ALAB.
79
15
ALAB.
80
15
ALAB.
81
18
SLATE
82
18
SLATE
83
21
SLATE
84
39
ALAB.
85
CALCITE
86
40
LIMESTONE
87
51
LIMESTONE
88
51
SLATE
89
51
SLATE
90
ALAB.
91
MAGNESITE

GIZEH. TOMB, POTTERY AND MARKS, IST DYNASTY. SEALINGS, IIND DYNASTY. VE.

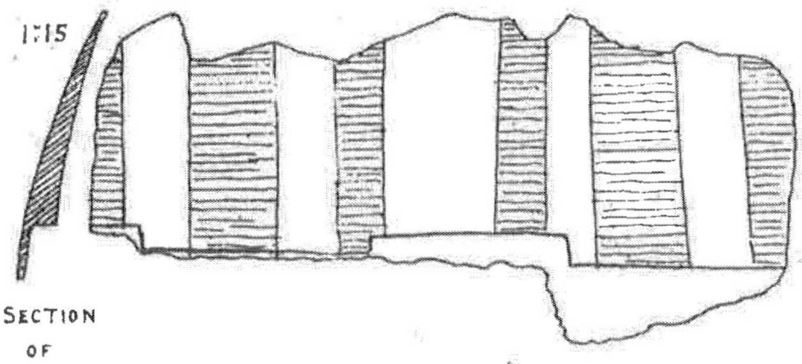

SECTION OF STUCCO. INNER FACE OF STUCCO, CAST OF TOMB OUTSIDE

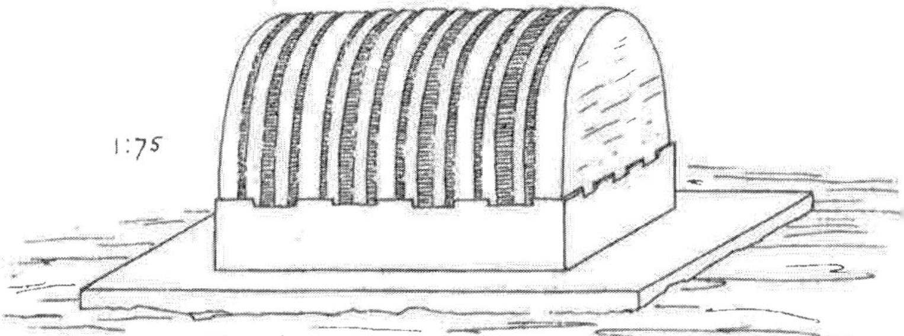

FORM OF TOMB, RESTORED FROM PIECE OF STUCCO

W. M. F. P.

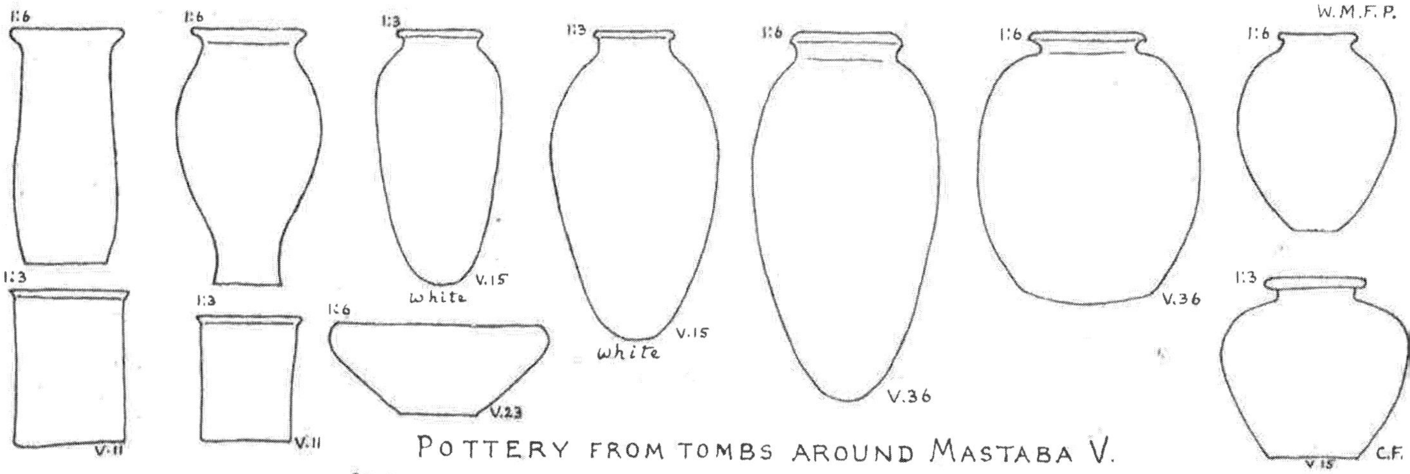

POTTERY FROM TOMBS AROUND MASTABA V.

MARKS ON POTTERY, MASTABA V.

SEALINGS OF NETEREN, TOMB OF IIND DYNASTY.

1:200 GIZEH. PLAN OF MASTABA V. AND GRAVES AROUND. ZET, Ist DYNASTY. VI.

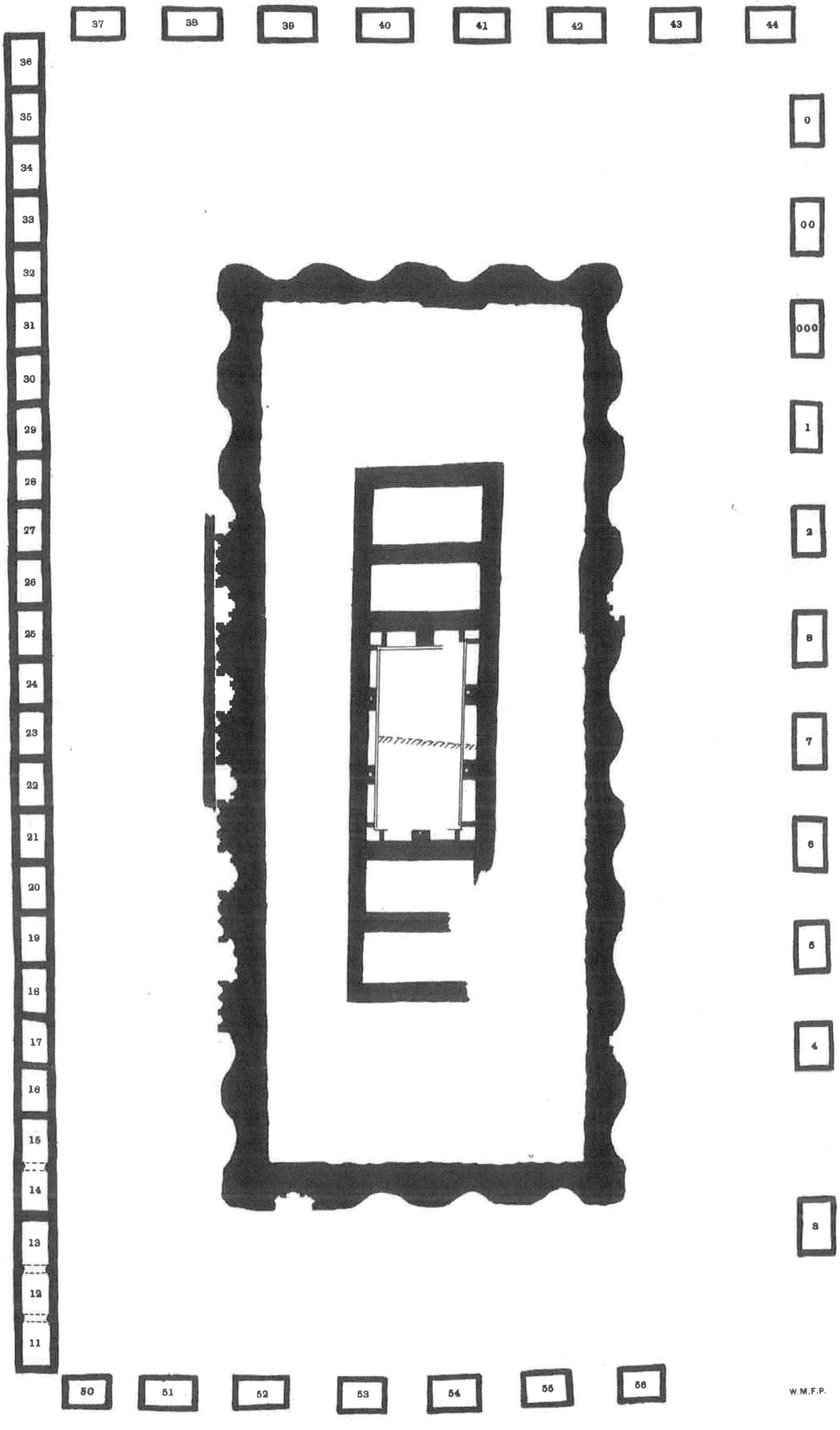

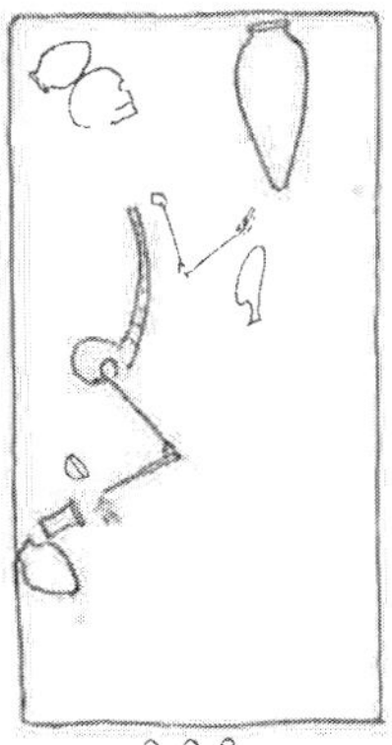

000

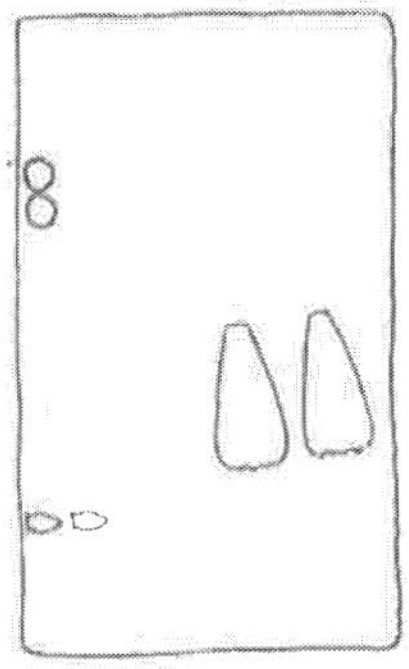

1

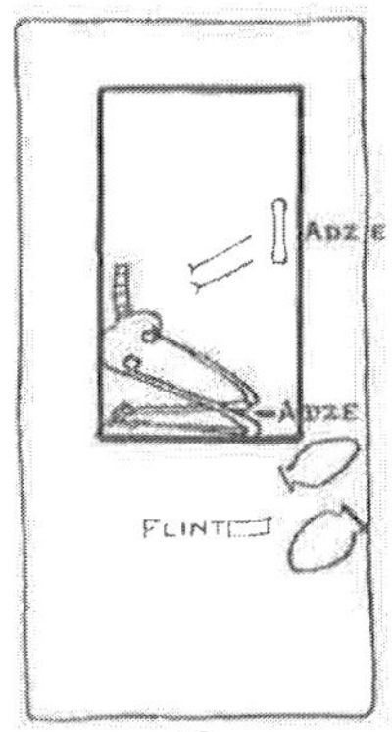

13

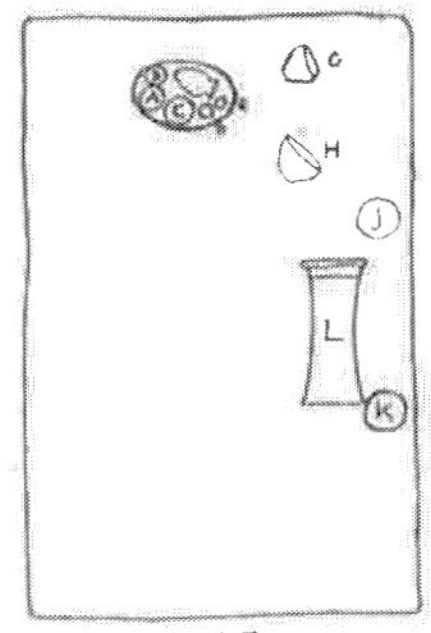

15
See view pl. II.

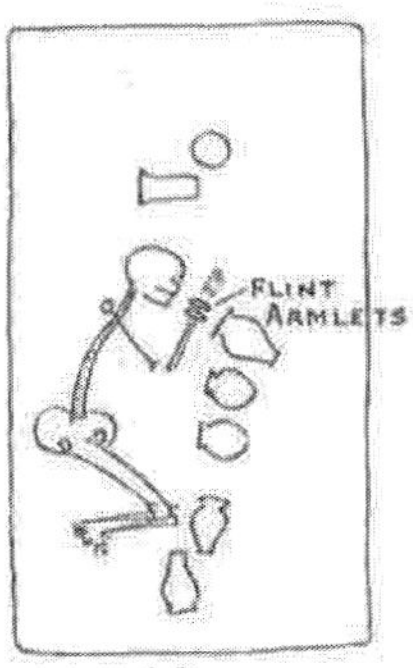

23

30

35

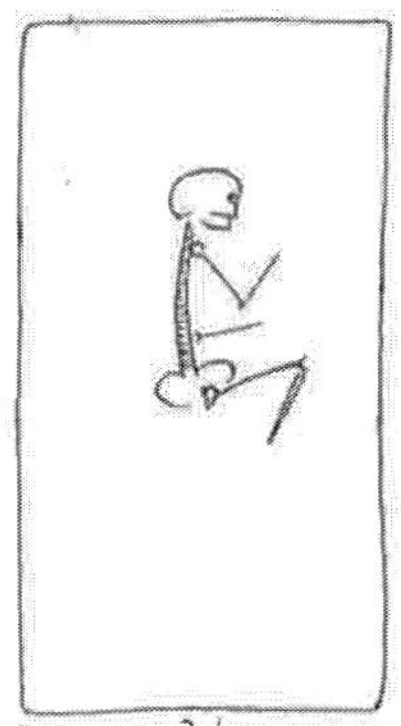

36

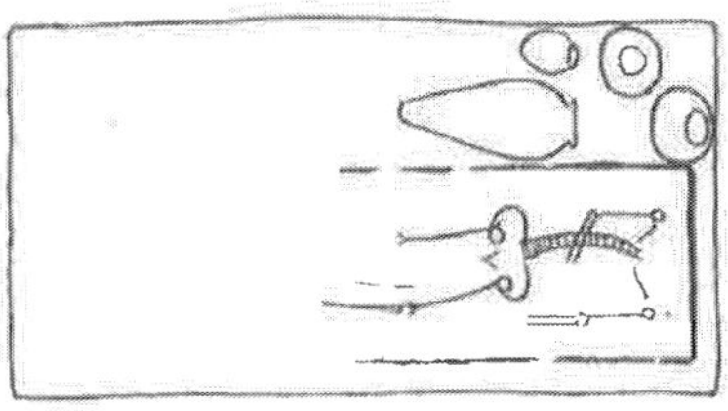

38. See view pl. III A

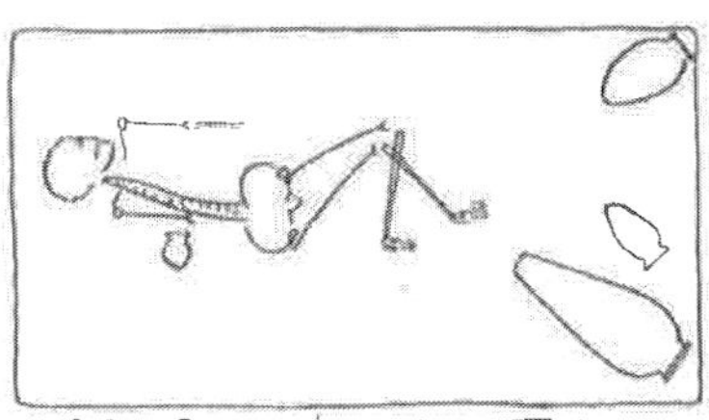

39. See view pl. III A.

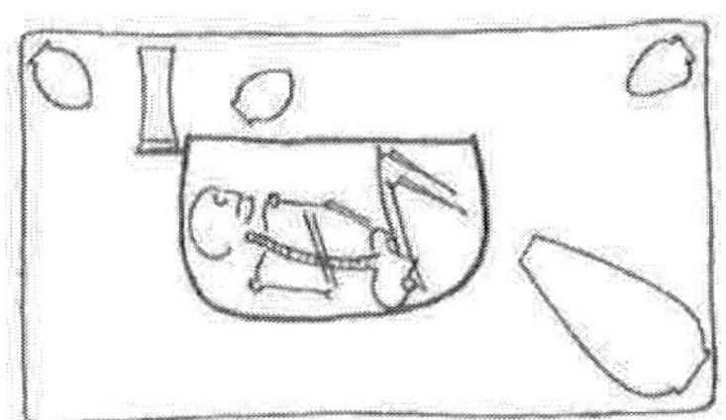

40

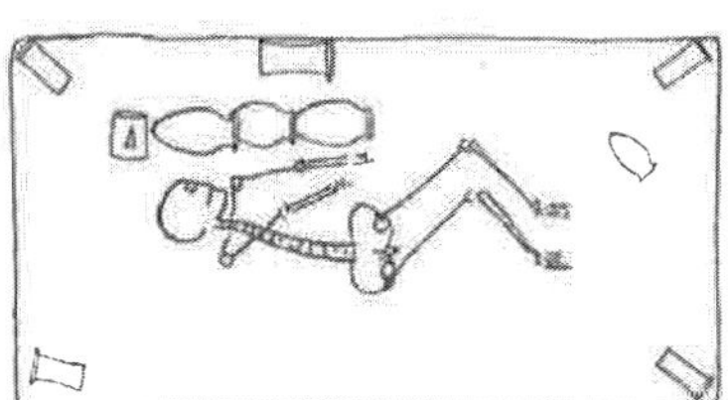

41

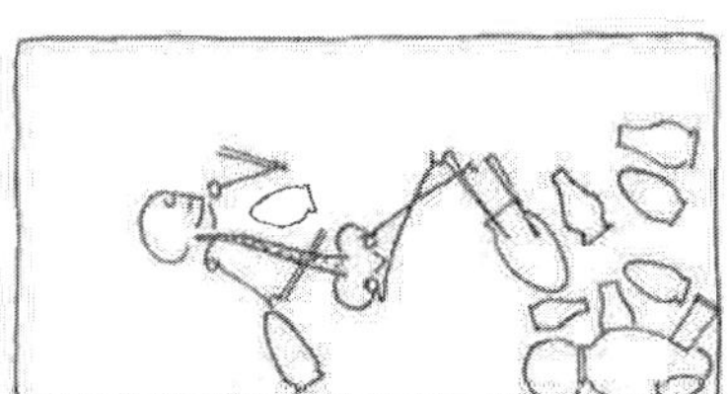

42

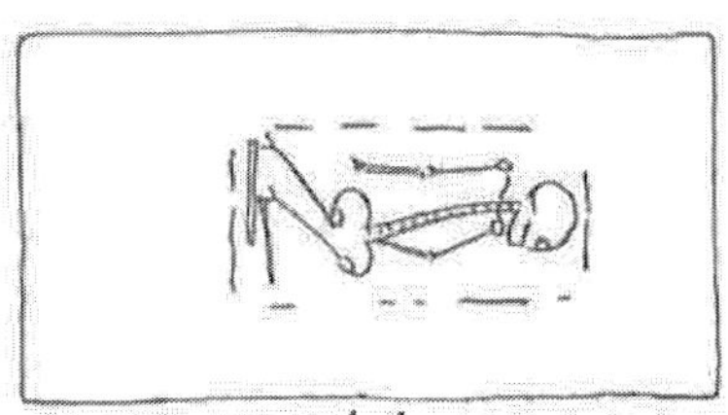

44

54

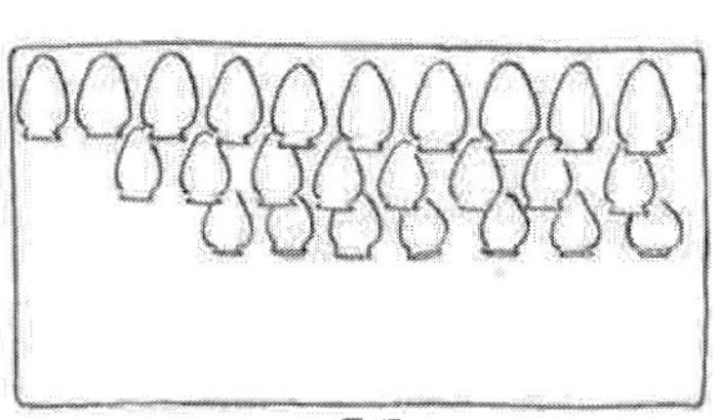

55

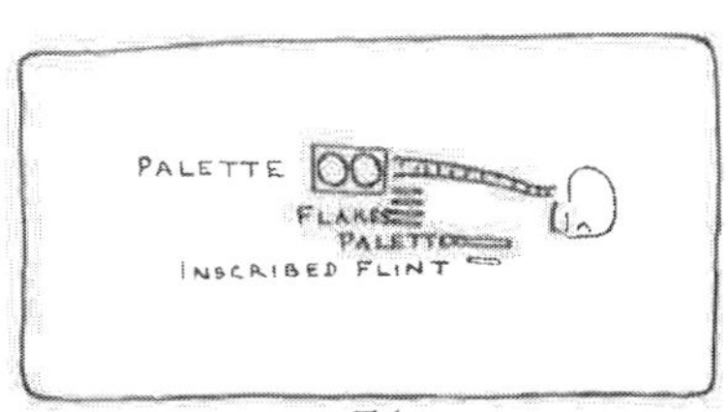

56

W.M.F.P.

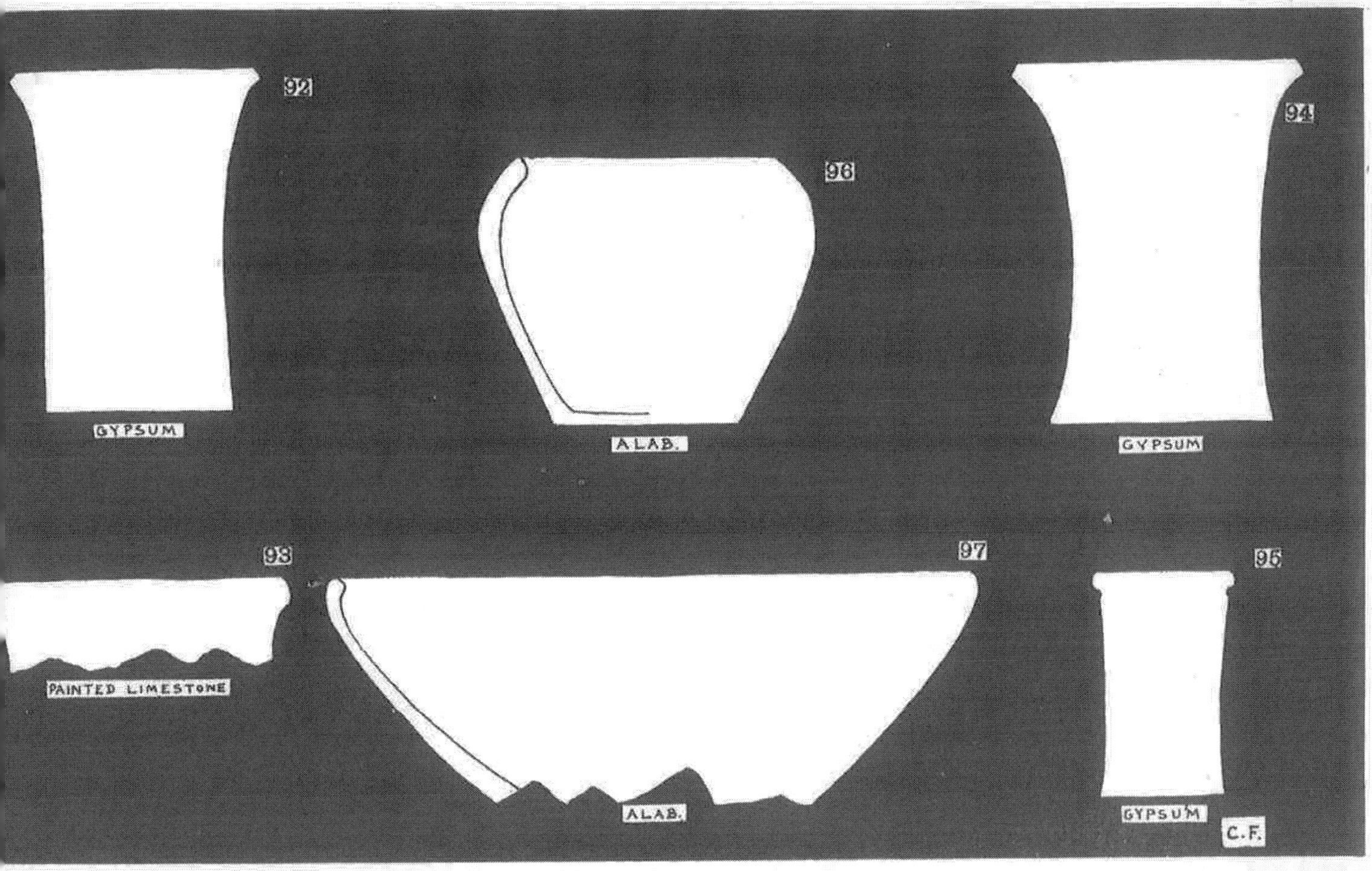
92
GYPSUM
96
ALAB.
94
GYPSUM
93
PAINTED LIMESTONE
97
ALAB.
95
GYPSUM
C.F.

1:20

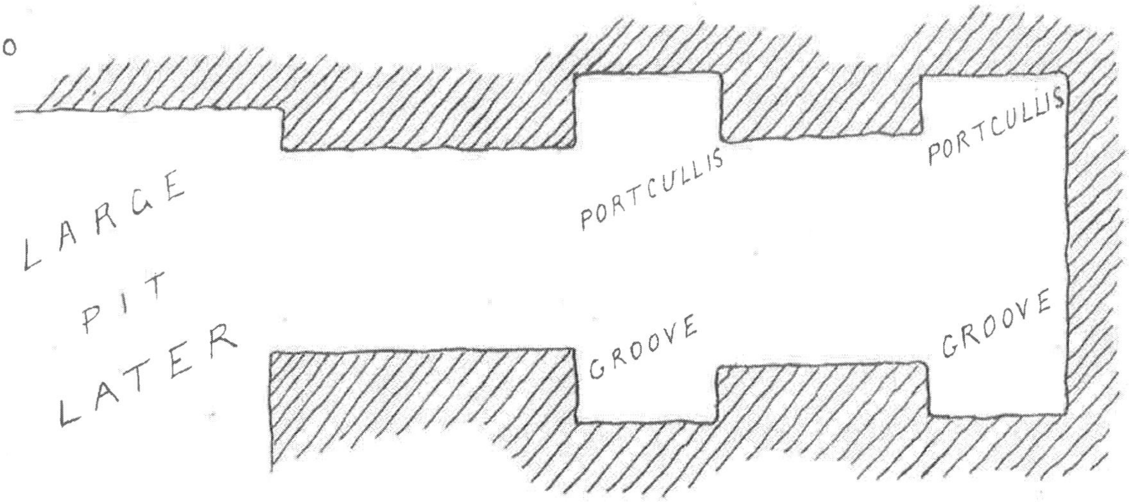
LARGE PIT LATER
PORTCULLIS
PORTCULLIS
GROOVE
GROOVE

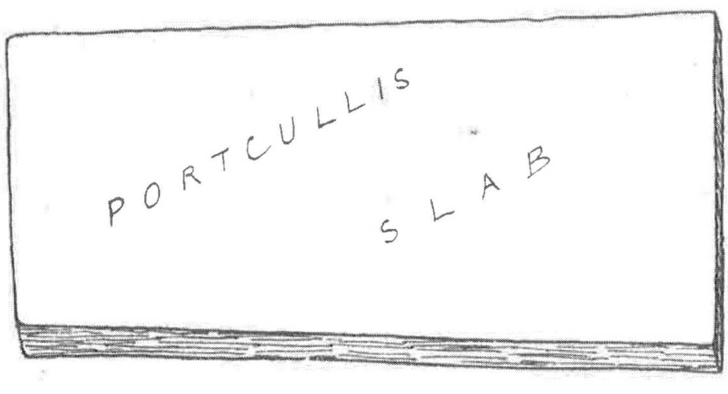
PORTCULLIS SLAB

E.M.
F.P.

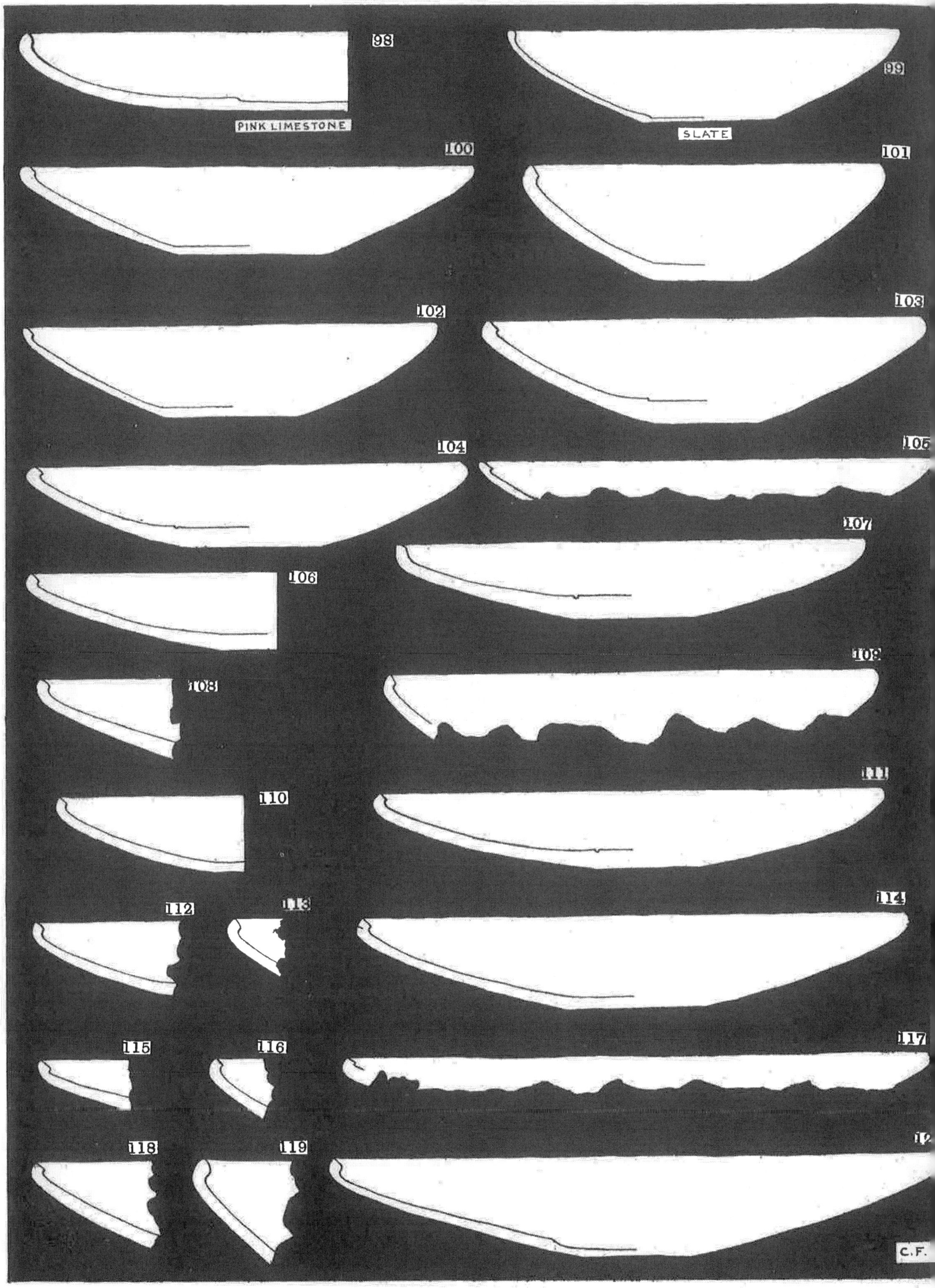
98
PINK LIMESTONE
99
SLATE
100
101
102
103
104
105
106
107
108
109
110
111
112
113
114
115
116
117
118
119
C.F.

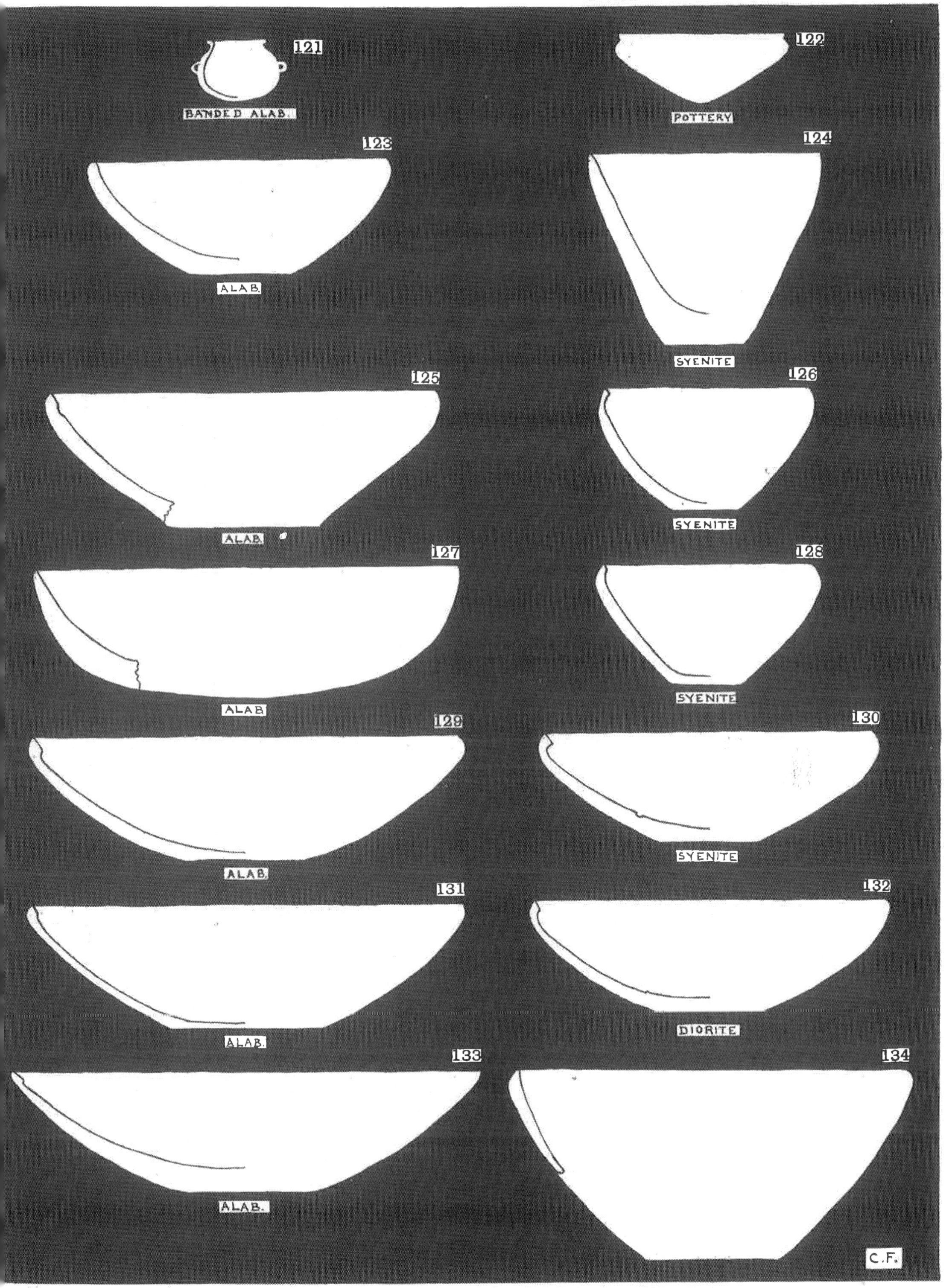
121
BANDED ALAB.
122
POTTERY
123
ALAB.
124
SYENITE
125
ALAB.
126
SYENITE
127
ALAB.
128
SYENITE
129
ALAB.
130
SYENITE
131
ALAB.
132
DIORITE
133
ALAB.
134
C.F.

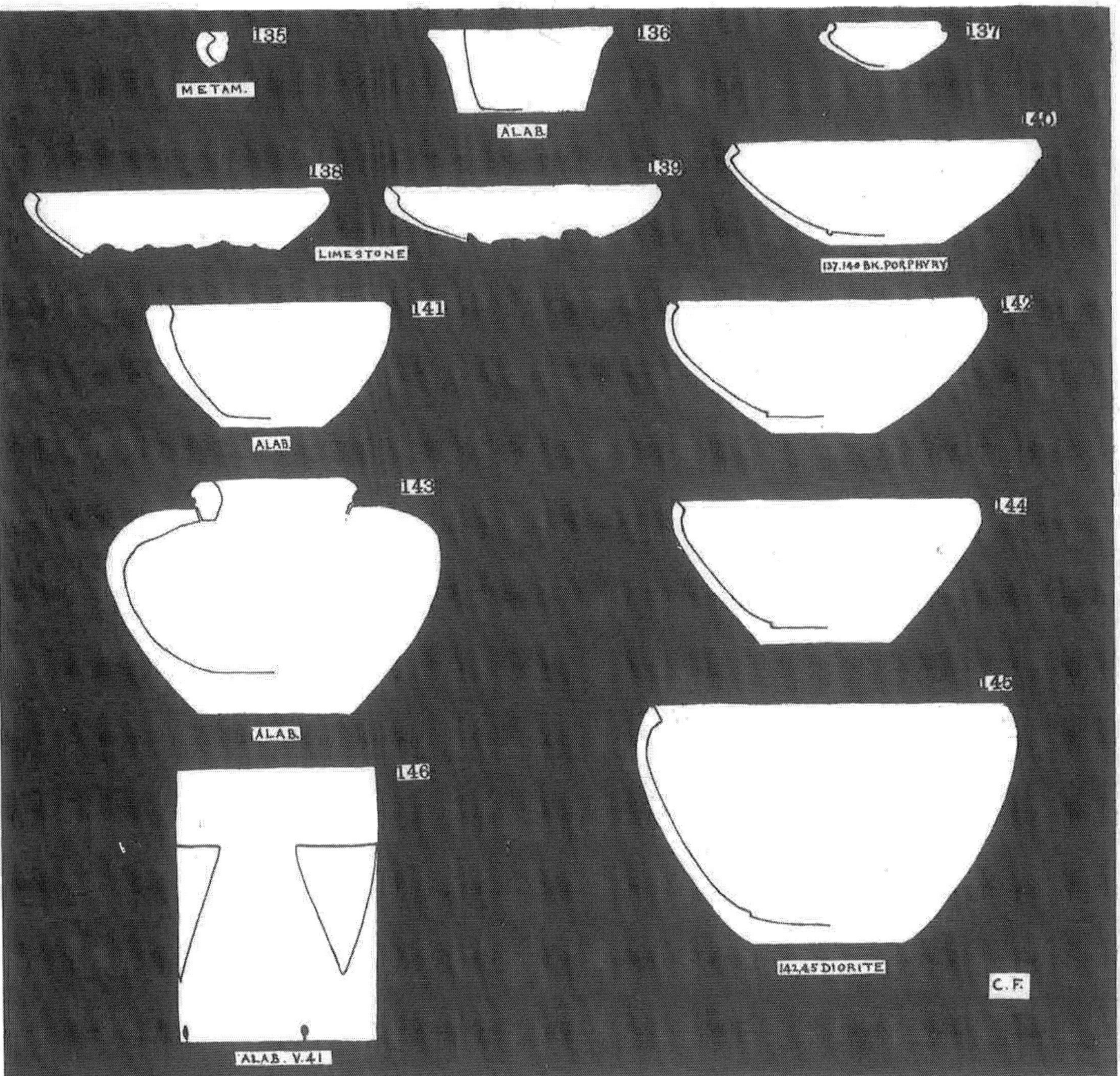

2:3
147

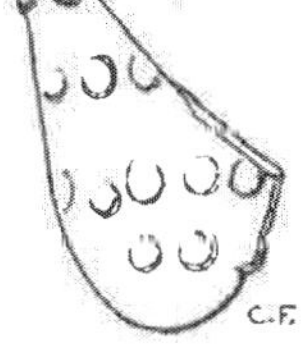

SLATE V.

2:3 148

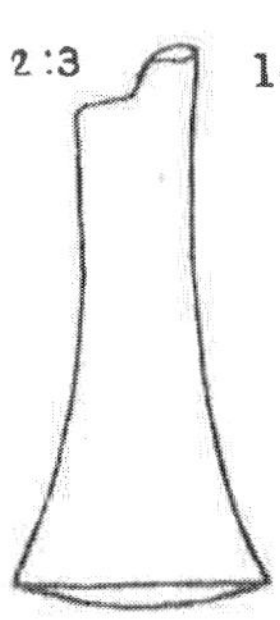

IVORY HANDLE
V.6

149

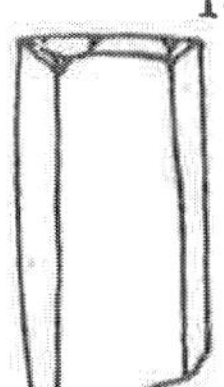

FLINT T.

150

COPPER CHISEL. MASTABA T.

151

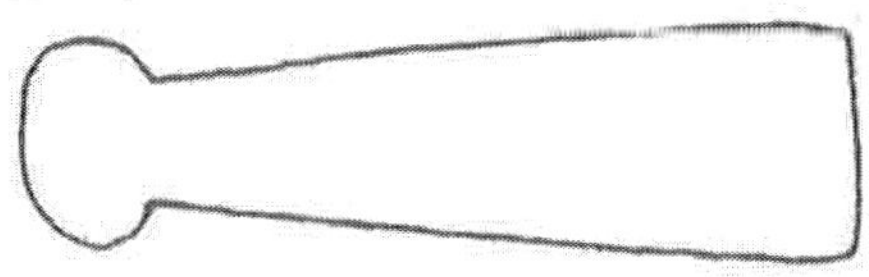

152

COPPER MODEL TOOLS. MASTABA T.

F.P.

NOFER-HER-NE-PTAH.

NOFER-HER-NE-PTAH.

AKHET-AB.

PER-NE-ANKH.

ERDU-NE-PTAH.

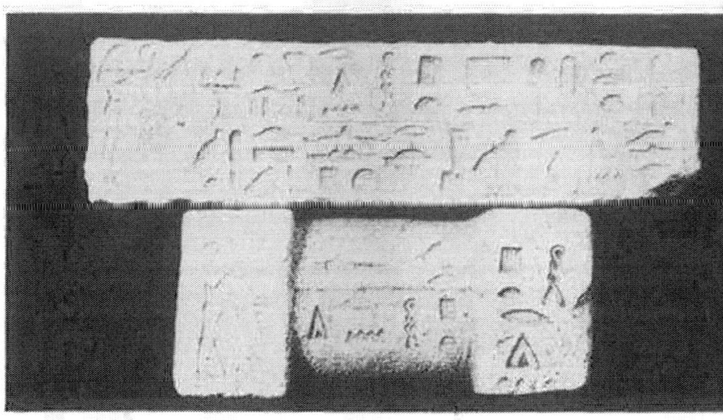

ERDU-NE-PTAH.

PLAIN LINTEL OVER TOMB.

FIGURE OF RES-HE-NOFER.

ROCK TOMBS.

HEAD, STONE PILLOW, INCENSE BURNERS.

NICHES WITH PITS.

TABLE ALTAR OF RA-HAPEF.

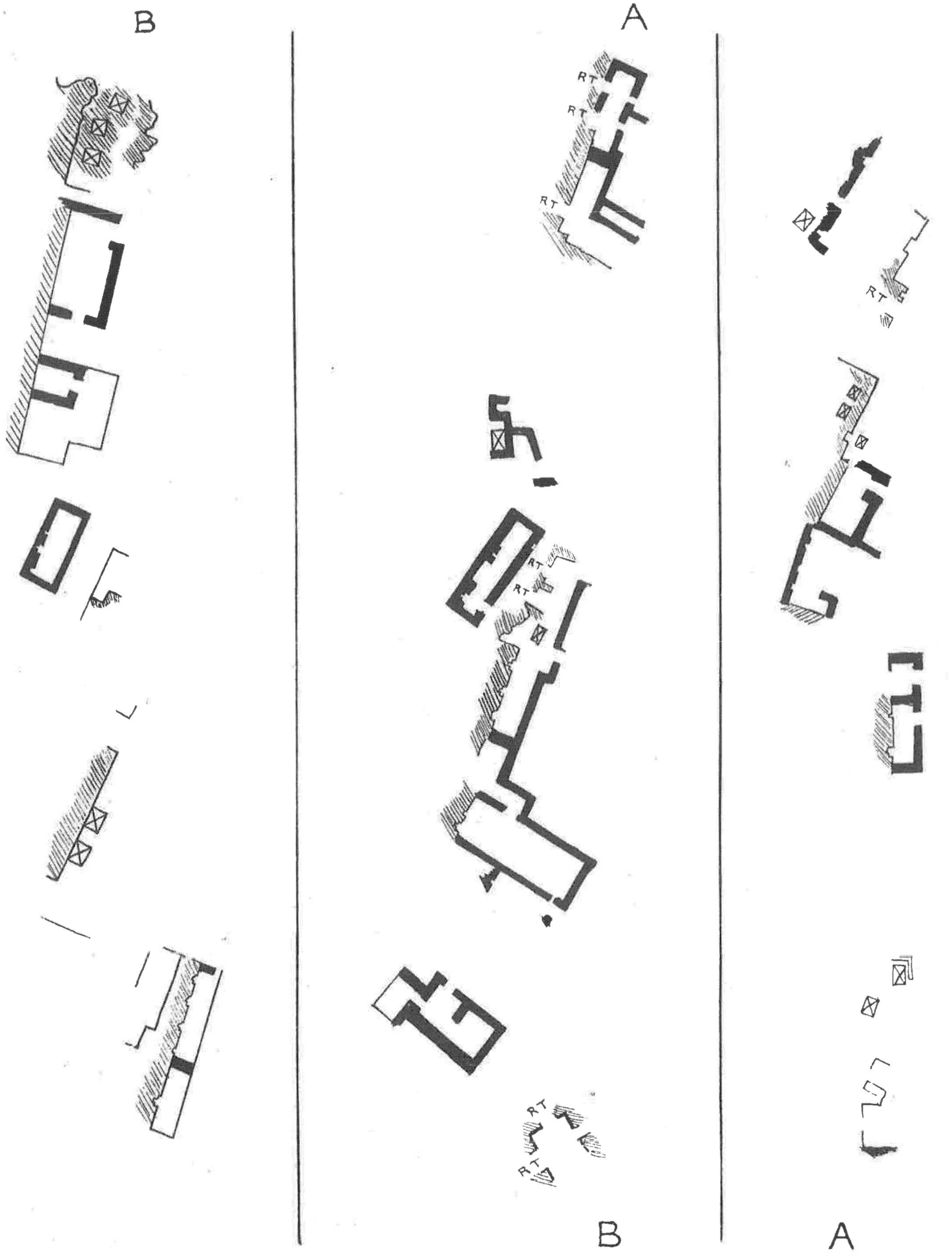

SHAFT. RT, ROCK TOMB BRICK WALL.

C.F.

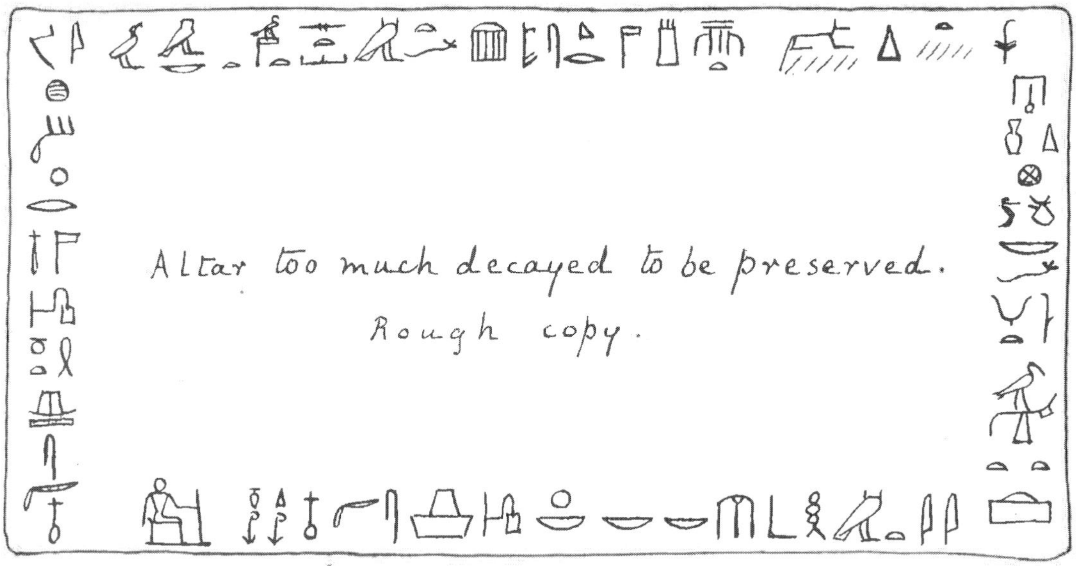
Altar too much decayed to be preserved.
Rough copy.

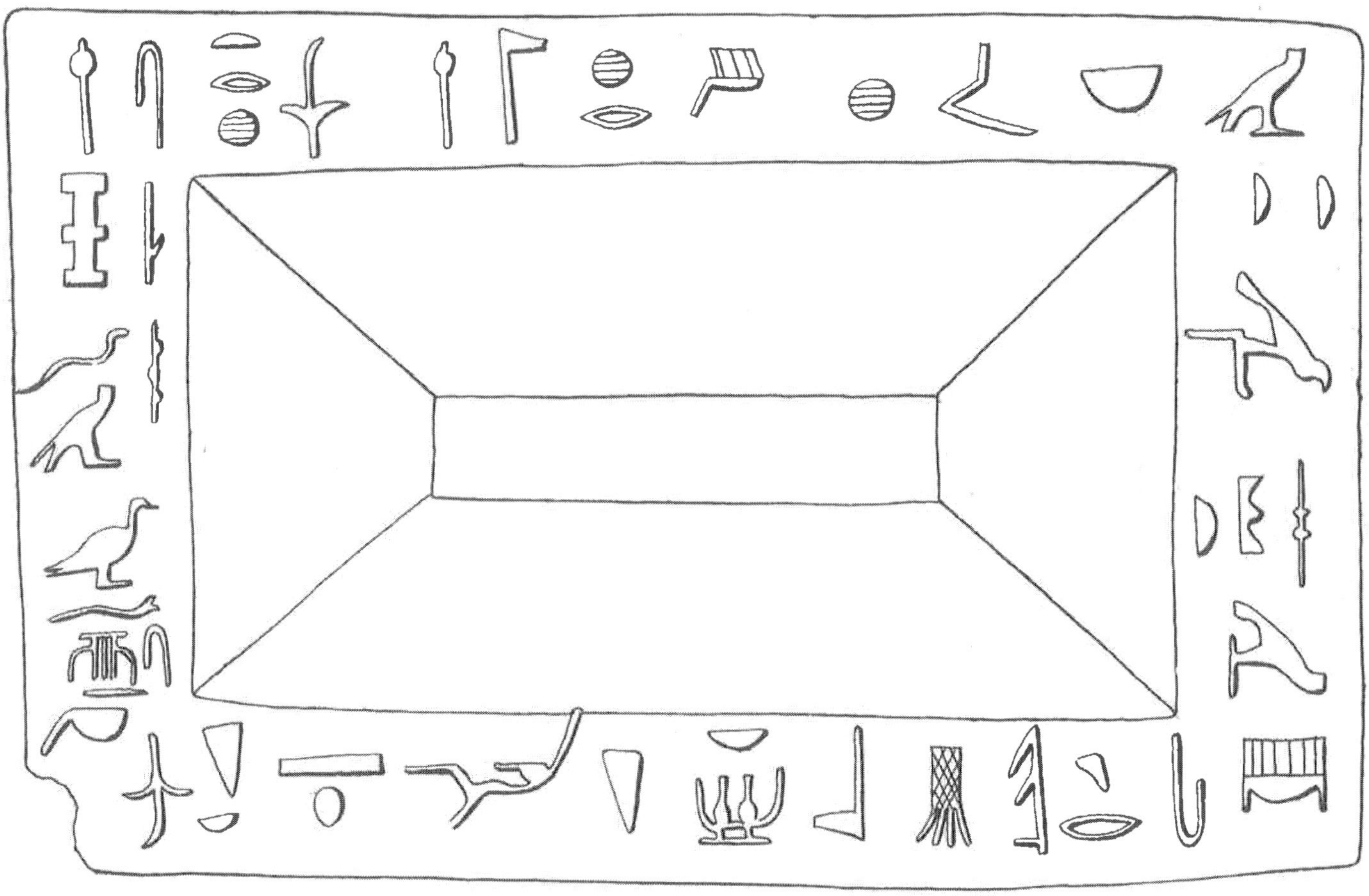

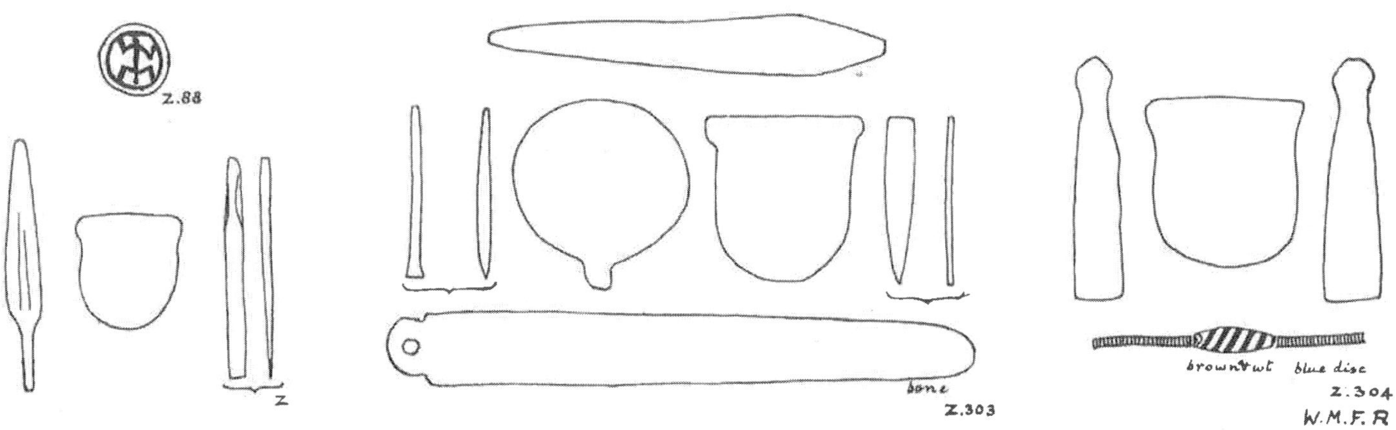
Z.88
Z
bone
Z.303
brown wt
blue disc
Z.304
W.M.F.R

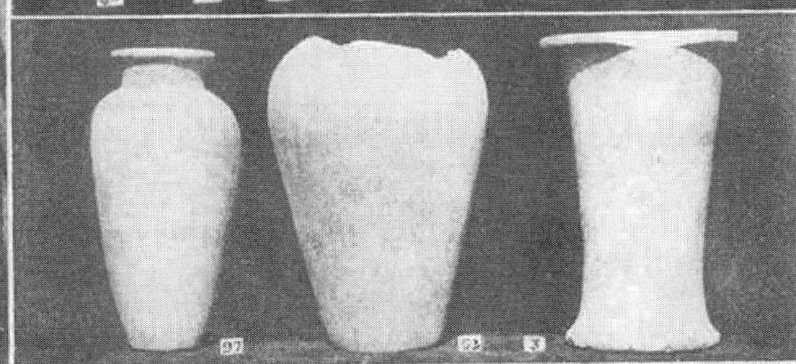

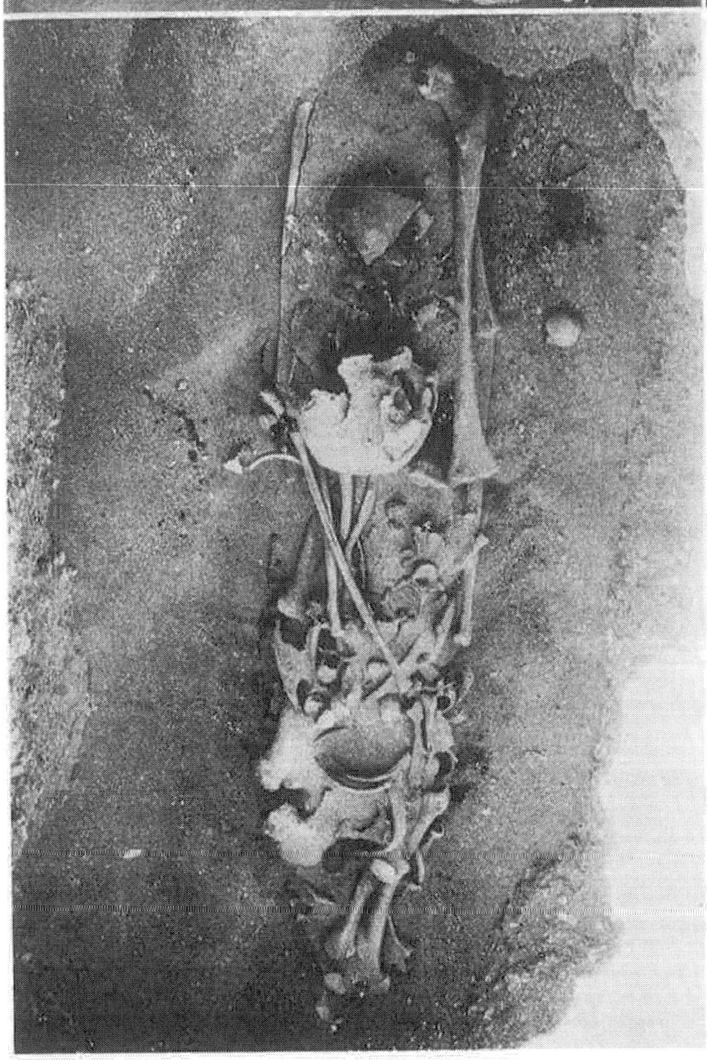

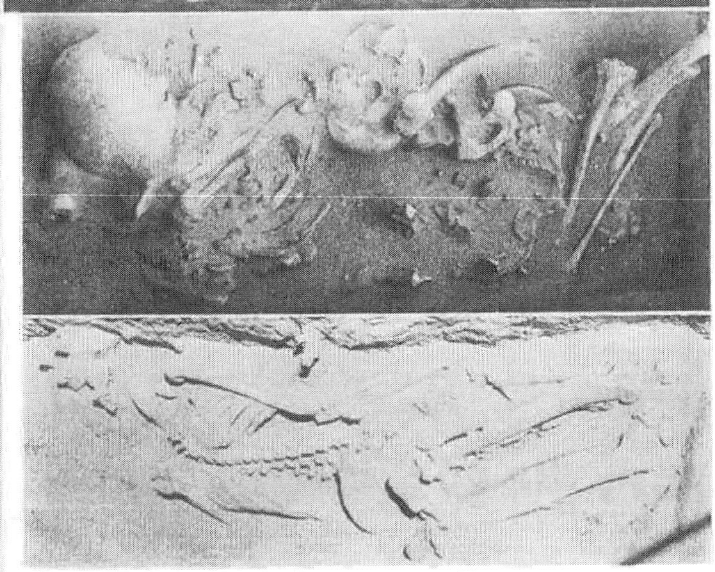

GRAVES 43 AND 60.

GRAVE 42.

VIth DYN. CEMETERY SOUTH OF RIFEH.

Numbers of Tombs. ZOW, Zowyeh by Rifeh. W. M. F. P.

MAP OF DISTRICT AND PLAN OF CEMETERIES.

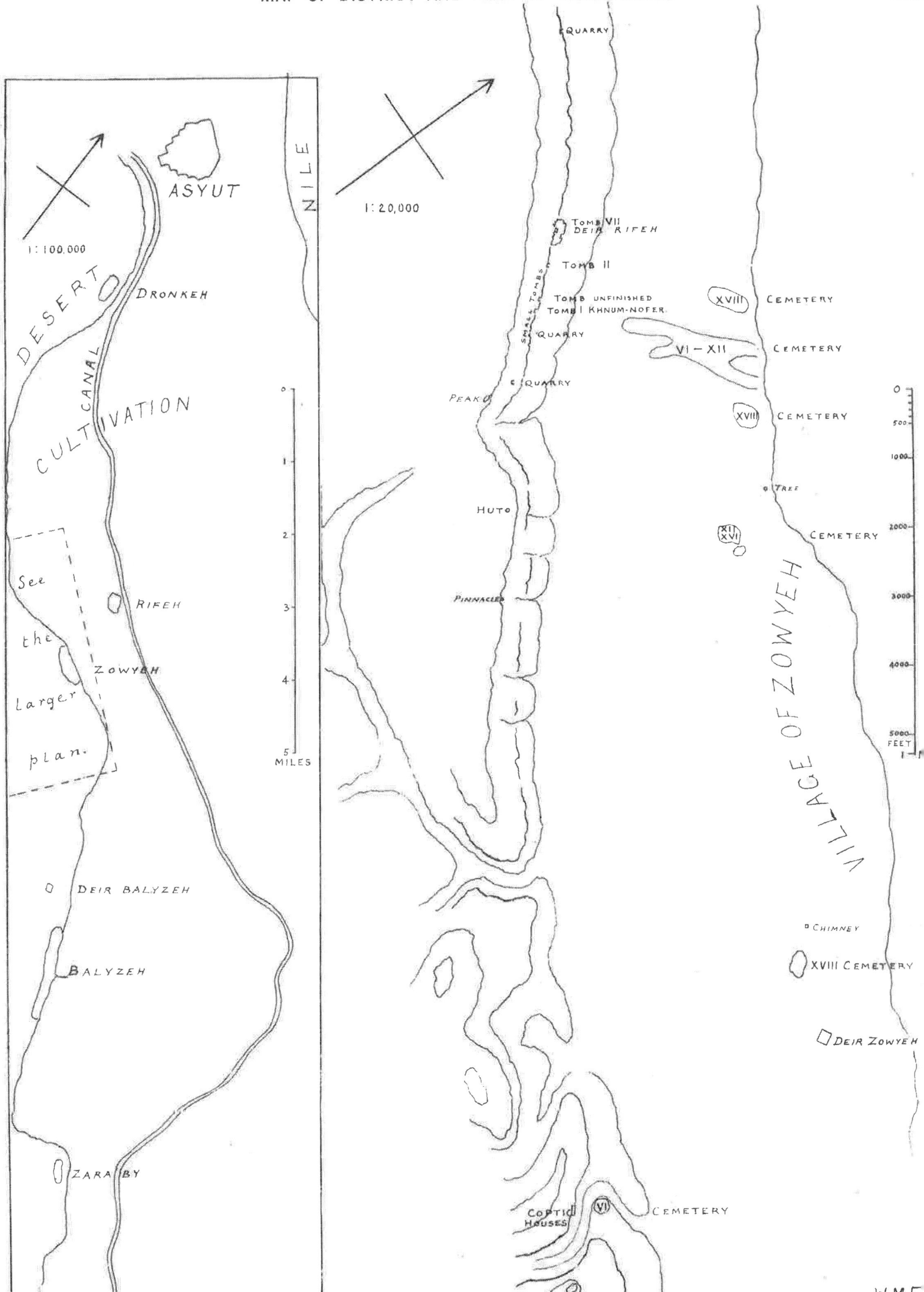

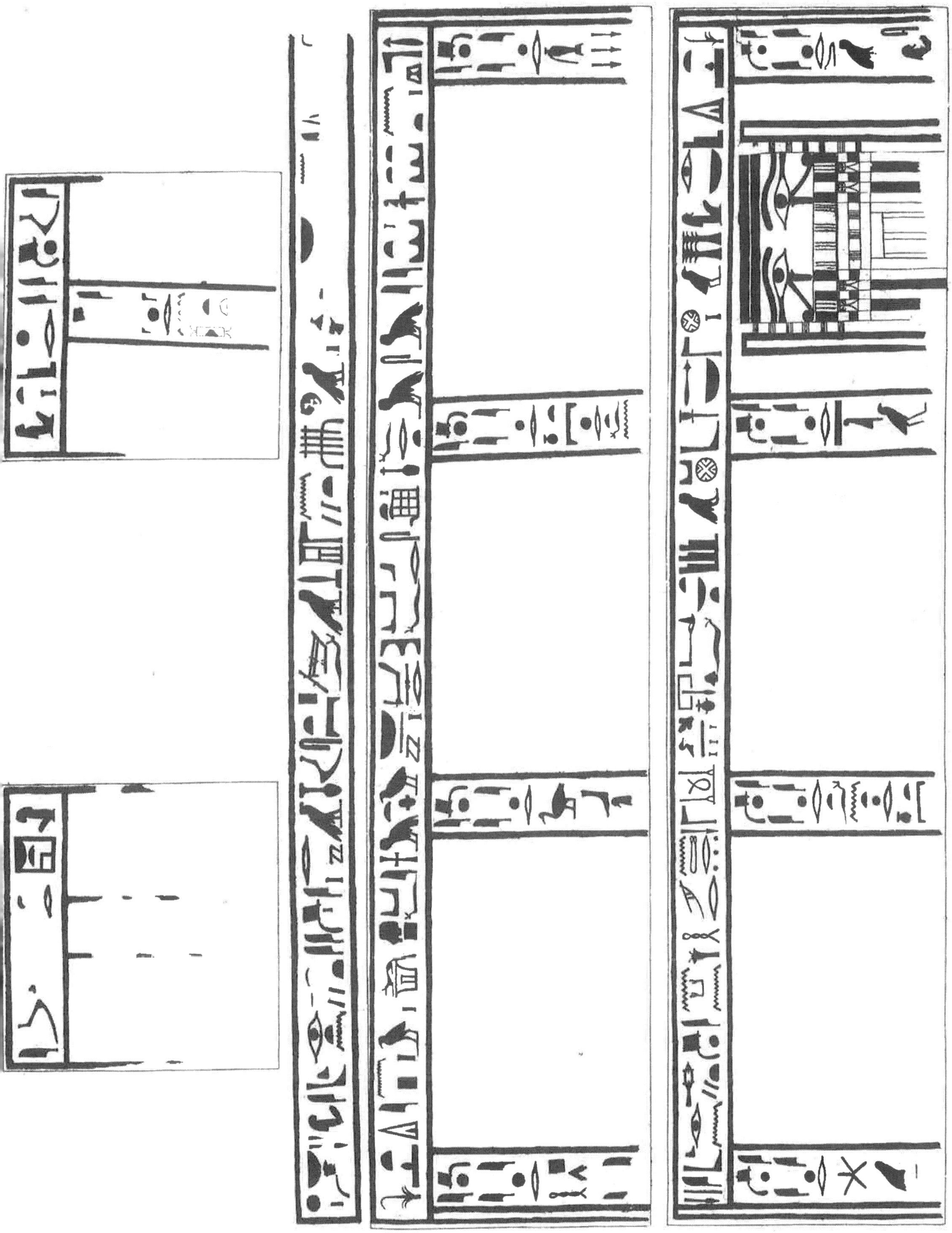

RIFEH. BLACK GRANITE FIGURE OF KHNUMU. XII DYNASTY.

COFFIN OF NEKHT-ANKH.

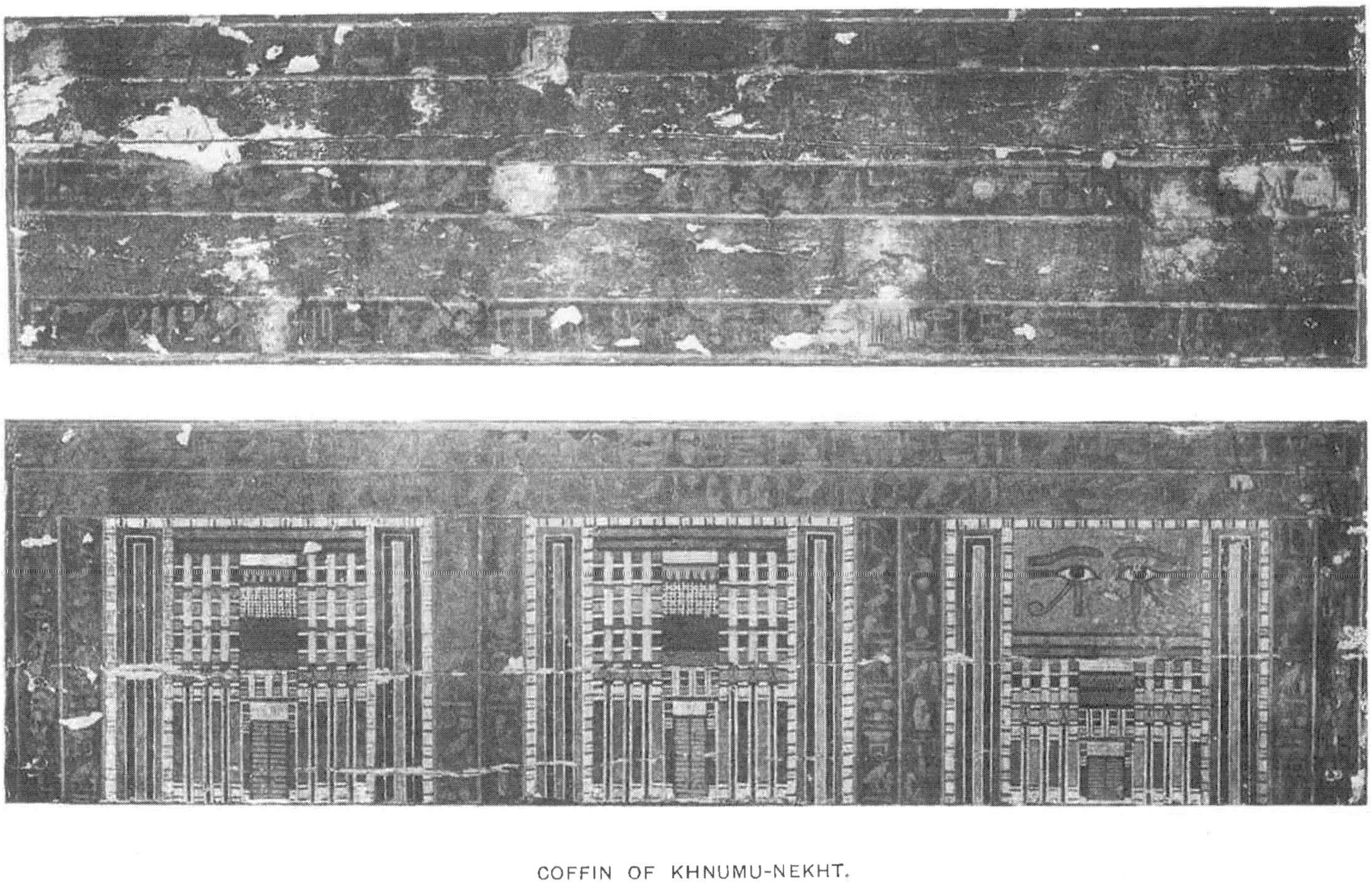

COFFIN OF KHNUMU-NEKHT.

NEKHT-ANKH.

KHNUMU-NEKHT.

GOING UP NILE.

GOING DOWN NILE.

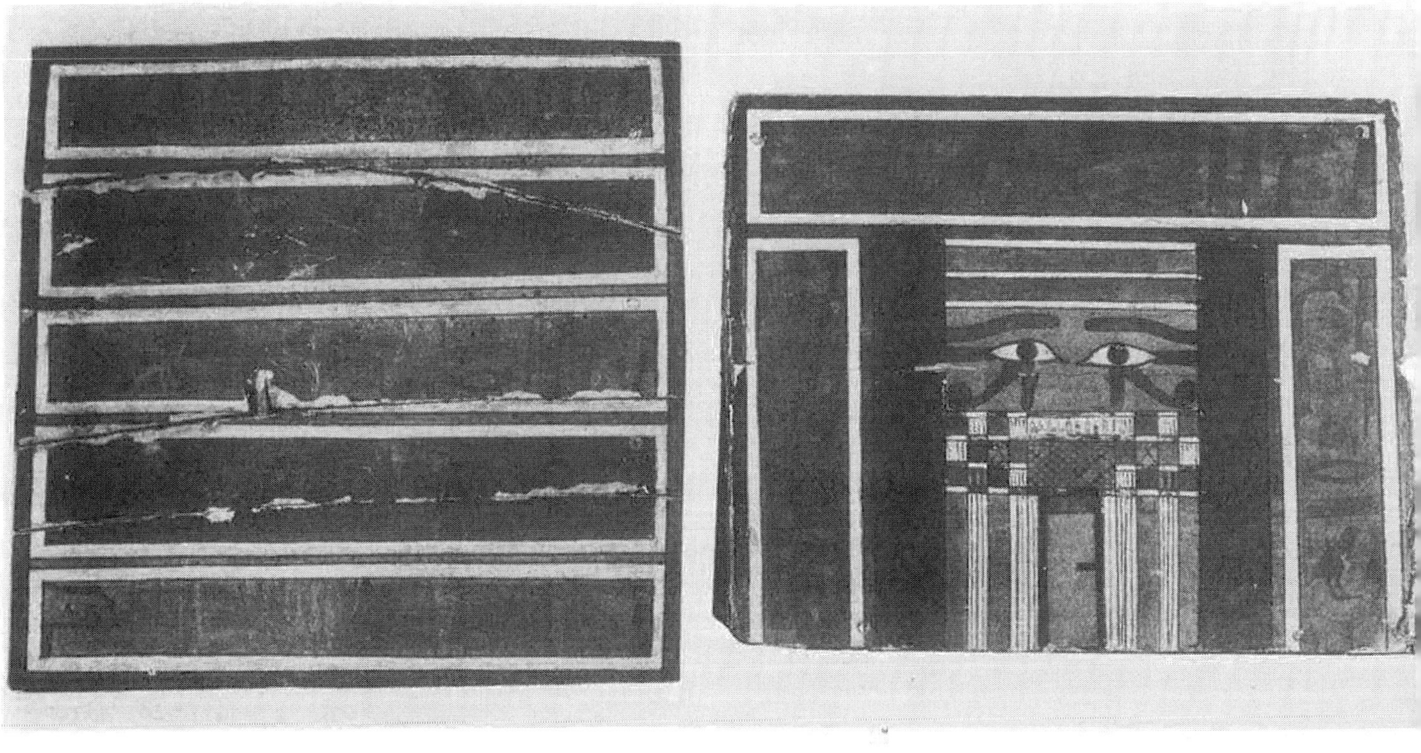

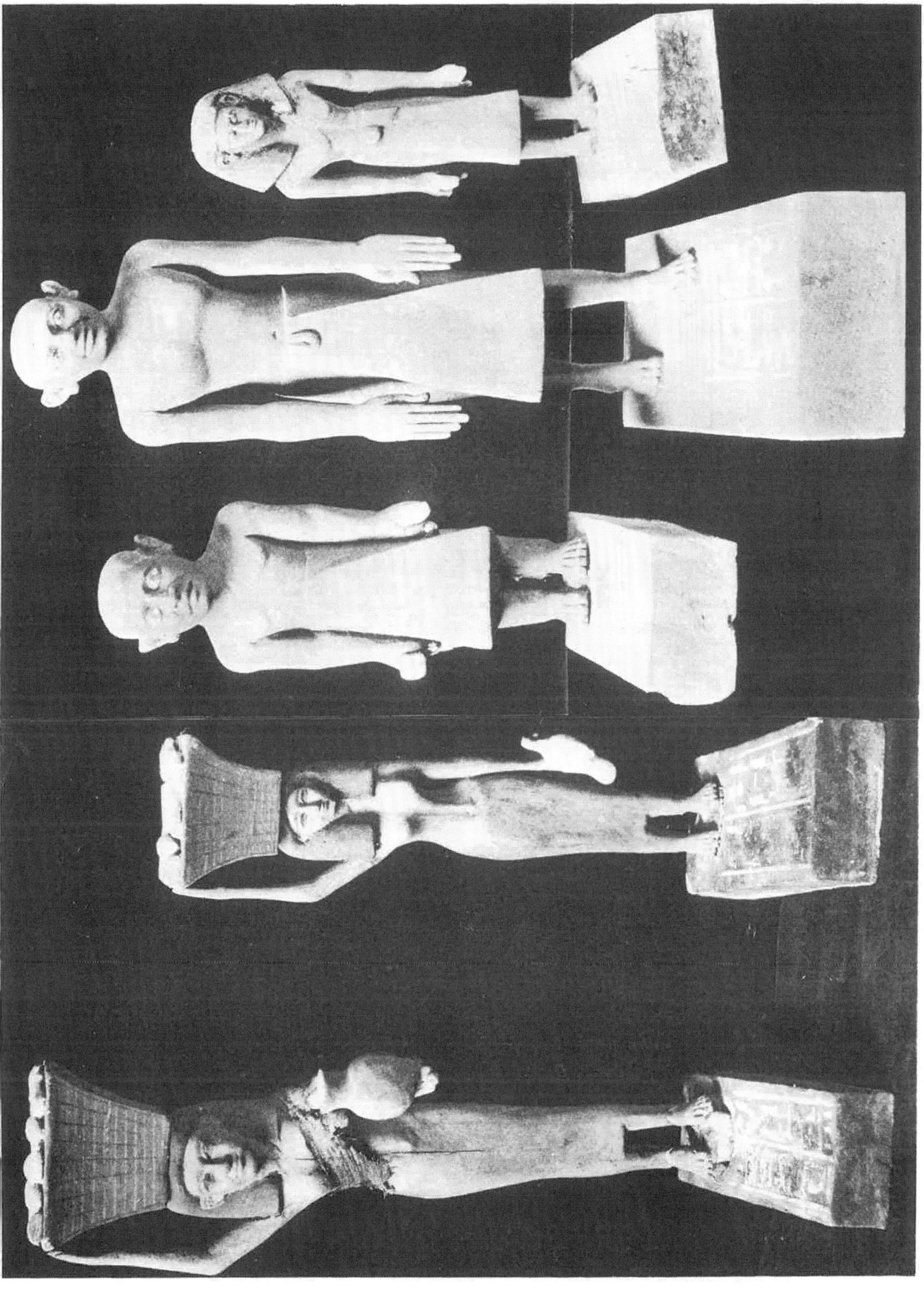

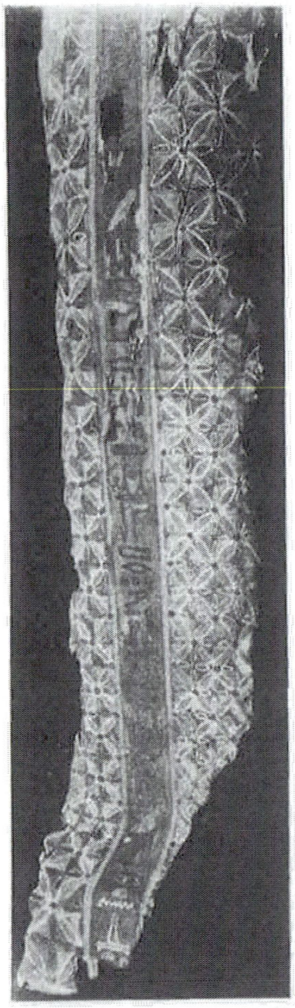

SILVER FACE. PL. XI.

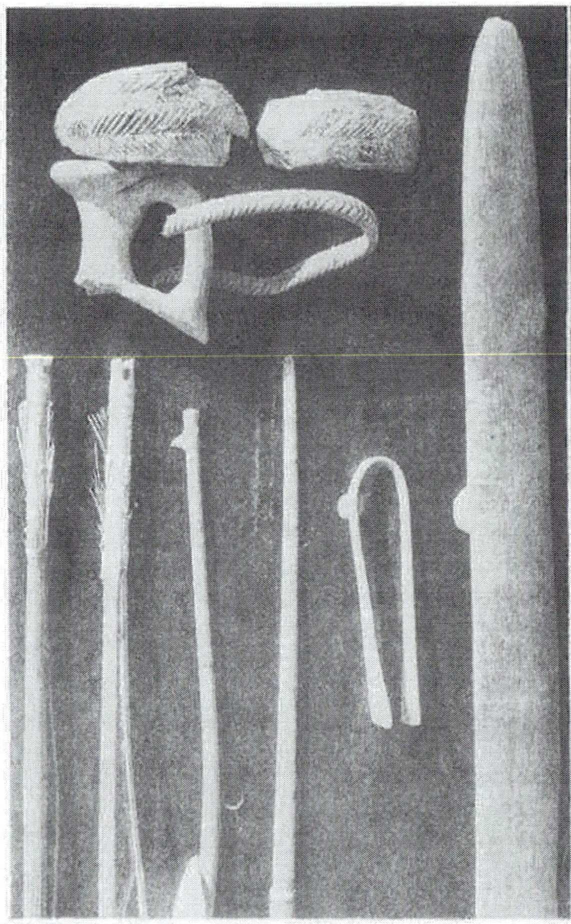

ARROWS, HORN AND LEATHER ARMLETS, WEAVERS SLAY, MATTING. XIII-XVI DYN.

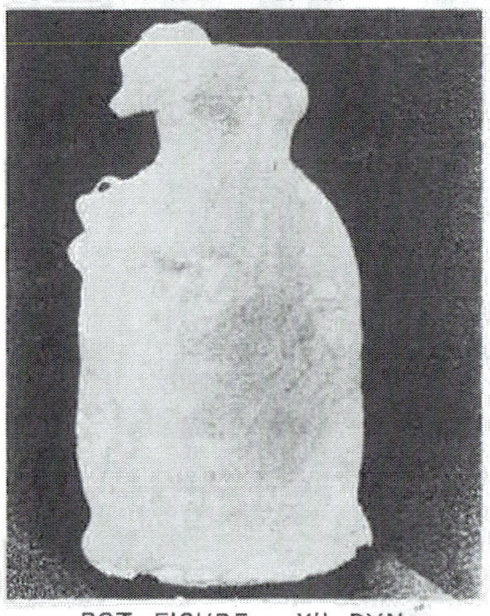

POT FIGURE. XII DYN.

PATTERN ON COFFIN 333. XII DYNASTY.

GROUP. XVIII. DYN.

A BASKET AND A COVER. XVIII DYNASTY.

CARTONNAGE OF ANKHET, DAUGHTER OF ATHA.

INNER CASE OF KHNUMU-HOTEP, BORN OF SITANHUR, SILVER FACE.

INNER CASE OF KHNUMU-HOTEP, SON OF KETU, GILT FACE.

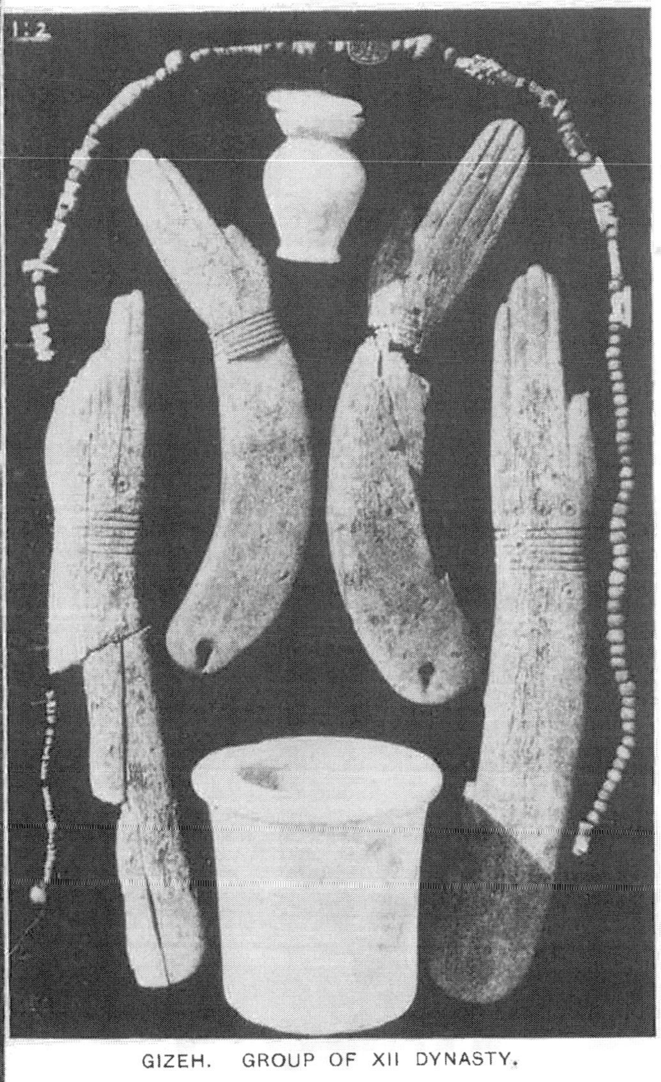

GIZEH. GROUP OF XII DYNASTY.

1:2 IVORY WAND.

2:3 WOODEN HEAD, LIMESTONE APES.

2:7 COPPER WEAPONS.

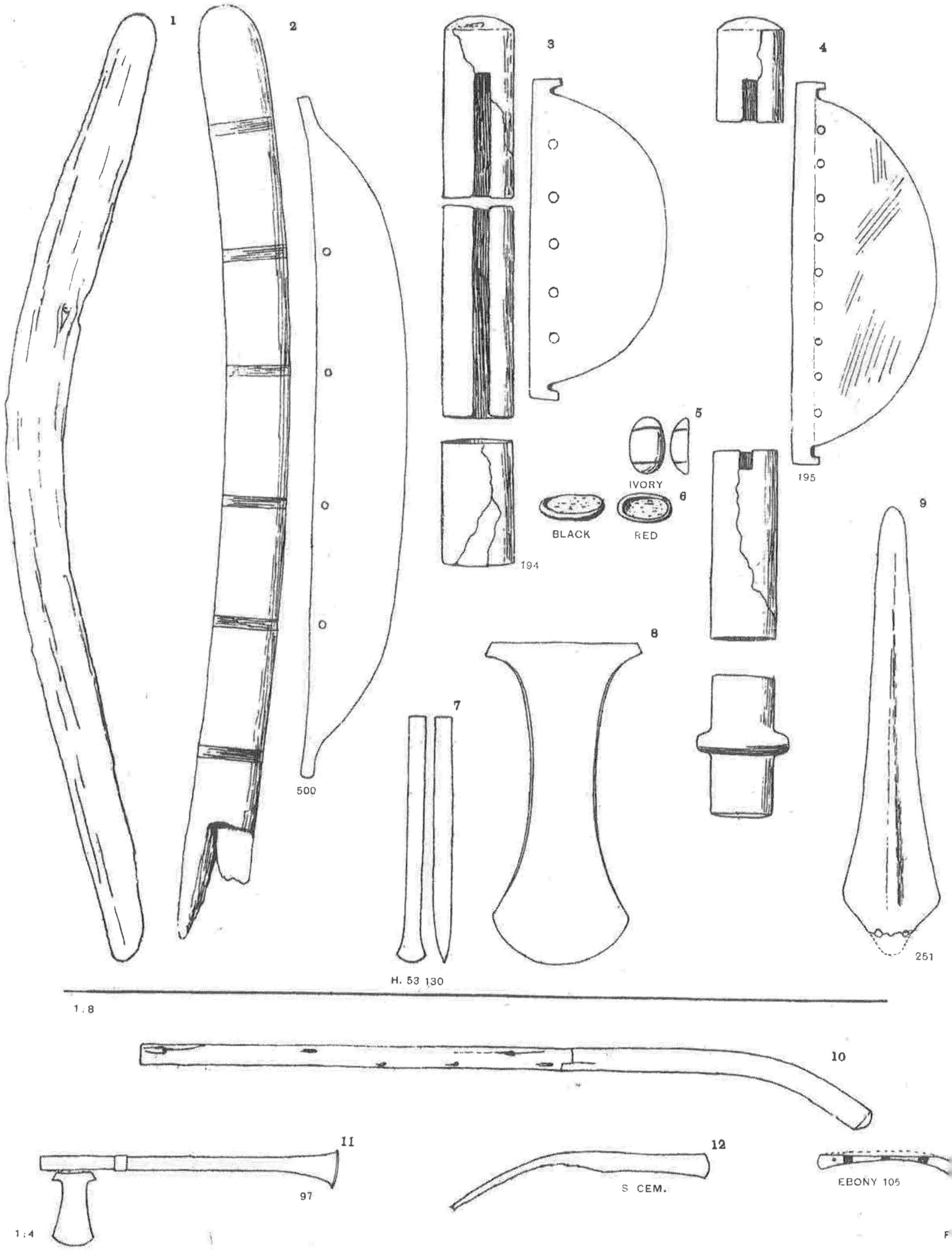
1
2
3
4
500
5
IVORY
6
BLACK
RED
194
195
8
9
7
H. 53 130
251
1.8
10
11
97
12
S CEM.
EBONY 105
1:4

1:6 RIFEH. POTTERY; IXTH–XTH DYNASTIES? XIII A.

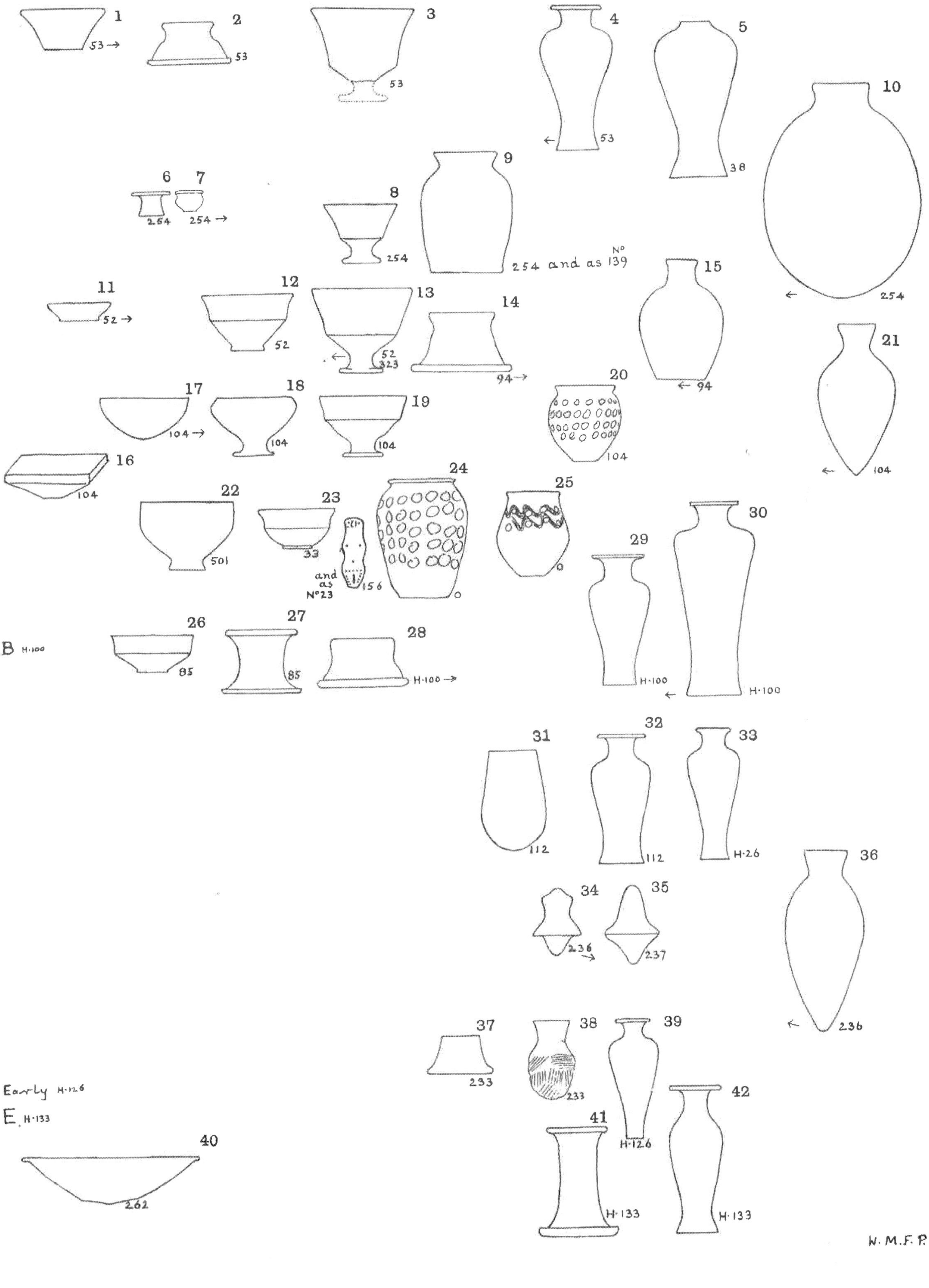

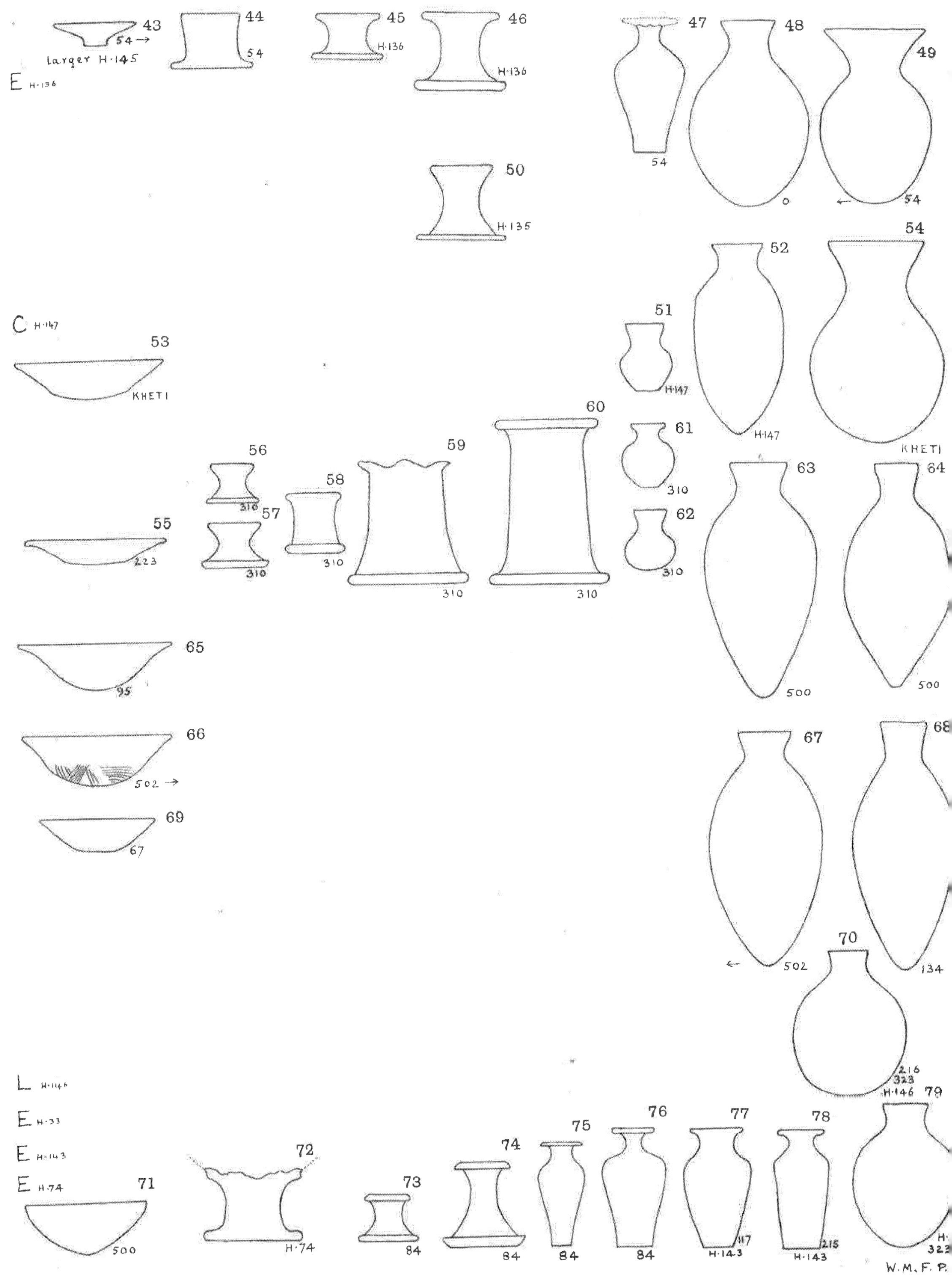

43
54 →
larger H·145
E H·136
44
54
45
H·136
46
H·136
47
54
48
o
49
← 54
50
H·135
52
54
C H·147
53
KHETI
51
H·147
H·147
KHETI
60
61
310
56
310
57
310
58
310
59
310
310
55
223
62
310
63
500
64
500
65
95
66
502 →
69
67
67
← 502
68
134
70
216
323
H·146
79
L H·146
E H·33
E H·143
E H·74
71
500
72
H·74
73
84
74
84
75
84
76
84
77
117
H·143
78
215
H·143
323
W.M.F.P.

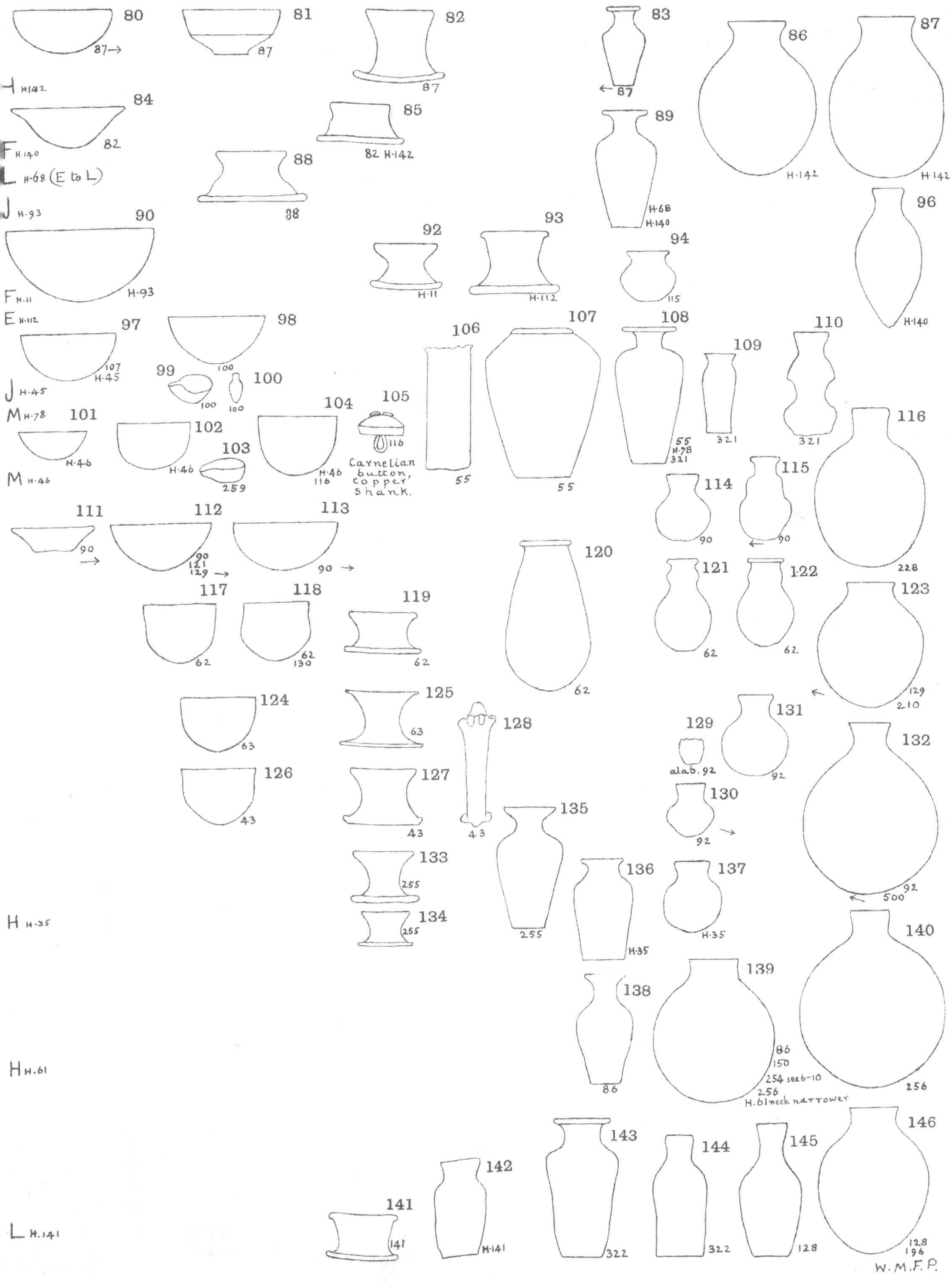

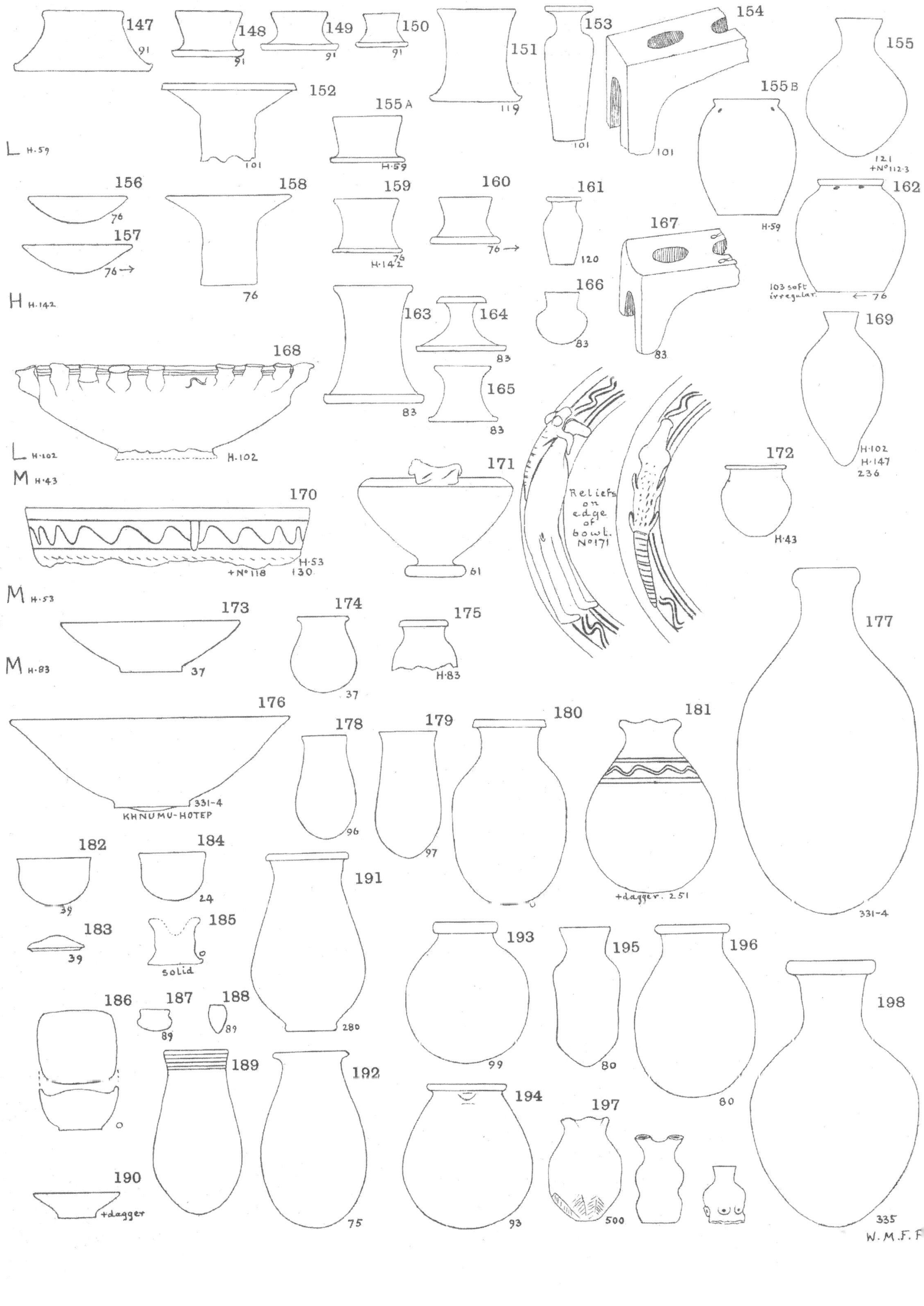

147
91
148
91
149
91
150
91
151
119
152
101
153
101
154
101
155
121 +No 112·3
155A
H·59
155B
H·59
L H·59
156
76
157
76→
158
76
159
H·142 76
160
76→
161
120
162
103 soft irregular.
←76
H H·142
163
83
164
83
165
83
166
83
167
83
168
H·102
L H·102
169
H·102 H·147 236
M H·43
170
H·53 +No 118 130
171
61
Reliefs on edge of bowl. No 171
172
H·43
M H·53
173
37
M H·83
174
37
175
H·83
176
331-4
KHNUMU-HOTEP
177
331-4
178
96
179
97
180
181
+dagger. 251
182
39
183
39
184
24
185
solid
186
187
89
188
89
189
190
+dagger
191
280
192
75
193
99
194
93
195
80
196
80
197
500
198
335
W. M. F. P.

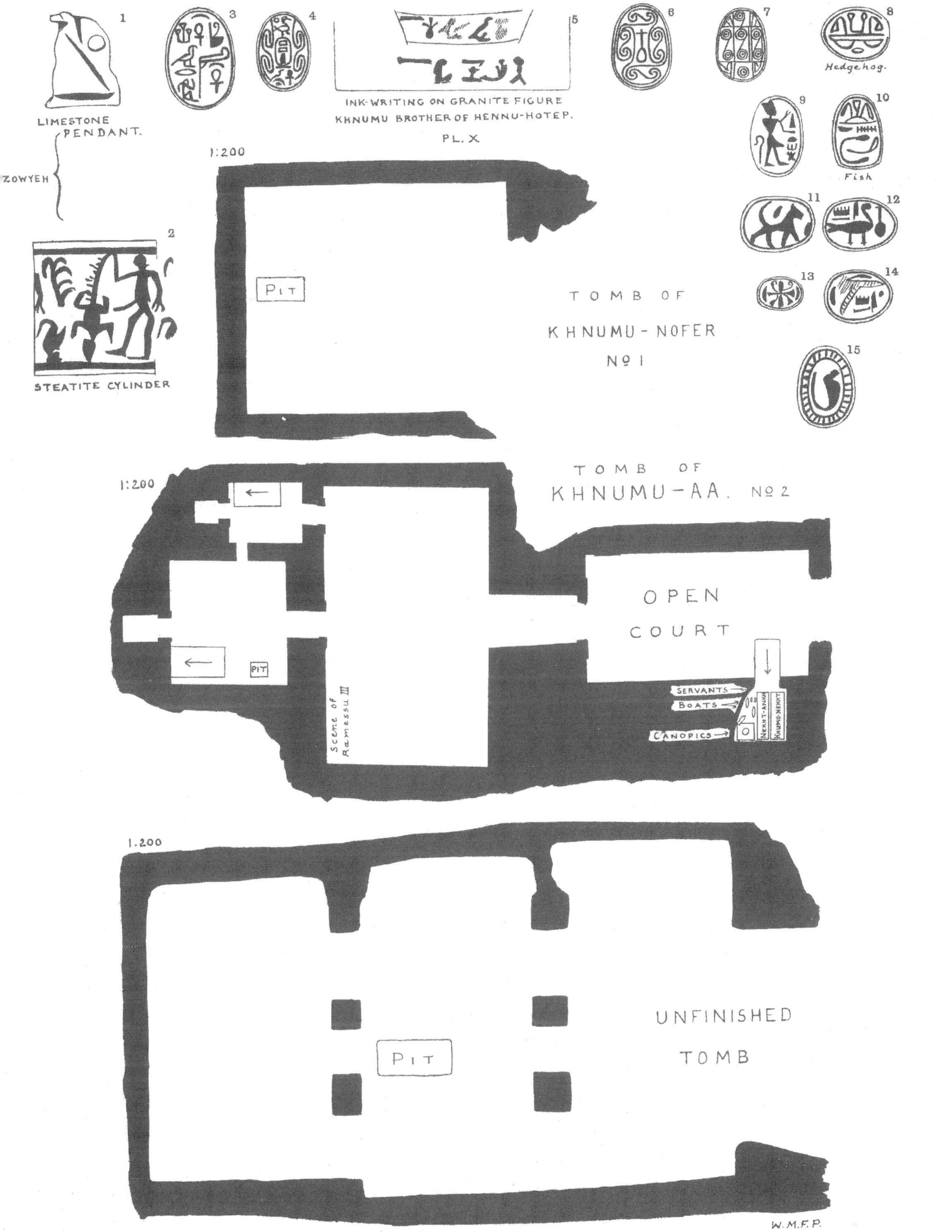
1
LIMESTONE PENDANT.
ZOWYEH
2
STEATITE CYLINDER
3
4
5
INK-WRITING ON GRANITE FIGURE
KHNUMU BROTHER OF HENNU-HOTEP.
PL. X
6
7
8
Hedgehog.
9
10
Fish
11
12
13
14
15
1:200
PIT
TOMB OF
KHNUMU-NOFER
Nº 1
1:200
TOMB OF
KHNUMU-AA. Nº 2
OPEN
COURT
PIT
Scene of Ramessu III
SERVANTS
BOATS
CANOPICS
NEKHT-ANKH
KHNUMU-NEKHT
1.200
PIT
UNFINISHED
TOMB
W.M.F.P.

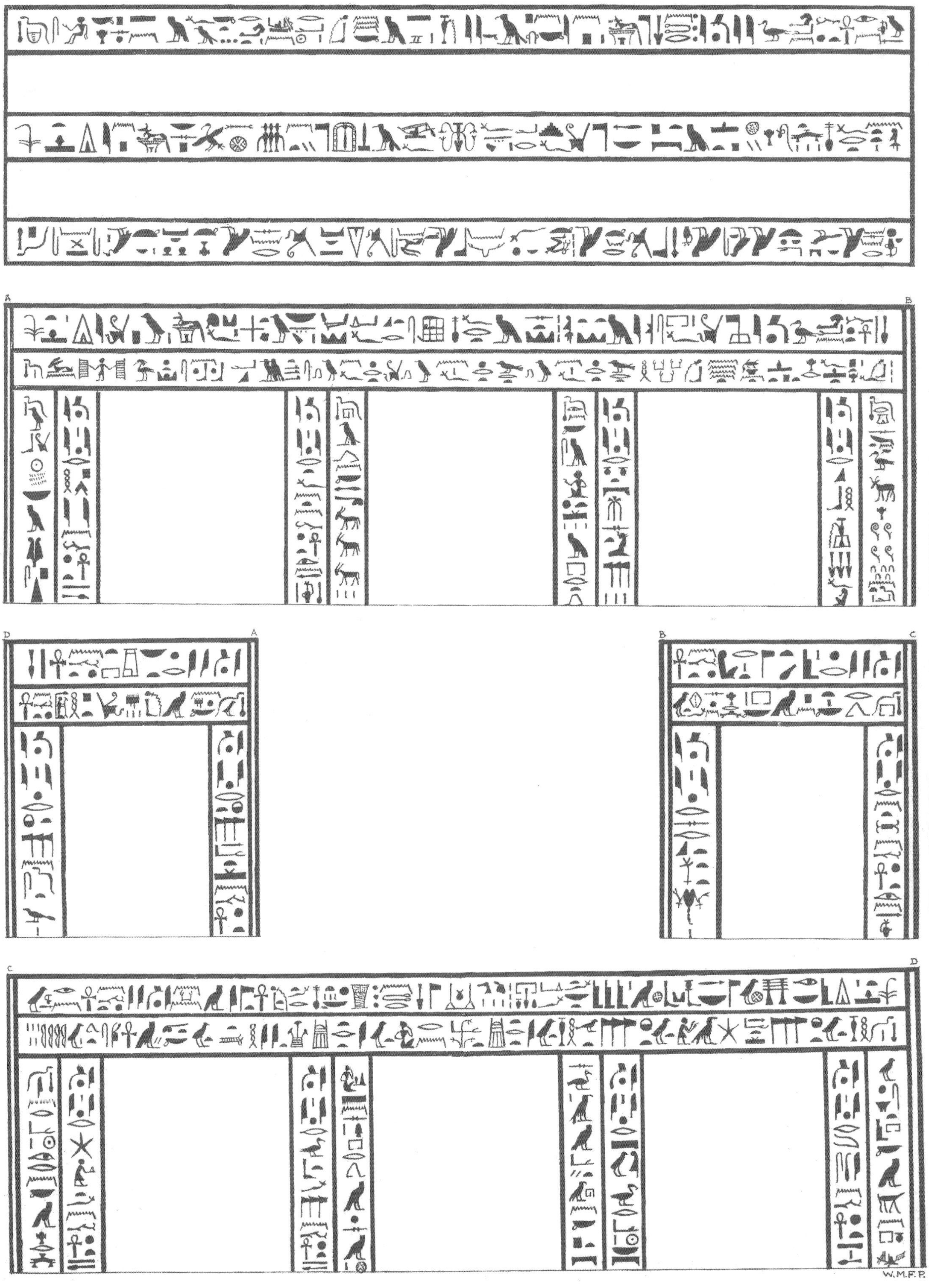
A
B
D
A
B
C
C
D
W.M.F.P.

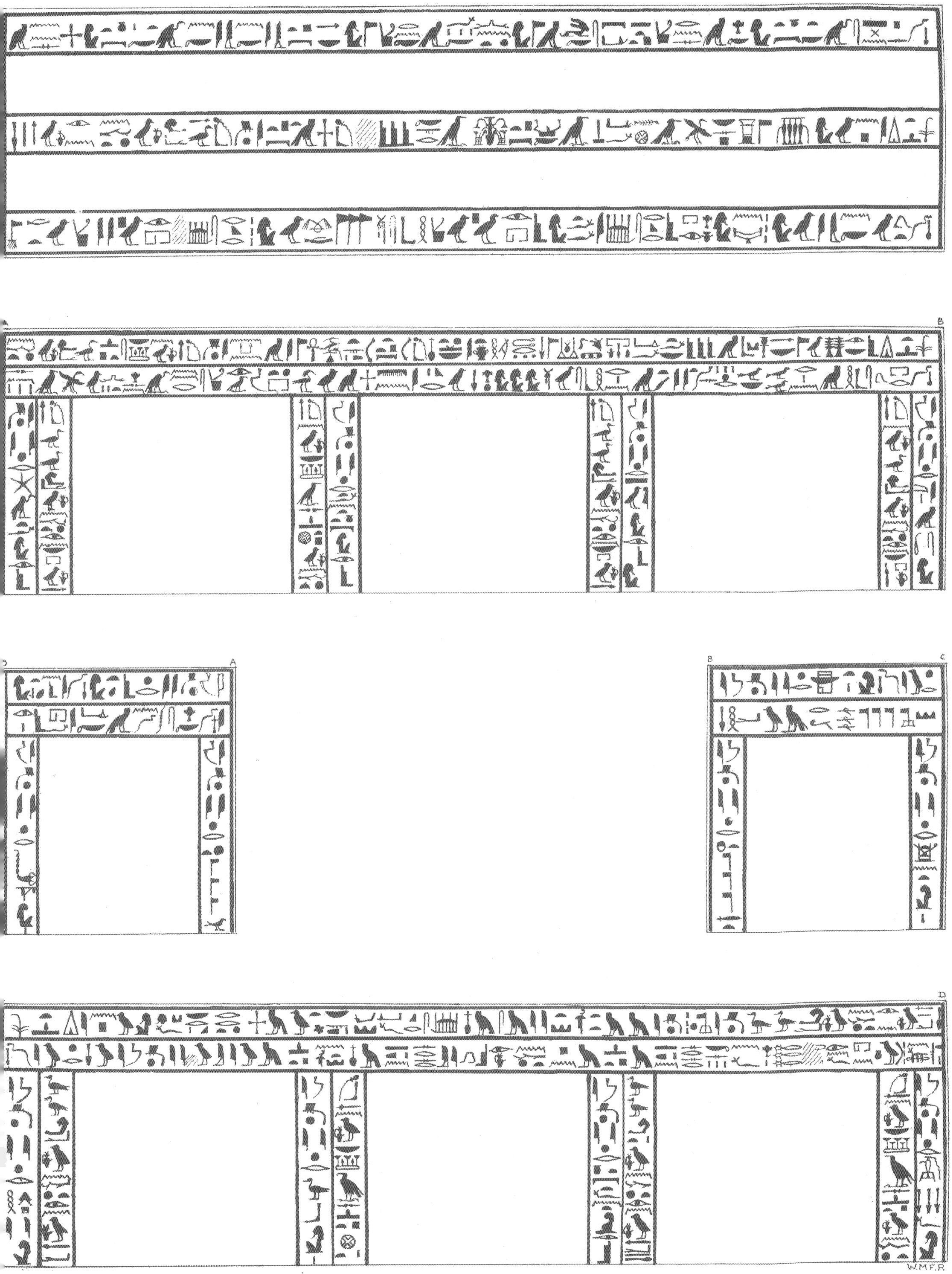

1:6 RIFEH. CANOPIC BOX AND JARS OF NEKHT-ANKH. COFFIN INSCRIPTIONS: SEE PL. XB. XIII H.

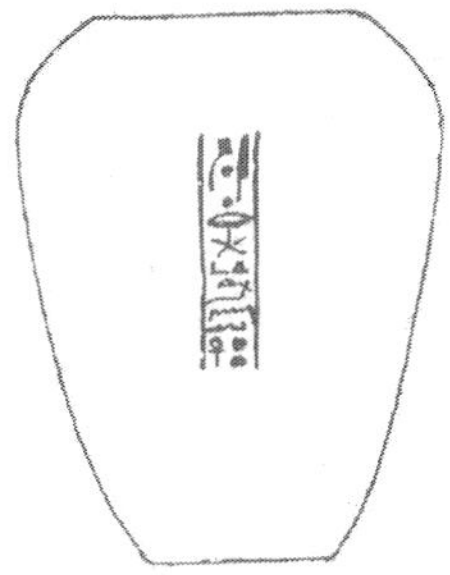

D

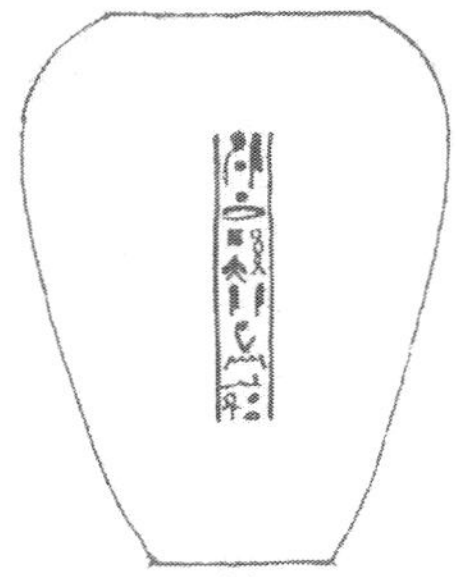

H

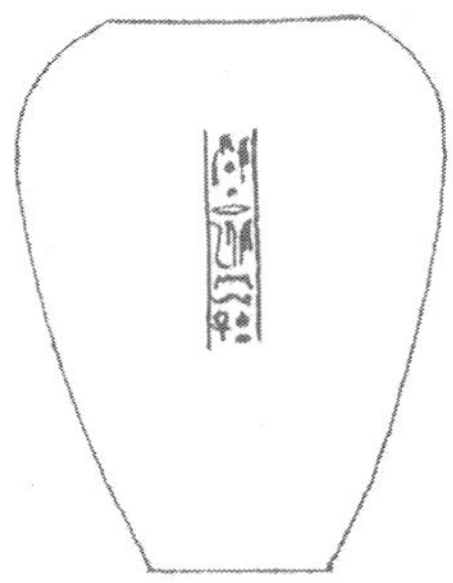

A

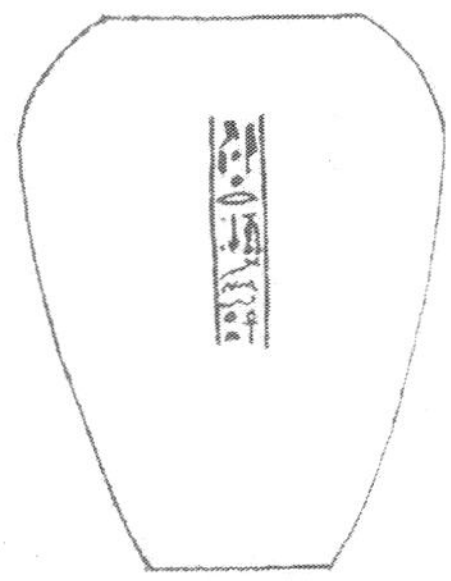

K

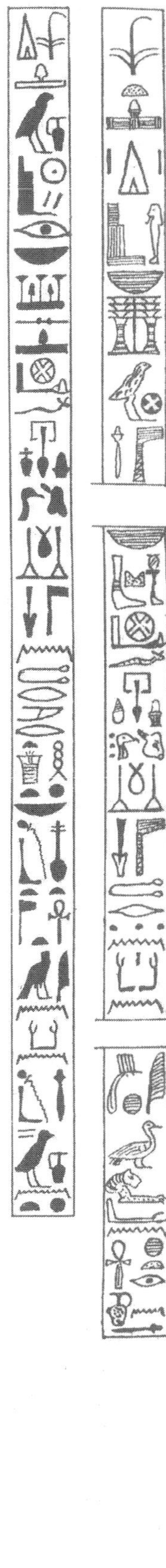

K D A

A H K

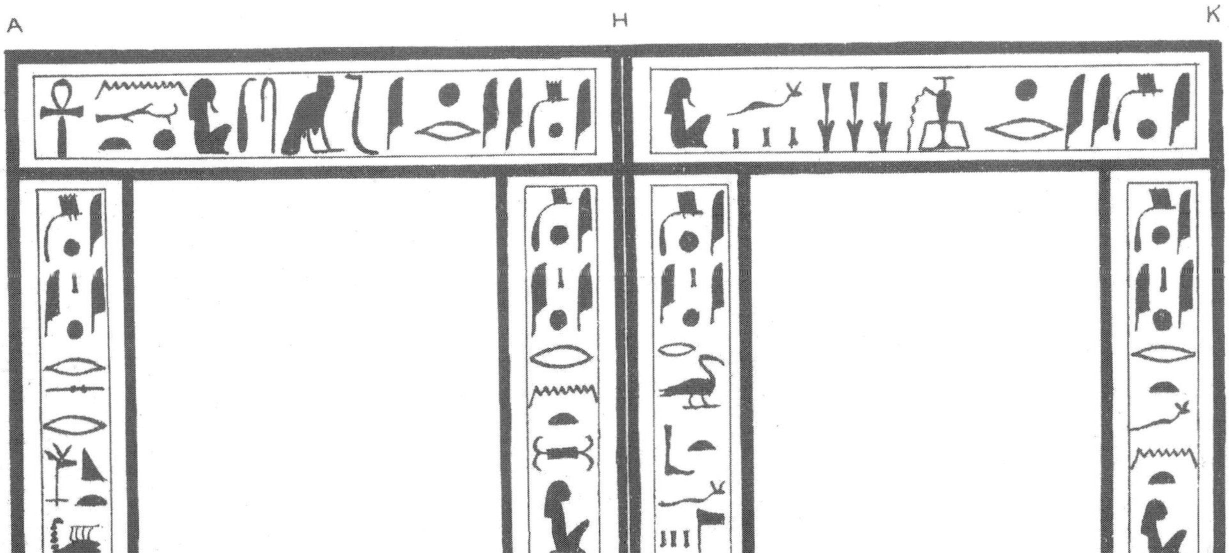

W.M.F.P.

Soul House
Soul House
same grave { Pot
Soul House
Soul House
Soul House
XIth dyn.
Soul House 77
Serrated Wall
Soul House
Soul Houses
Soul House
XII
Soul House
Invert?
W.M.F.P.

1 3 EARLIEST. 2 4 5 GOOD RELIEFS. 6 7

8 9 COARSE. 10 11

12 13 DECADENT. 14 15

TYPE A. SHELTER WITHOUT SATAH ON ROOF.

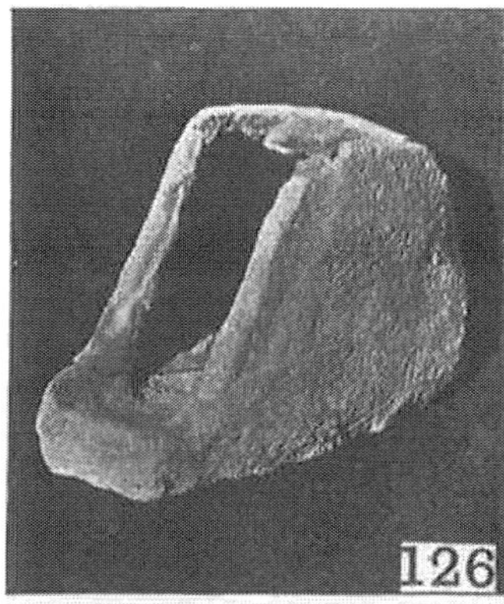

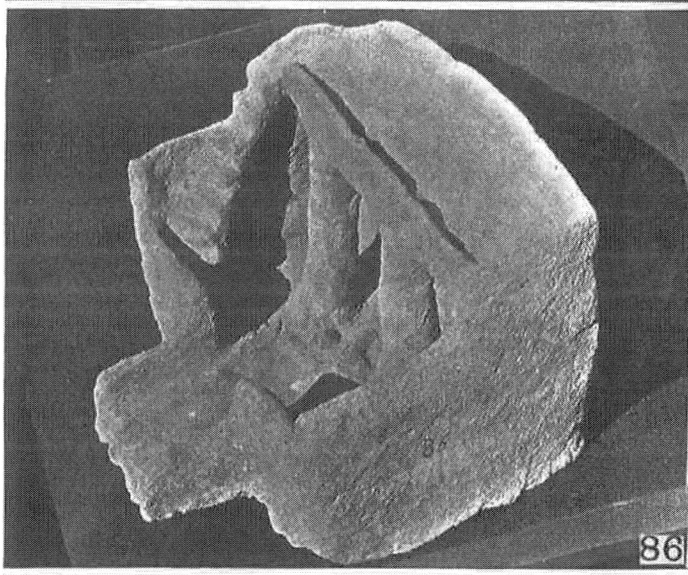

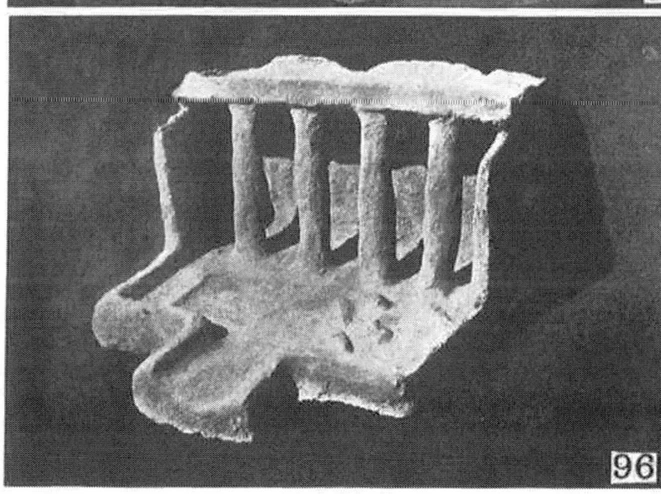

TYPE B. SHELTER WITH SATAH ON ROOF.

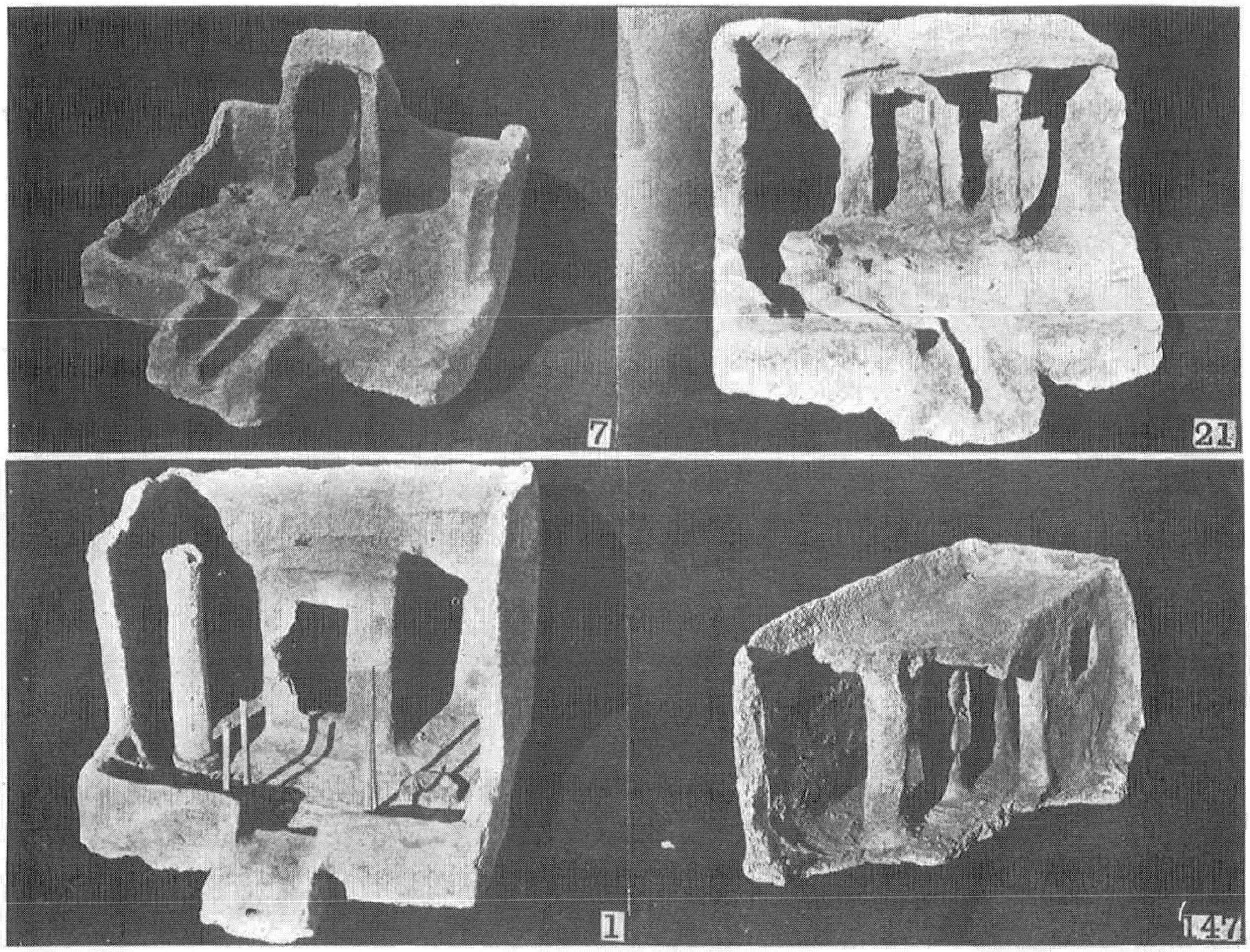

TYPE C. HUT CHAMBER ADDED.

TYPE D. LONG CHAMBER, PORTICO IN FRONT.

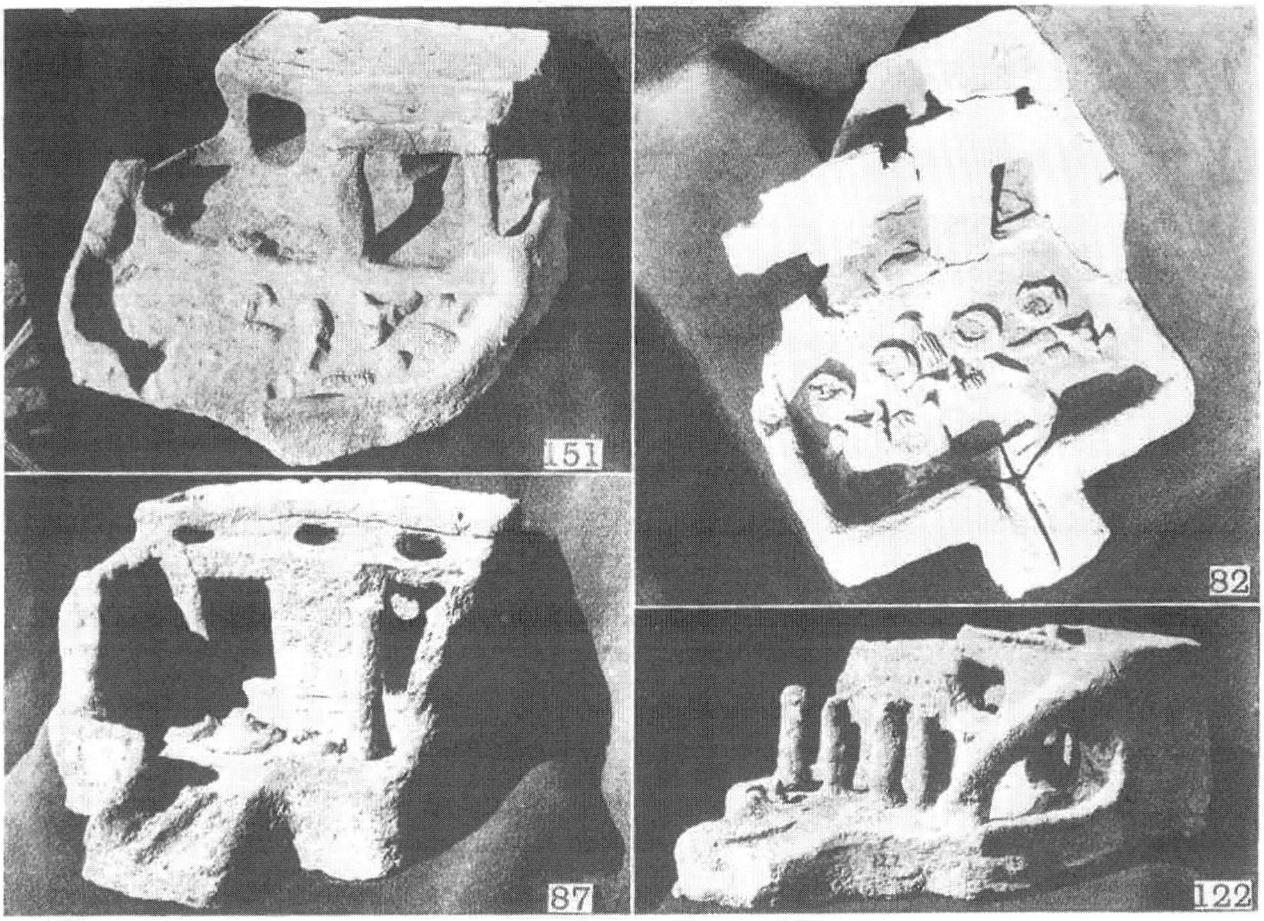

TYPE D.

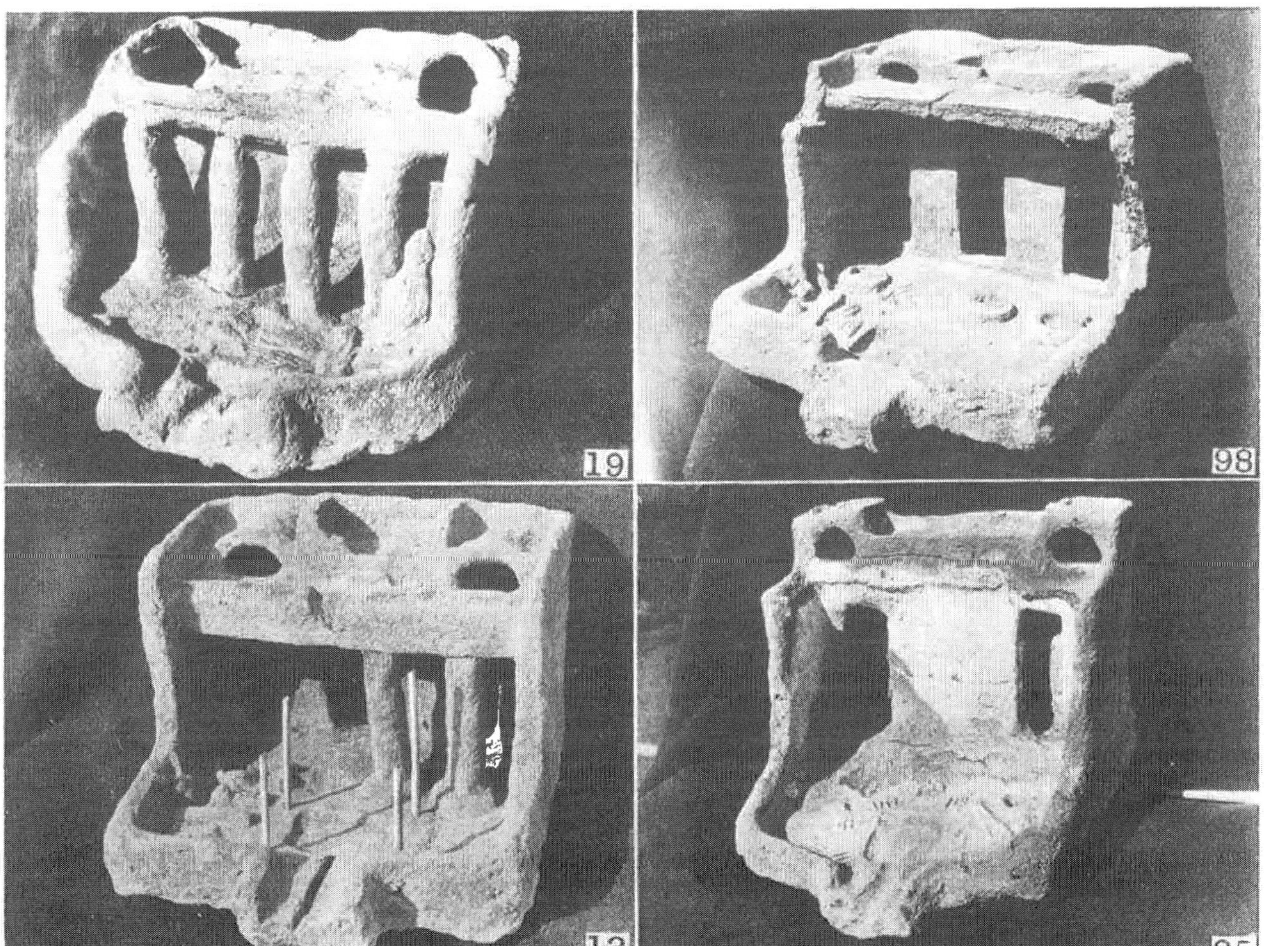

TYPE E.

150

67

74

29

TYPE E. MULQAFS WITH SATAH BETWEEN.

95

69

TYPE F. SEPARATE CHAMBERS AT BACK OF COURT.

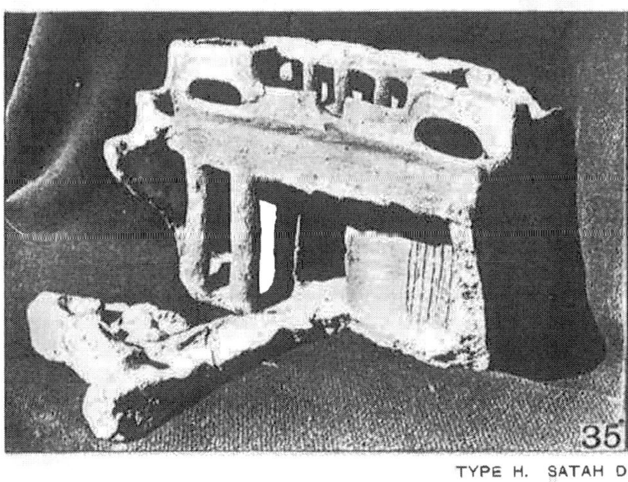
35

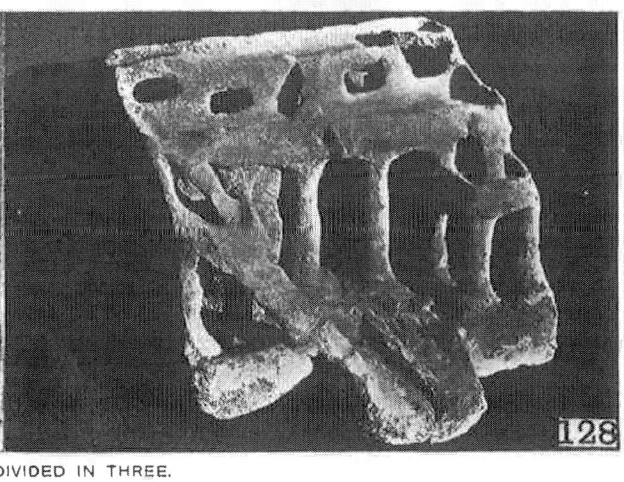
128

TYPE H. SATAH DIVIDED IN THREE.

69

55

65

3

TYPE F.

85

TYPE G.

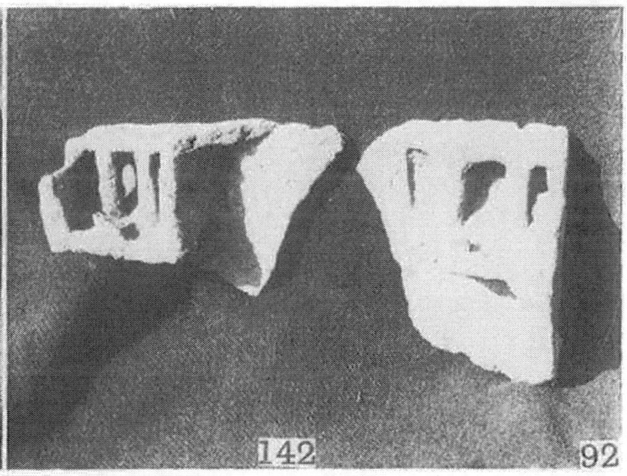
142 92

TYPE H.

153

121

TYPE H.

TYPE J. 42, 101. TWO MULQAFS WITH SATAR OVER EACH.

TYPE K. 80, 84, 107. CLOSED DOORS AND UPPER STOREY.

TYPE L. FIGURES AND FURNITURE BEGIN.

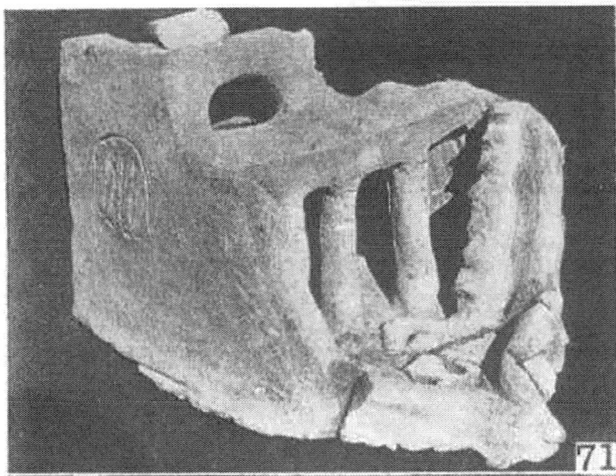
71

93

4

16

TYPE J.

16 TYPE K.

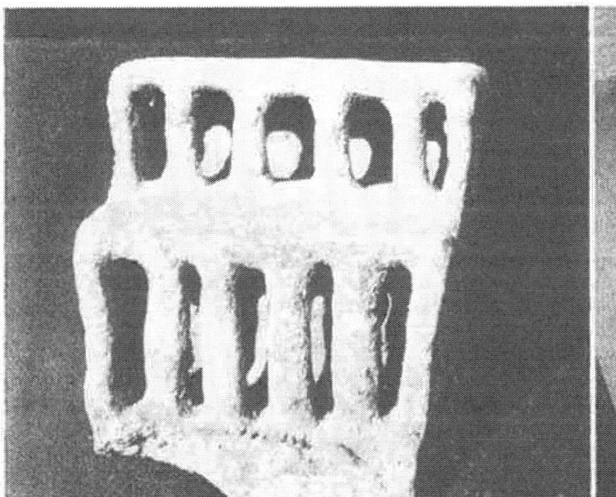
20

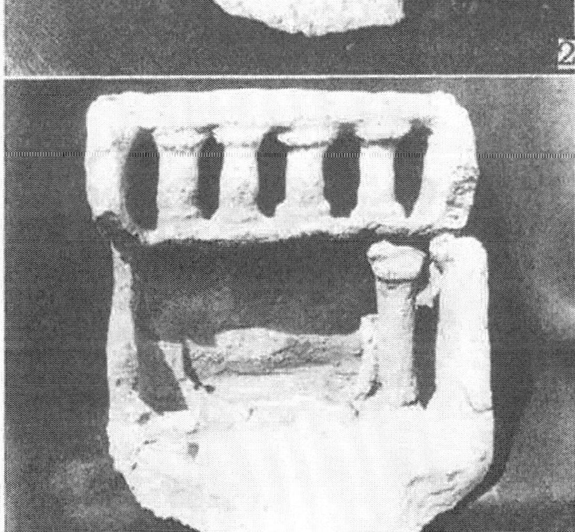
59

2

TYPE L.

TYPE L.

83, 22, 32 TYPE M.

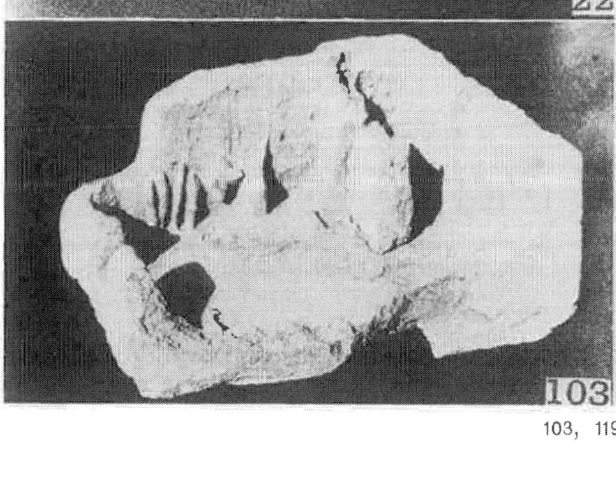

103, 119 TYPE N.

TYPE M. CLOSED COURT WITH DOORWAY, FURNITURE.

TYPE N. STRIPS ON WALL.

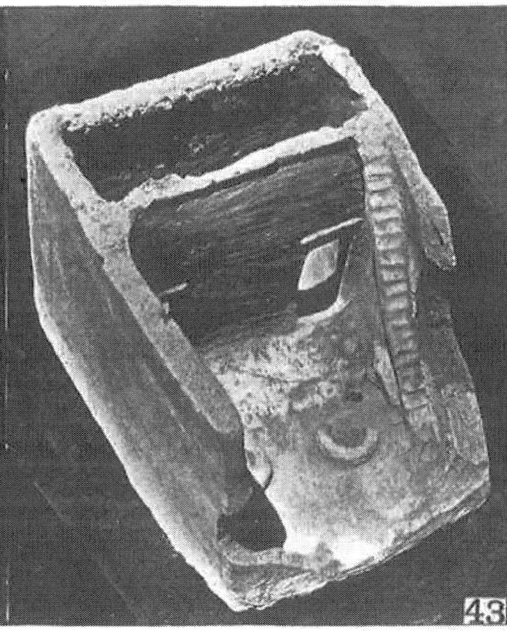

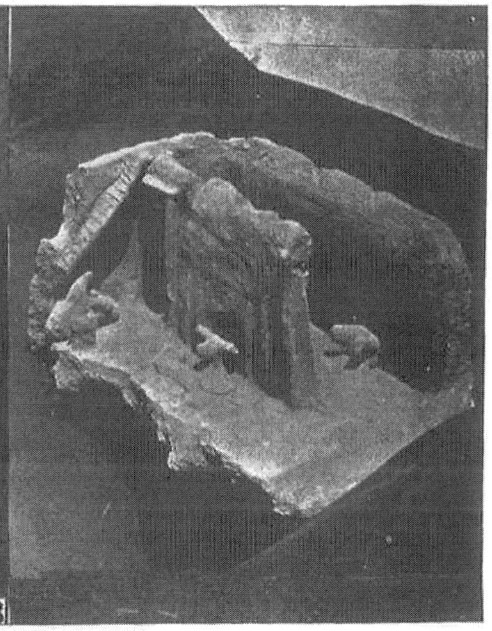

TYPE M.

ABOVE 77.

TYPE M.

TYPE N.

ARCHED ROOFS.

SMALL ROOF-CHAMBERS.

STAIRCASES.

BARRED WINDOWS, BLACK BAND FLOOR.

WINDOWS, DOORWAYS, SERRATED WALLS

COLUMNS, TYPE N., STRIPS, DOOR CHAIR.

SERRATED WALLS AND MODERN TOMB.

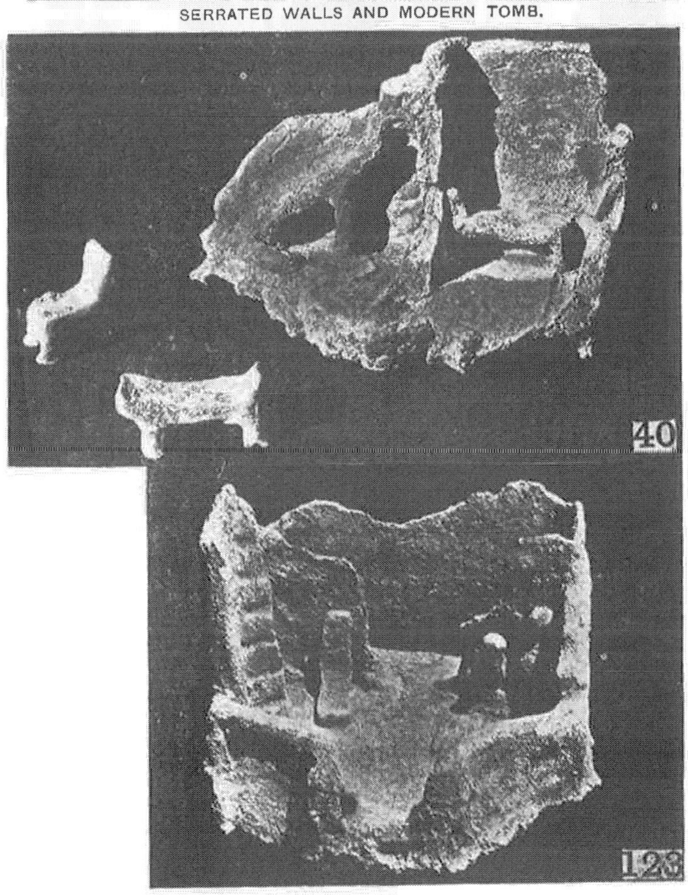

COUCHES, CHAIRS, AND WATER-STANDS.

TYPE M. WATER-STAND AT BACK.

TYPE L. WATER-STAND AND OFFERINGS.

DOOR, AND GRANARIES FROM ROOF.

FIGURES.

TYPE L.

SEATED FIGURES.

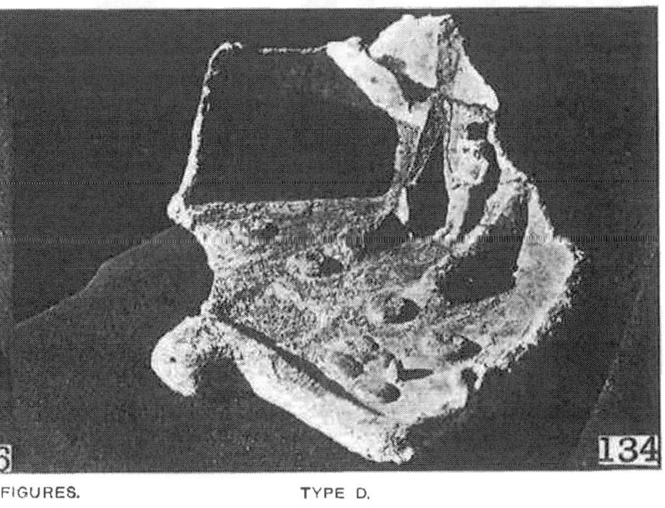

TYPE D.

No.	Type	Levels 2	3	Columns 0	1	2	3	4	5	6	7	8	Chambers 0	1	2	3	4	5	Satahs 0	1	2	3	Mulqafs 0	1	2	3	4	Stair O	L	R
6	A	all	·	·	·	1	·	5	·	·	·	·	all	·	·	·	·	·	all	·	·	·	all	·	·	·	·	all	·	·
9	B	all	·	·	·	3	2	4	·	·	·	·	all	·	·	·	·	·	·	all	·	·	8	·	·	·	·	6	1	1
5	C	all	·	1	·	2	1	·	·	1	·	·	·	hut	·	·	·	·	3	1	·	·	all	·	·	·	·	all	·	·
9	D	all	·	·	·	1	·	8	·	·	·	·	·	7	·	2	·	·	4	3	1	·	3	1	4	1	·	6	2	0
31	E	30	1	·	1	5	4	20	·	·	·	·	·	all	·	·	·	·	·	all	·	·	·	·	24	1	3	18	9	4
9	F	all	·	·	2	2	1	4	1	1	·	·	·	·	4	4	1	1	·	1	1	1	3	·	·	·	1	6	·	1
1	G	·	1	·	·	·	1	1	·	·	·	·	·	1	·	·	·	·	·	1	·	·	·	·	1	·	·	·	1	·
11	H	9	1	·	·	3	1	8	·	·	·	·	1	5	·	3	·	·	·	·	·	9	·	·	7	·	2	2	6	2
9	J	1	7	·	1	1	8	3	·	·	·	·	·	7	3	·	·	·	·	·	7	·	·	·	6	1	·	·	7	2
7	K	2	4	·	·	3	4	2	·	·	·	1	·	6	1	·	·	·	·	?	·	·	4	·	·	·	·	1	4	1
26	L	4	17	·	5	12	5	6	·	·	·	·	4	16	3	·	·	·	3	6	·	·	12	·	1	·	·	1	18	5
17	M	2	7	·	5	10	·	2	·	·	·	·	1	12	2	·	·	·	·	1	1	·	6	·	1	·	·	4	3	5
4	N	·	1	1	·	1	·	·	·	·	·	·	·	all	·	·	·	·	·	·	·	·	·	·	·	·	·	1	1	·
144		86	39	2	14	44	27	63	1	2	0	1	21	94	13	9	1	1	16	53	10	10	47	1	44	3	6	56	52	21

No.	Type	Open Door 0	1	2	3	Closed Door O	L	M	R	Window O	side	back	front	Chair Low L	M	R	Chair High L	M	R	Couch Low L	M	R	Couch High L	M	R	Head rest L	front	R	Grinder
6	A	all	·	·	·	all	·	·	·	all																			
9	B	all	·	·	·	all	·	·	·	all																			
5	C	·	all	·	·	all	·	·	·	4	·	·	2	·	2														
9	D	1	3	2	3	all	·	·	·	7	1	2	·	1	1														
31	E	·	4	14	12	28	1	·	1	all																			
9	F	·	6	1	2	7	·	·	1	4	·	6	1																
1	G	·	·	·	1	1	·	·	·	1																			
11	H	1	1	3	4	7	·	·	2	9	·	2																	
9	J	·	1	7	·	all	-	·	·	5	3																		
7	K	1	2	4	·	·	2	4	2	all																			
26	L	5	4	12	1	19	·	1	·	13	14	3	5	3	3	1	0	5	1	3	4	3	2	1	·	2	2	4	
17	M	1	6	6	·	all	·	·	·	7	5	6	·	1	2	·	·	·	·	3	2	1	1	1	1	7	·	2	1
4	N	·	·	all	·	all	·	·	·	3	·	·	·	·	·	1	·	·	·	1	·	·	·	·	·	·	·	·	1
144		24	32	53	23	121	3	5	6	106	23	19	8	5	8	2	0	5	1	7	6	4	3	2	1	9	2	6	2

No.	Type	Zyr Left side	Middle doors	Middle back	Right court	Right chr	Tank 0	1	2	3	4	'esh sha	clos'd chair	Bull's head 0	Left corn.	Left side	Mid	Right corn.	Right side	Haunch O	L	M	R	Ribs O	L	M	R	Front tray			
6	A	·	·	·	·	·	·	2	2	·	·	·	·	·	1	·	1	·	1	·	2	1	1	1	1	3	·	2	1	·	·
9	B	·	·	·	·	·	1	7	1	·	·	1	·	2	1	1	·	1	4	2	1	3	3	4	1	2	1	9	·	·	·
5	C	·	·	·	·	·	·	4	1	·	·	1	1	1	1	1	·	1	·	·	2	·	2	·	2	1	2	4	·	·	·
9	D	·	·	·	·	·	3	3	·	1	·	2	1	1	·	·	·	1	3	2	·	3	2	2	·	1	3	5	1	·	·
31	E	·	·	·	·	·	1	24	·	·	·	5	4	1	3	9	1	5	4	4	11	·	7	3	8	4	7	14	2	3	·
9	F	·	·	·	·	·	3	4	·	·	1	·	·	1	2	·	·	1	3	1	3	1	2	1	1	1	3	6	1	1	·
1	G	·	·	·	·	·	·	1	·	·	·	·	·	·	·	·	·	·	·	·	·	·	·	·	·	·	·	·	·	·	·
11	H	·	·	·	·	·	·	5	2	·	·	·	·	2	1	1	·	·	1	1	2	1	2	1	3	2	1	6	1	·	·
9	J	·	·	·	·	·	2	1	2	·	·	·	·	1	·	2	·	1	·	1	1	2	1	2	2	2	·	1	2	1	·
7	K	·	·	·	·	·	2	5	·	·	·	·	·	1	1	2	·	2	1	1	2	·	4	1	2	1	3	6	·	1	·
26	L	1	1	1	3	1	8	6	1	·	1	·	·	4	1	3	·	2	3	6	3	1	6	5	1	6	3	5	1	6	1
17	M	1	·	·	·	·	6	3	·	·	·	·	·	6	·	3	·	·	·	6	1	·	2	5	1	3	·	2	·	3	5
4	N	·	·	·	·	·	1	·	·	·	·	·	·	·	1	·	1	·	·	·	·	2	·	·	2	·	·	·	1	·	2
144		2	1	1	3	1	27	65	9	1	2	9	6	20	12	22	3	14	20	24	28	14	32	25	24	26	23	60	10	15	8

Type	No.	Levels	Column	Chamber	Satah	Mulqaf	Stair	Open Door	Closed Door	Window	Chair	Couch	Head rest	Grinder	Tank 'eshsha	Channl closed	Bull's head	Haunch	Ribs
A	126	2	o	o	o	o	o	o	o	o	o	o	o	o	o	o	o	o	o
	5	2	4	o	o	o	o	o	o	o	o	o	o	o	1		L corn.	L	M
	88	2	4	o	o	o	o	o	o	o	o	o	o	o	Lost	– –	– –	– –	– –
	89	2	4	o	o	o	o	o	o	o	o	o	o	o	Lost	– –	–	– –	– –
	106	2	2	o	o	o	o	o	o	o	o	o	o	o	2		R	M	M
A–B	108	2	4	o	o	Lost		o	o	o	o	o	o	o	1	?	?	L	M–R
	144	2	4	o	?	o	o	o	o	o	o	o	o	o	2		M	R	L
B	6	2	4	o	1	o	o	o	o	o	o	o	o	o	2		R	M–R	o
	31	2	2	o	1	o	o	o	o	o	o	o	o	o	o		o	o	o
	72	2	3	o	1	o	R	o	o	o	o	o	o	o	1		L corn	L	L
	86	2	2	o	1	o	L	o	o	o	o	o	o	o	1		M–R	M	o
	96	2	4	o	1	o	o	o	o	o	o	o	o	o	L		R wall	R	R
	100	2	4	o	1	o	o	o	o	o	o	o	o	o	1 'esh.		bad, L	R	R·M·L
var.	113	2	3	o	1	2	?	o	o	o	o	o	o	o	1		R corn	R	?
	148	2	4 to end	o	1	o	o	o	o	o	o	o	o	o	1		o	o	o
	149	2	2	o	1	o	o	o	o	o	o	o	o	o	L		R	M	M
C	1	2	2	hut	?	?	o	1	o	o	o	o	o	o	1 'esh.	cl.	L	L	L
	7	2	o o o o	hut	o	o	o	1	o	o	M back	o	o	o	1		o	L	M·R
	21	2	2	hut	o	o	o	1	o	o	o	o	o	o	1		L corn.	R	L
	91	2	o	hut	o	o	o	1	o	o	M back	o	o	o	1		R corn.	R	R
var.	147	2	3 inside	'1	1	o	o	1	o	2 Fr.	o	o	o	o	2 ?		?	?	R
D	10	2	4	1	o	2 ends	o	3	o	o	o	o	o	o	lost	– –	– –	– –	– –
	12	2	4	3	o	2	o	1	o	o	o	o	o	o	lost	– –	– –	– –	– –
	82	2	4	1	o	2, small	o	3	o	R	o	o	o	o	3		3	RML	RML
	105	2	4	1	o	2	?	3	o	o	o	o	o	o	1 'esh.		Lost	– –	– –
	115	2	4	1	2	o	o	1	o	o	o	o	o	o	o		R	M	o
	116	2	2	1	1	1 end	o	1	o	o	o	o	o	o	o		o	o	o
var.	134	2 ?	4	3	?	o	o	o	o	o	fig. back fig. L.	o	o	o	1 'esh.	cl.	R	o	R
	151	2	4	1	1	o	L	2	o	2 back	o	o	o	o	o		R	M	R
D–E	87	2	4	1	1	3	L	2	o	o	o	o	o	o	1		R corn.	R corn.	R
E	9	2	4	1	?	2	o	3	o	o	o	o	o	o	1		L	L	L
	13	2	4	1	1	2	o	3	o	o	o	o	o	o	1 'esh.		L	L	L
	14	2	4	1	1	2	L	2	o	o	o	o	o	o	1		R corn.	R	R
	15	2	4	1	?	4	o	3	o	o	o	o	o	o	1		R pillar	R	M
	17	2	4	1	1	2	L	2	o	o	o	o	o	o	1		R	o	R·M
	18	2	2	1	1	2	R	2	o	o	o	o	o	o	1		L	o	o
	19	2	4	1	1	2	L	2	o	o	o	o	o	o	1 'esh.		R	R	R
	25	2	3	1	1	2	o	2	o	o	o	o	o	o	1		R corn.	R	M
	29	2	4	1	1	2	o	2	L	o	o	o	o	o	1 'esh		o	L	R·L
	33	2	2	1	?	2	L	3	o	o	o	o	o	o	1	½ cl.	M	o	o
?	38	3	?	1 ?	1	{2 2	L L	?	?	o	o	o	o	o	lost	– –	– –	–	– –
	67	2	2	1	1	4	o	1	o	o	o	o	o	o	Lost	– –	–	– –	– –
	70	2	3	1	1	2	o	?	o	o	o	o	o	o	1		L corn.	L corn.	o
	74	2	4	1	1	2	o	1	o	o	o	o	o	o	1		L wall	L	L.R.
E–J	75	2 or 3	4	1	?	?	L	3	o	o	o	o	o	o	1		{R Lost {L none		– –
	81	2	4	1	1	3	o	3	o	o	o	o	o	o	Lost	– –	– –	– –	– –
	98	2	4	1	1	2	o	3	o	o	o	o	o	o	1	cl.	L	before head	
	104	2	4	1	over porch	2	o	3	o	o	o	o	o	o	1		Lost	– –	– –
?	109	2	3	1	?	?	o	2	o	o	o	o	o	o	o		L	L 3λ	goat R
	112	2	4	1	?	2	L	2	R	o	o	o	o	o			R corn.	R	L

Type	No.	Levels	Column	Chamber	Satah	Mulqaf	Stair	Open Door	Closed Door	Window	Chair	Couch	Head rest	Grinder	Tank 'eshsha	Channel closed	Bull's head	Haunch	Ribs
E	114	2	4	1	1	2	o	2	o	o	o	o	o	o	1		L corn.	L	L
	117	2	4	1	1	2	R	2	o	o	o	o	o	o	lost	—	—	—	—
	129	2	{2 fr. / 1 chr.	1	1	2	L	1	o	o	o	o	o	o	1		R corn.	L	M
	133	2	?	1	1	4	R	2	o	o	o	o	o	o	lost	—	—	—	—
	136	2?	4	1	?	2?	L	3	o	o	o	o	o	o	1		R corn.	o	L
	137	2	4	1	?	?	o	3	o	o	o	o	o	o	1		L	L	M
	138	2	4	1	1	2	R	3	o	o	o	o	o	o	lost	—	—	—	—
	139	2	3	1	1?	2	o	3	o	o	o	o	o	o	1		L corn.	L	L
	143	2?	4	1	?	?	o	1	o	o	o	o	o	o	L 'esh.		R	R	R
	150	2	2	1	1	2	o	2	o	o	o	o	o	o	1	cl.	L	R	R
	152	2	4	1	1	2	o	2	o	o	o	o	o	o	1 'esh	cl.	L	L	L
F	3	2	4	3	1	4	o	1	o	o	o	o	o	o	1		R	R	R
	11	2	5	3	?	?	?	1	o	o	o	o	o	o	1		R	R	R
	55	2?	{4 fr. / 2 chr.	4	?	?	o	1	o	?	o	o	o	o	o		R corn.	L fr.	o
	65	2	6	2	?	o	o	1	R	3 back	o	o	o	o	o	forked	R	M	M
	69	2	oo court oo / 1 chr.	2 open / 2 shut	2	o	o	1	o	3 back	o	o	o	o	4	o	L corn.	L	bird L-M / cakes R
	95	2?	4	5	?	?	o?	2	o	o	o	o	o	o	o		open	flat	court
	110	2	2	3	?	?	o	3	o	o	o	o	o	o	1		o	o	o
	122	2	{3 fr. / 1 chr.	2	3	o	R	1	o	front	o	o	o	o	1		L corn.	L	R
	140	2?	?	3	?	?	?	3	?	?	o	o	o	o	lost	—	—	—	—
G	85	3	3 top / 4 porch	1	1	2	L	3	o	o	o	o	o	o	1		lost	—	—
H	35	3	4 / 4	1	3	2	L	2	R	o	o	o	o	o	1		?	L	L
	61	2	4	1 mid	3	2	R	3	o	o	o	o	o	o	1		lost	—	—
	92	2	2 top / ?	?	?	o	R	?	?	o	Lost	—	—	—	—	—	—	—	—
	111	2	2	1	3	4	O	3	o	o	o	o	o	o	lost	—	—	—	M
	120	2	4	3	3	2	o	3	o	2 back	o	o	o	o	2		R	M	M
	121	2	4	1	3	2	L	2	o	o	o	o	o	o	1		L corn.	L corn.	L corn.
	128	2	4+2	1	3	4	L	1	o	o	o	o	o	o	L		o	o	R
	132	2	3	o	3	2	L	o	o	o	o	o	o	o	1		o	R	L
	142	fragment of top.				—	—		—	—	—	—	—	—	—	—	—	—	—
	153	2	4	3	3	2	L	2	R	o	o	o	o	o	2		L	R	o
	154	2	4	3	3	2	L	3	o	o	o	o	o	o	Lost	—	—	—	—
J	4	3	{3 / 3	1 / 1	2	3	L	2	o	o	o	o	o	o	2		R corn.	L, M-R	L, M.
	27	3	{3 / 3	1	?	?	L	2	o	o	o	o	o	o	o		o	o	o
	42	3	1 chr.	2	2+x	2	L?	?	?	o	lost	—	—	—	—	—	—	—	—
	45	3	{4 / ?	?	2	2	{L / L	?	?	?	lost	—	—	—	—	—	—	—	—
	71	2	3	2	2	2	R	2	o	sides	o	o	o	o	2		L	M	L
	73	2 or 3	4	1	2	2	o?	1	o?	o	Lost	—	—	—	—	—	—	—	—
	93	3	{4 / 3	{2 / ?	2	2	L	{2 / ?	?	o?	lost	—	—	—	—	—	—	—	—
	101	3	{3 / 2	{1 / 1	2	2	R	{2 / 2	o	2 sides	o	o	o	o	1		L	R	R·M·L
G–J	131	3	3	1	?	?	L	2	o	o	o	o	o	o	o		o	o	o
K	8	3	{2 / 4	1	?	o	L	2	M	o	o	o	o	o	1		R corn	R	M
	16	2	8	2	?	?	L	1	R	o	o	o	o	o	1		R	R	R
	37	3	{3 / 2	1	?	?	?	2	M	o	o	o	o	o	1		L?	R	R
	80	3	{3 / 3	1	?	o	R	1	L	o	o	o	o	o	o		L corn	L	cakes R
	84	2 or 3	3	1	?	o	L	2	M	o	o	o	o	o	1		R corn.	L corn	L
	107	2	2	1	?	?	o	o	R 2 L	o	o	o	o	o	o		o	o	o
	156	3	4	1	?	o	L	2	M	o	o	o	o	o	1		L	R	L
L	? 2	3	{3 / 2	2	o	o	L	o	o	o	o	o	o	o	o		R	o	R
	20	3	{4 / 4	1	o	o	L	o	M	{2 / 2 front	o	o	o	o	1		lost	R	R-M

Type	No.	Levels	Column	Chamber	Satah	Mulqaf	Stair	Open Door	Closed Door	Window	Chair	Couch	Head rest	Grinder 2 yrs	Tank 'eshsha	Channel closed	Bull's head	Haunch	Ribs
L	28	2?	2	1	lost	—	—	2	o	2 sides	top?	ground 'tween doors	R	o	1		L?	M	M·R
	30	3	2 / 3	1	?	?	L	2	o	o	up M. back	up L	?	o	0		o	o	o
-M	36	2?	?	lost	—	—	—	—	—	2 back	L mid low	R mid	R	?	lost	—	—	—	—
	39	3	?	1 top	1	o	lost	—	—	top front	lost	—	—	—	—	—	—	—	—
	40	2	?	1?	?	2	L	lost	—	—	—	L end.	front	?	lost	—	—	—	—
	41	3	1 chr. / 1 chr.	1+x / 1+x	o	o	R / R	lost	—	—	—	—	—	—	—	—	—	—	—
	44	3	3	o	1	o	R	R / o	o	o	o	o	o	o	1		L corn.	R	L
	56	2?	2	1	?	?	L	3	o	?	court L 'tween doors	R wall court	front	2 yrs R 'tween doors	0		R corn.	L front	M
-M	57	2?	?	1	?	?	R	2	o	o	L back	o	o	2 yrs back M	lost	—	—	—	—
	59	3	4 / 4	0 / 1	1	o	L	2	o	o	o	o	o	o	0		R corn.	L	M
	60	2	1	o	?	o	L	o	o	o	M back	L back	L	2 yr L side	0		R front	R	o
var.	64	3	?	?	arched roofs	?	L	1?	?	L top / low, back low	lost	—	—	—	—	—	—	—	—
	68	3?	4	2	?	?	L	2	o	R court	o	o	o	o	lost	—	—	R-M	?
	76	3	2	2	1	o	L	2	o	ends 2 top 2 low	top porch	court 'tween doors	?	o	1		L	L	M·R
	97	3	3 / 2	1	?	o	L	2	o	o	top R back	do.	R	2 yrs R court	spongy		mass only		
	99	2 or 3	1?	1	?	?	R	2	o	o	L low back	R back	L	o	o?		o?	o?	o?
	102	3	2 / 2	1 / 1	1	o	L	2 / 2	o	sides top low	top 'tween doors	court 'tween doors	o	o	1		L	R	M
	118	3	1	1	?	?	L	2	o	o	R back low	L back low	o	under stair	0		o	o	o
	123	2	2	1	?	?	L	1	o	R side	L door	o	o	2 yr R door	o		o	o	R [illegible] 4 ends
	124	2	2	1	?	?	o	1	o	o	o	o	o	o	2		o	o	o
?	130	3	3 / ?	1	?	o	L	?	?	o	top M back	top L back	R	2 yr R top	lost	—	—	—	—
	141	3?	2	1	?	?	L	1	o	o	o?	top back	o	2 yr R court	o		o	o	o
	146	3	?	2	1	?	L	2 / ?	o	ends	M top front	lost	—	—	—	—	—	—	—
	155	3	2 / 4	0	?	o	L	o	o	o	o	o	o	o	1 'esh.		R	R	M
M	?22	2?	4	1	?	?	R	1	o	?	o	o	o	o	o		o	o	o
	23	2?	2	1	?	?	o?	2	o	?	o	court 'tween doors	R	o	1		L	R	M
	24	2?	2	1	?	?	o?	2	o	o	o	do.	?	o	1		L	R	M
	32	3	2 / 2?	0 / 1	?	o	R	1	o	2 court / back low / back top	o	L top	L	o	lost	—	—	—	—
	34	3	2 left	1	?	?	o?	2	o	o	court 'tween doors	o	o	o	lost	—	—	—	—
	43	3	1 chr.	2 side by side	2+x	2	L?	?	?	o	lost	—	—	—	—	—	—	—	—
	46	3	?	2	?	?	o	o	o	3 back	o	o	o	o	lost	—	—	—	—
	53	2 or 3	?	?	deep	?	?	?	?	?	?	lost	—	—	—	—	—	—	—
	54	2 or 3	lost	—	—	—	—	—	—	—	—	—	—	—	—	—	—	—	—
	63	3	4 / ?	?	?	o	R / ?	?	?	R back } top	?	R top back	L	lost	—	—	—	—	—
	66	3	2 / 1	1	?	o	R	2	o	R top	o	L back top	L	o	o		o	o	o
	78	2	1	1	1?	o	o	1	o	o	o	L	L	2 yr L court	o		o	o	o
	79	2	1	1	?	o	o	1	o	o	o	L chr.	L	o	L court		o	o	o
	83	3	2 / 1	1	?	o	R	1	o	R high	M back low	L low back M high	L R	under stair	o		o	o	o
	90	2 or 3	2	1	?	?	o	1	o	o	o	o	o	o	lost		L	L corn.	L
	127	2 or 3	2	1	?	?	L	2	o	o	L back low	R back	?	o	o		?	?	?
	145	2?	2	1	?	?	L	2?	?	?	?	?	?	?	o		o	o	M
N	58	?	?	1	?	?	?	2	o	o	lost	—	—	—	—	—	—	—	—
	77	3	2	1	?	?	L	2	o	o	R back	L back	L	under stair	?		M back	M	
	103	2 or 3	o	1	?	?	o	2	o	o	o	o	o	o	o		L wall	M	L
	119	?	?	1	?	?	?	2 or 3	?	?	?	?	?	?	?		?	?	L
?	50	2?	?	o	?	?	R	?	?	?	lost	—	—	—	—	—	—	—	—
?	51	roof chamber																	
?	52	roof chamber																	
?	62	pieces of side					L												
?	135	3	?	1 top ? base	3	2	?	1 / ?	?	o?	?	lost	—	—	—	—	—	—	—

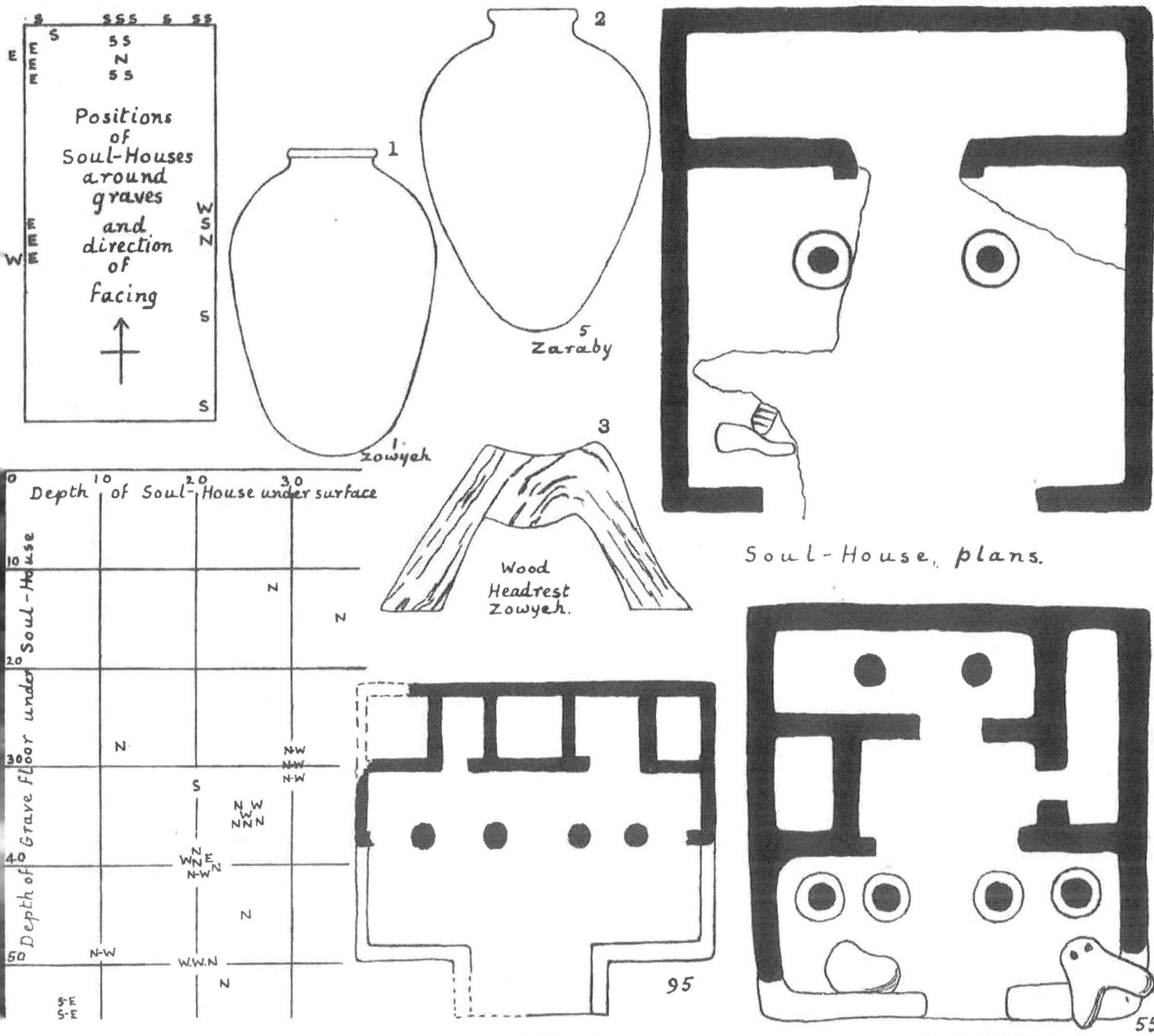

1:6 Ptolemaic & Roman Pottery.

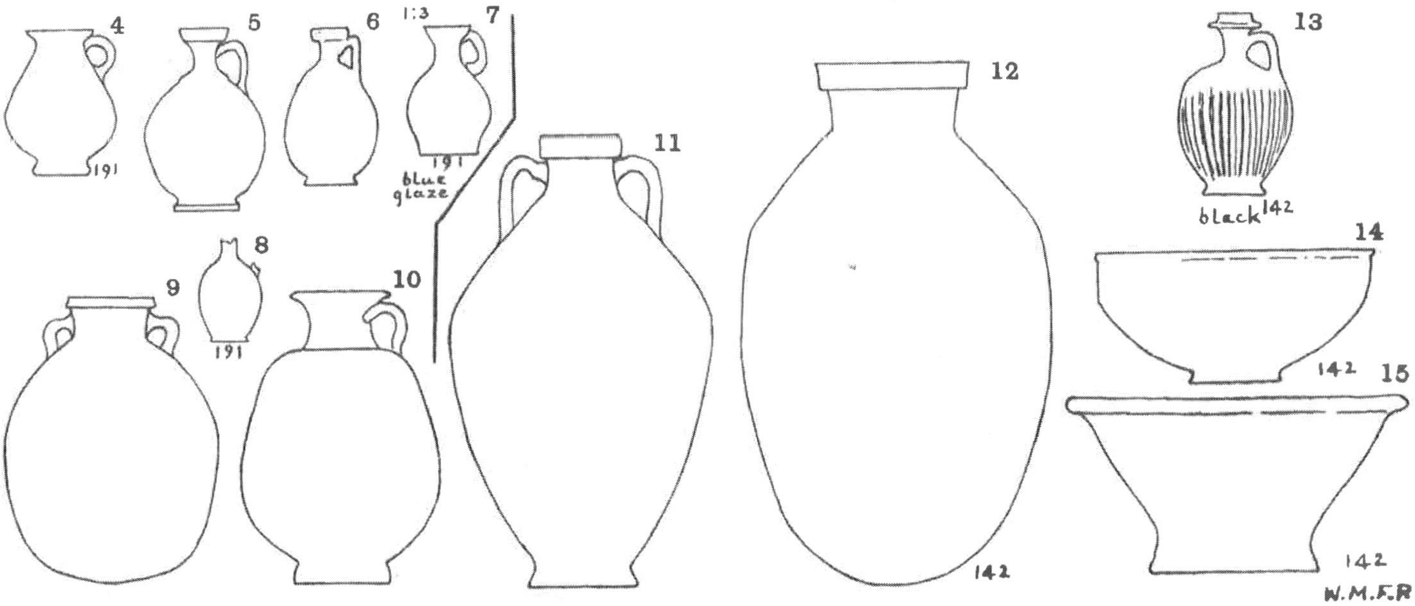

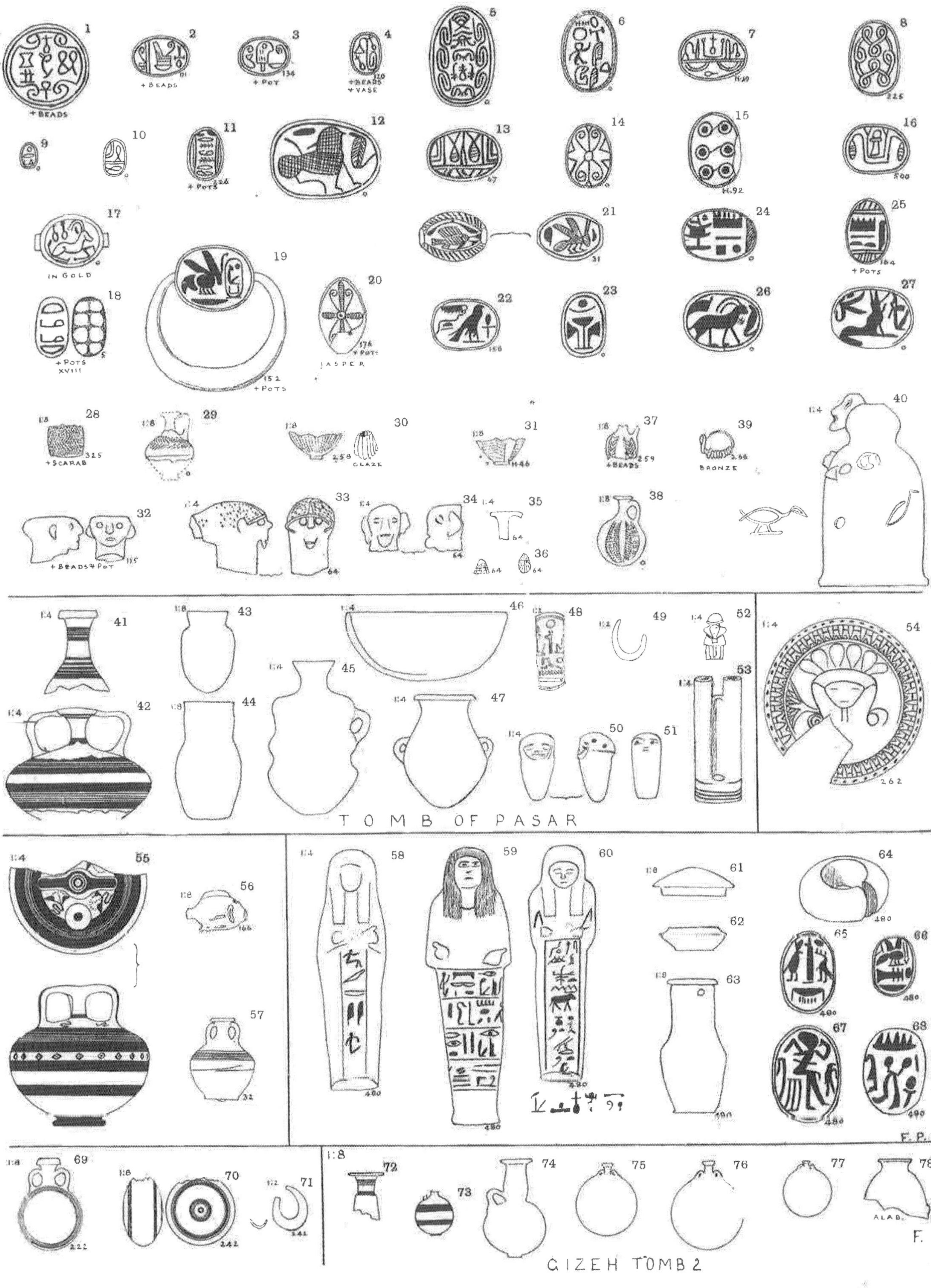
+ BEADS
+ BEADS
+ POT
+ BEADS
+ VASE
+ POTS
IN GOLD
+ POTS
XVIII
JASPER
+ POTS
+ POTS
+ SCARAB
GLAZE
+ BEADS
BRONZE
+ BEADS + POT
TOMB OF PASAR
ALAB.
GIZEH TOMB 2
F. P.

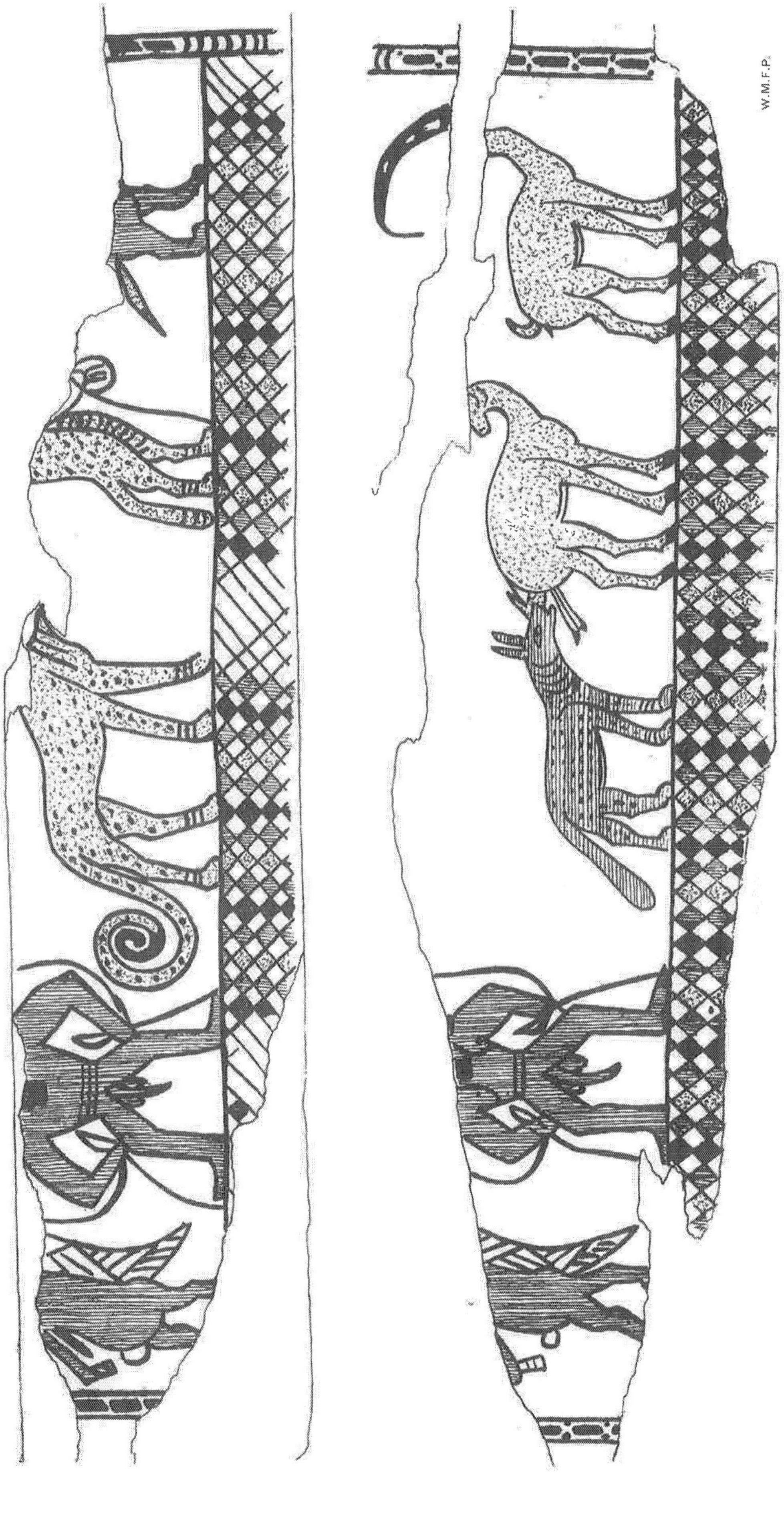
W.M.F.P.

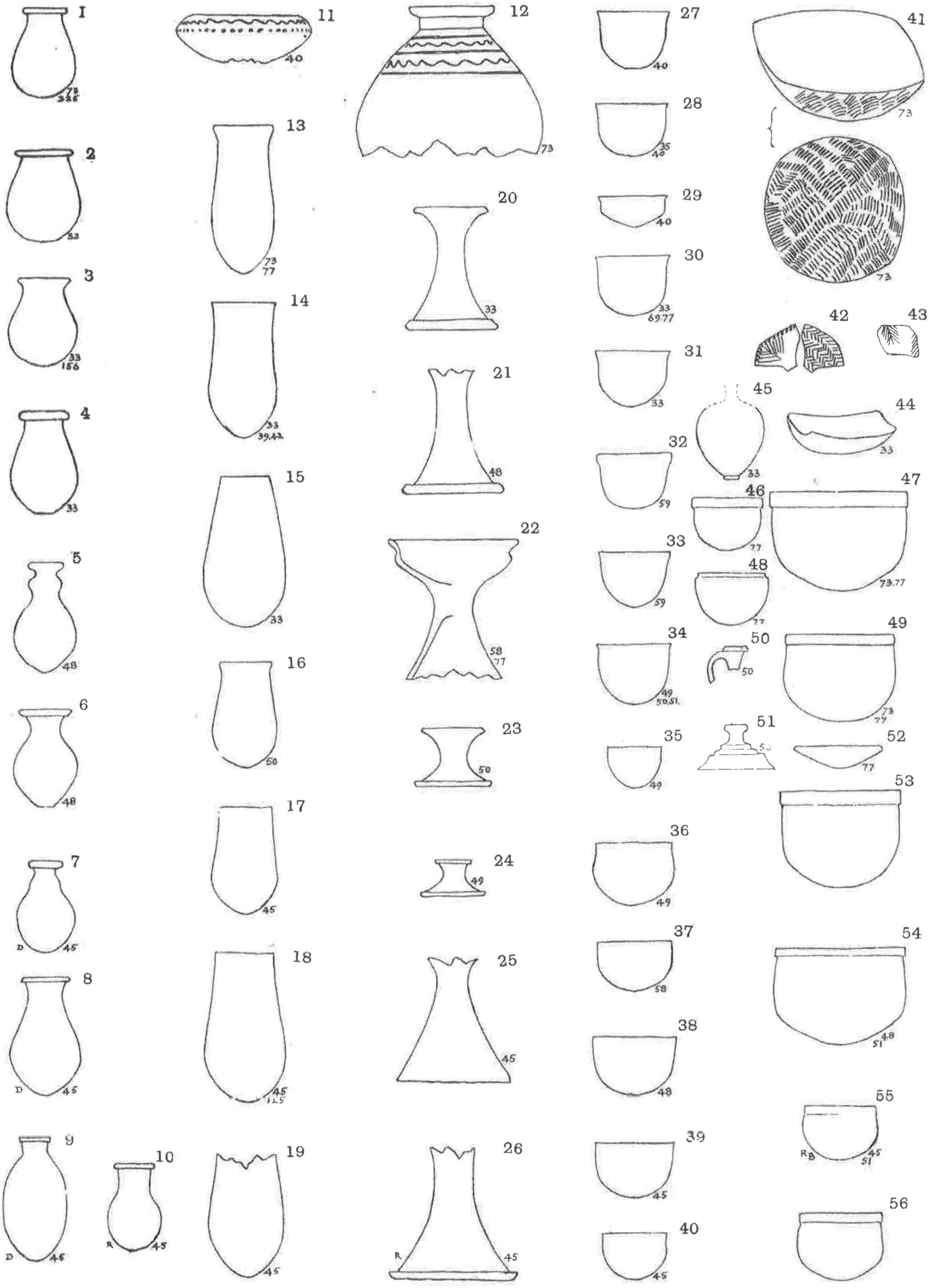

W.M.F.P.

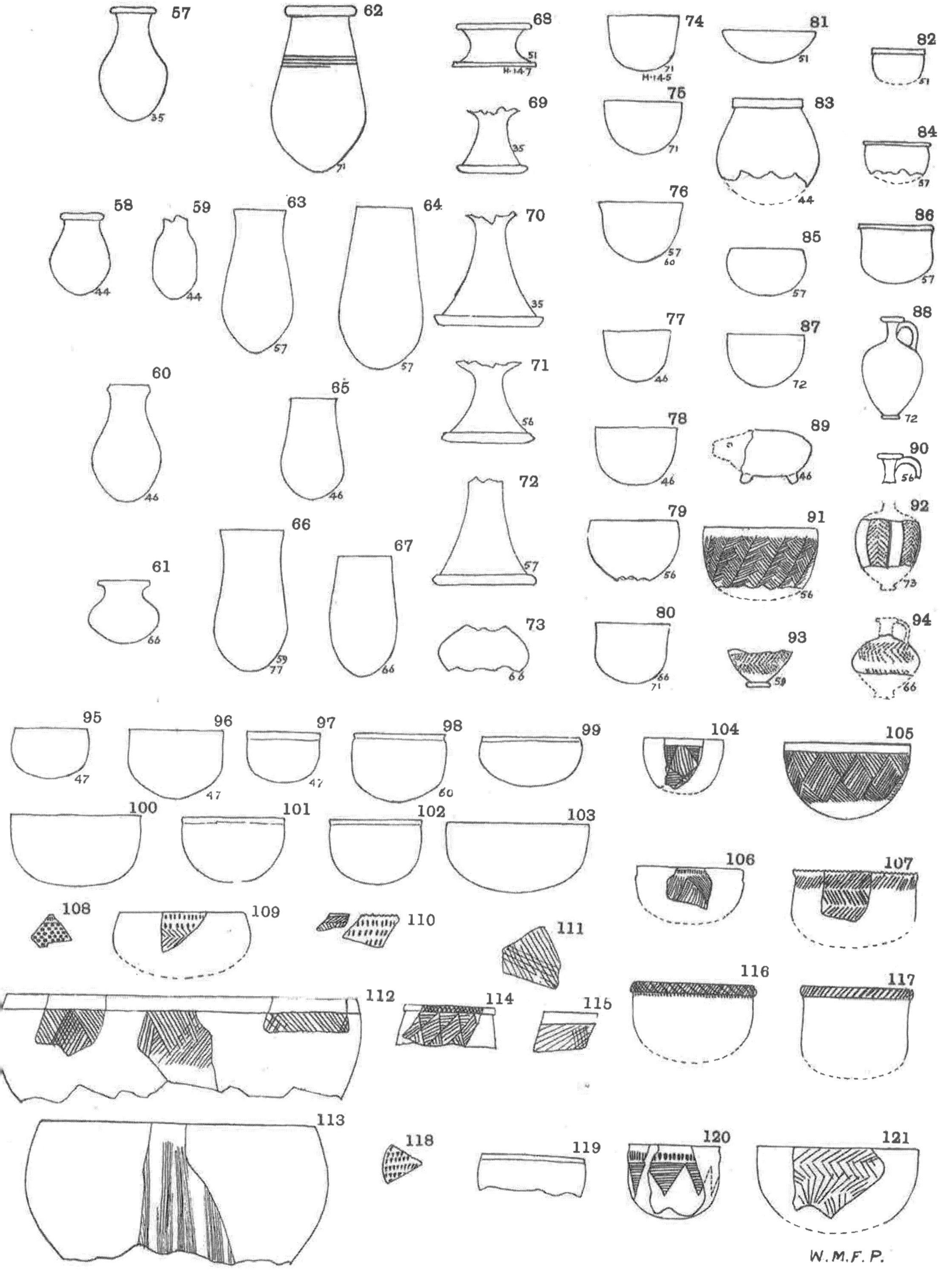
57
62
68
74
81
82
69
75
83
84
58
59
63
64
70
76
86
85
77
87
88
60
65
71
78
89
90
72
79
91
92
66
67
61
73
80
93
94
95
96
97
98
99
104
105
100
101
102
103
106
107
108
109
110
111
112
114
115
116
117
113
118
119
120
121
W.M.F.P.

POTTERY COFFIN HEAD.

THREE VASES (20), DOG (223), AND FISH.

USHABTI OF PASAR.

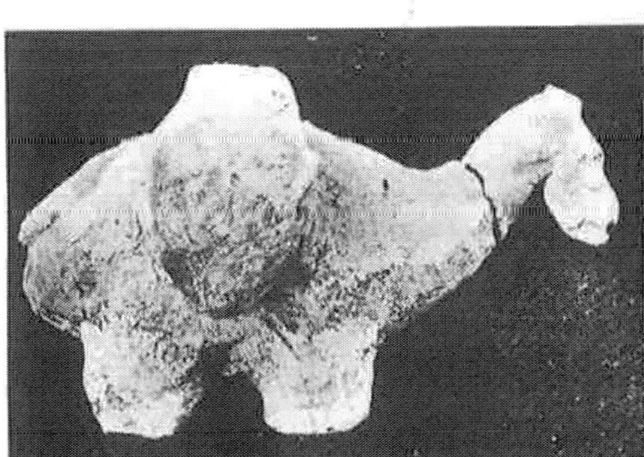

CAMEL WITH WATER JARS.

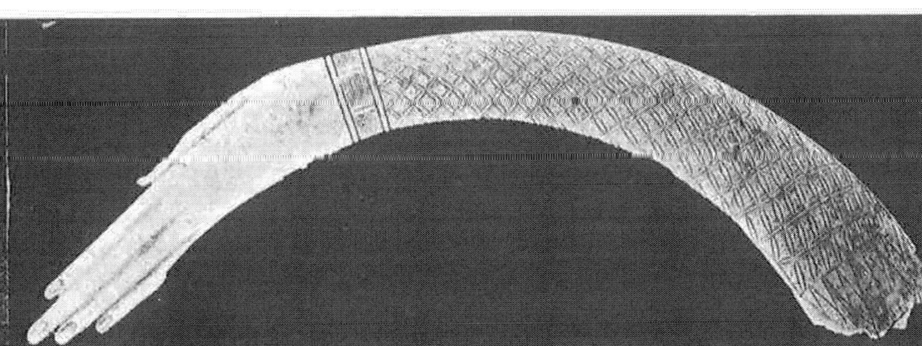

IVORY ARM WAND.

12 TAHUTM. III
28
29 END XVIII
21

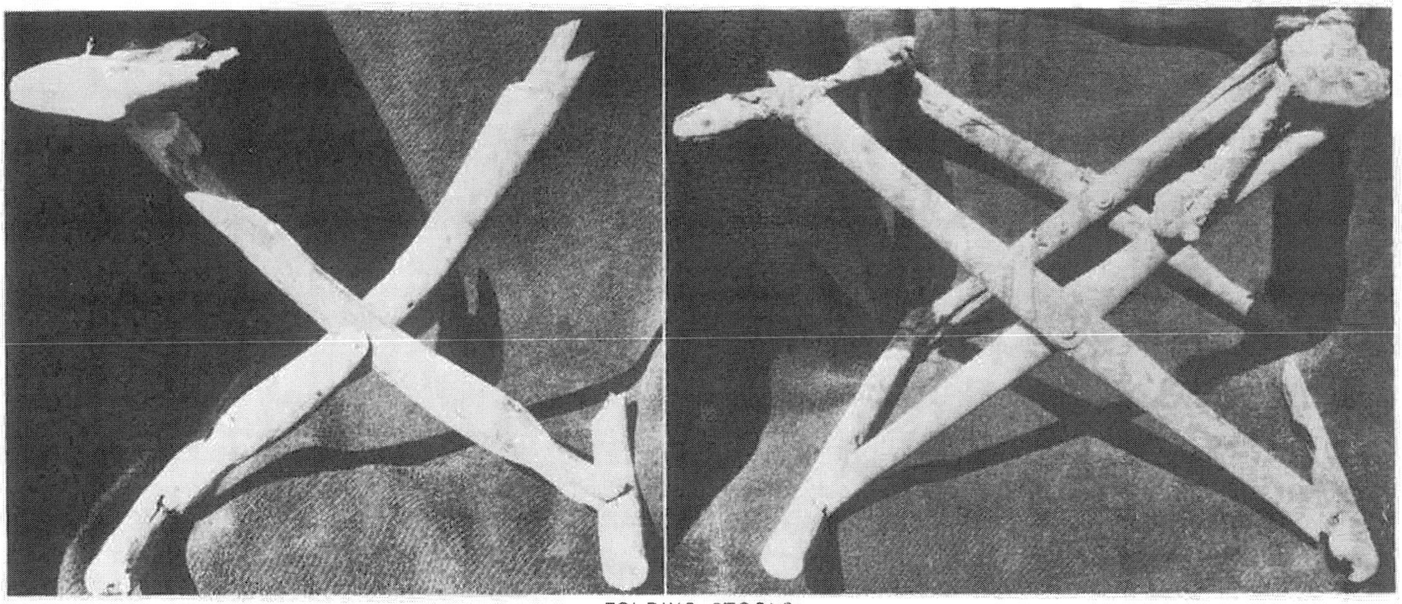

FOLDING STOOLS.

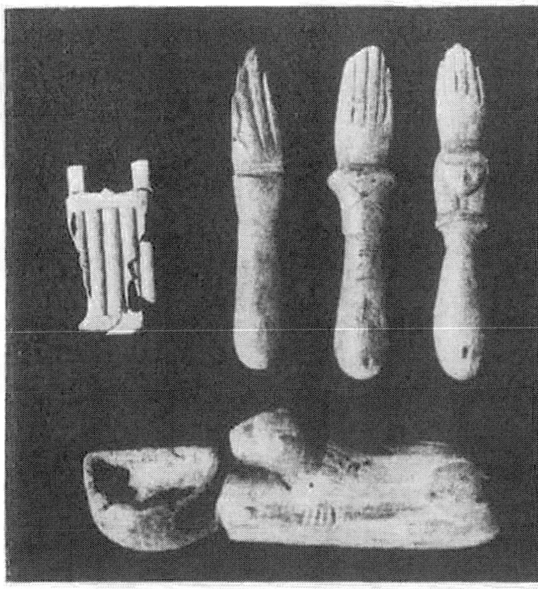

WOODEN WANDS AND LION DISH.

ALABASTER CANOPIC JARS OF HUY.

LIMESTONE HEAD OF HATHOR.

COFFIN LID.

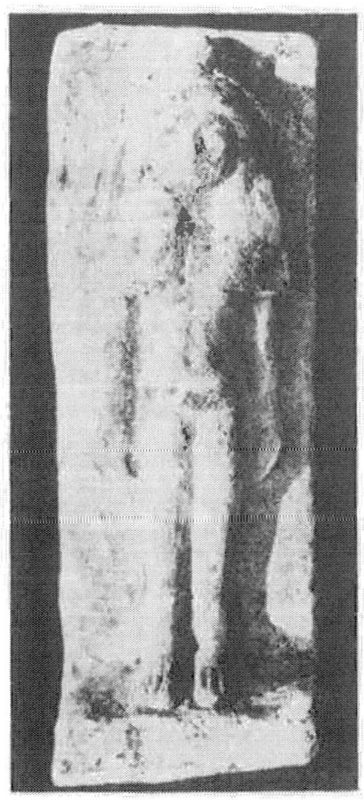

LIMESTONE GIRL.

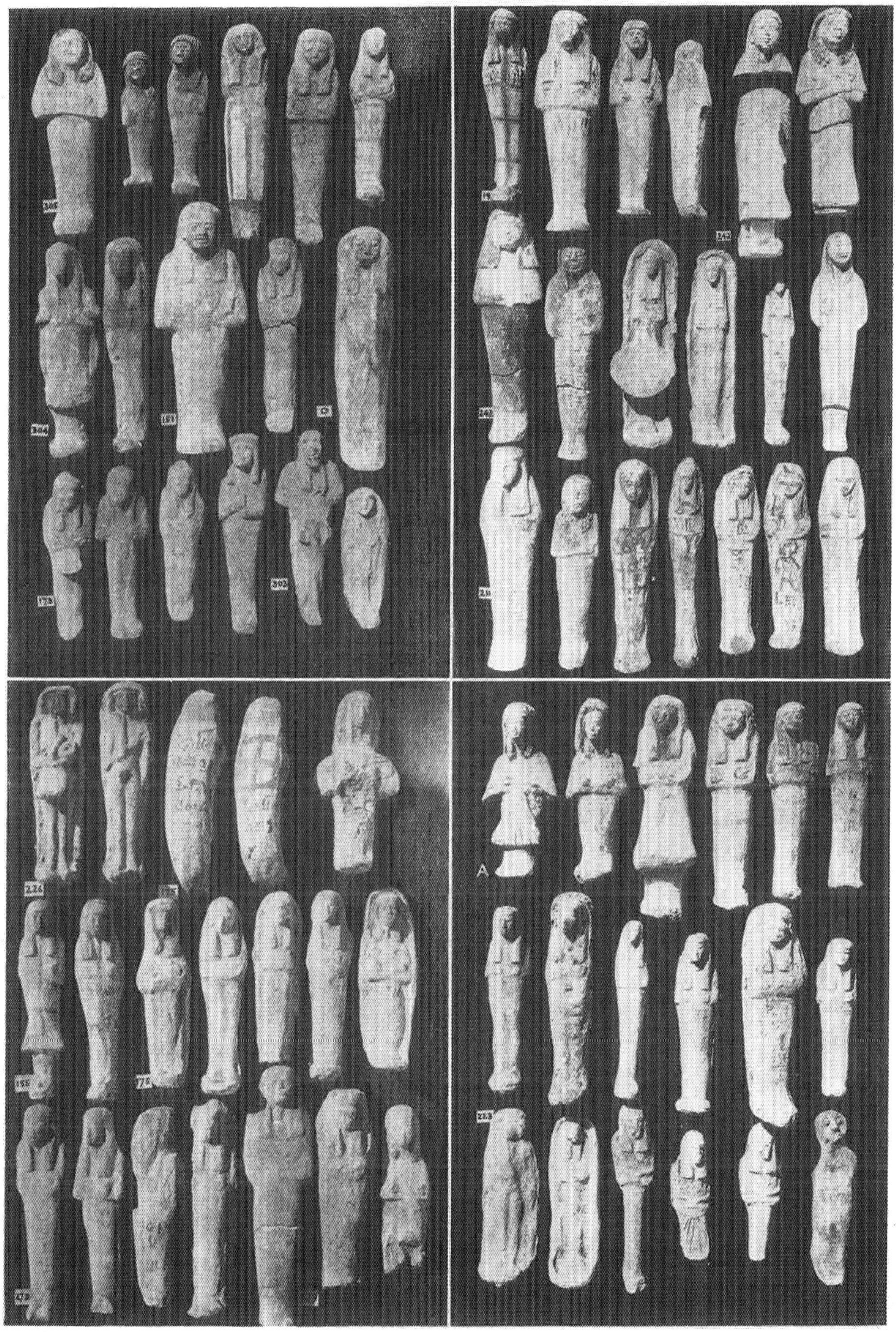

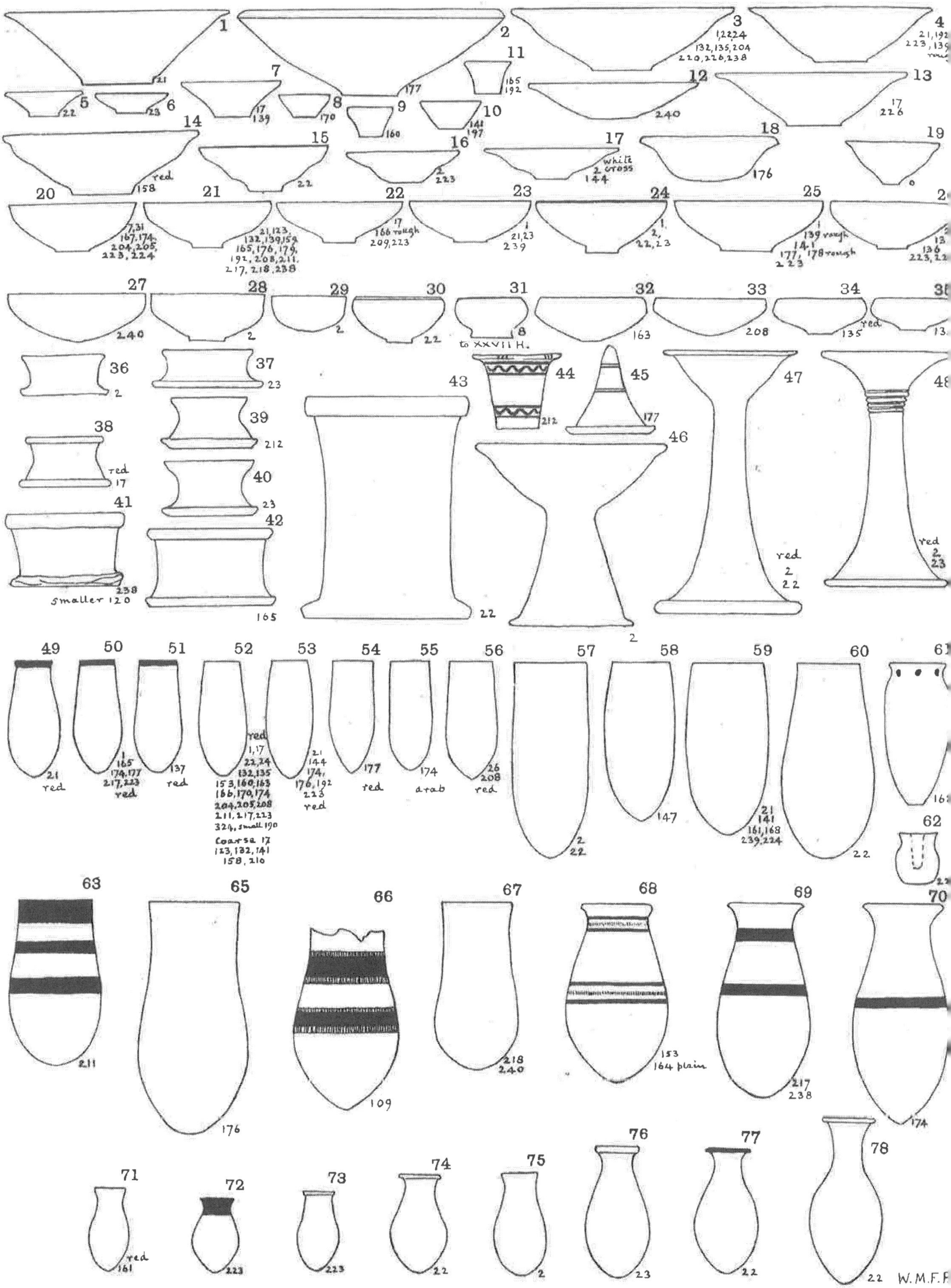
W. M. F. P.

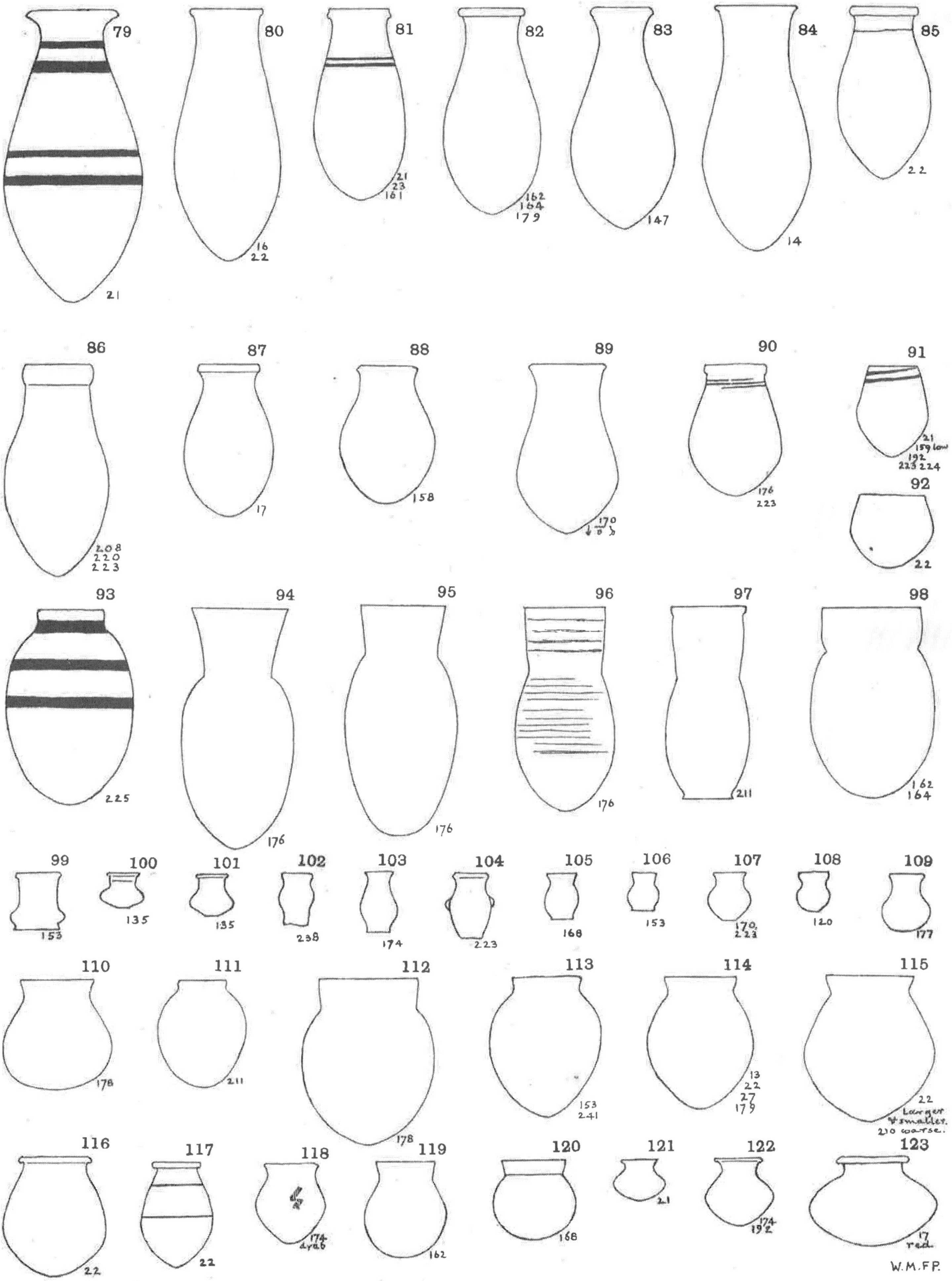
79
21
80
16
22
81
21
23
161
82
162
164
179
83
147
84
14
85
22
86
208
220
223
87
17
88
158
89
170
90
176
223
91
21
159 low
192
223 224
92
22
93
225
94
176
95
176
96
176
97
211
98
162
164
99
153
100
135
101
135
102
238
103
174
104
223
105
168
106
153
107
170
223
108
120
109
177
110
178
111
211
112
178
113
153
241
114
13
22
27
179
115
22
Larger & smaller.
210 coarse.
116
22
117
22
118
174
drab
119
162
120
168
121
21
122
174
192
123
17
red.
W.M.F.P.

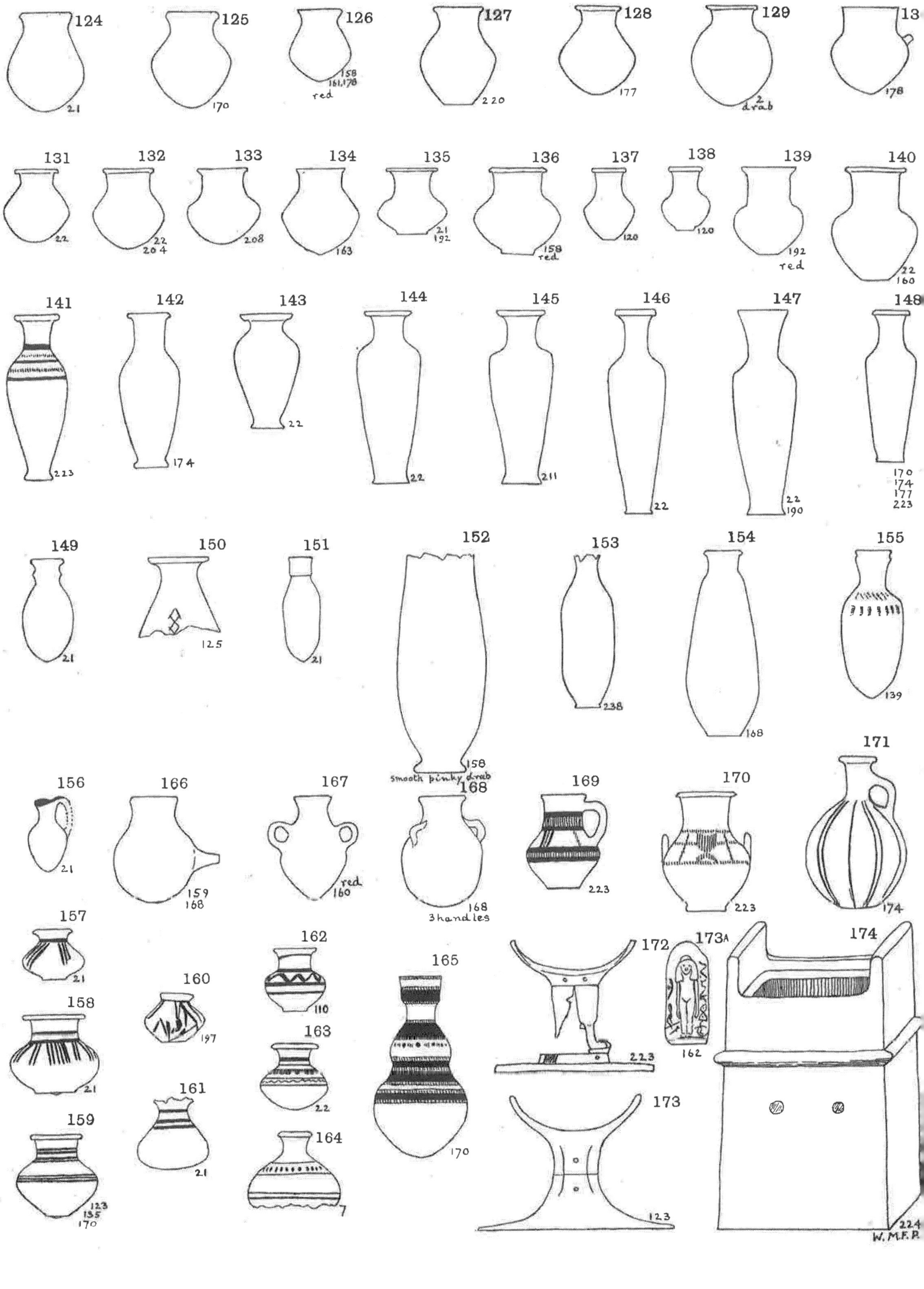

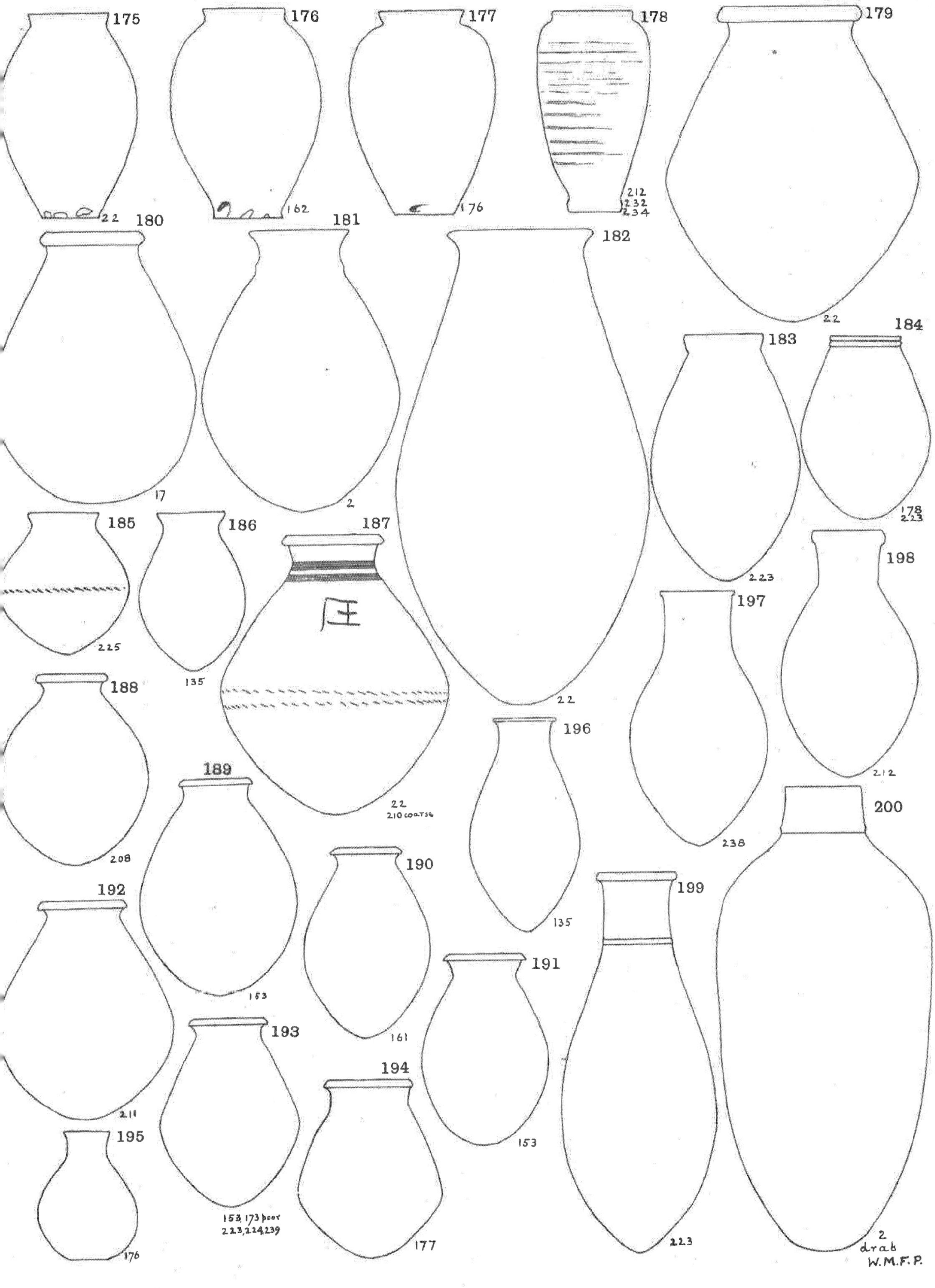
175
22
176
162
177
176
178
212
232
234
179
22
180
17
181
2
182
22
183
223
184
178
223
185
225
186
135
187
22
210 coarse
188
208
189
163
190
161
191
153
192
211
193
153, 173 poor
223, 224, 239
194
177
195
176
196
135
197
238
198
212
199
223
200
2
drab
W.M.F.P.

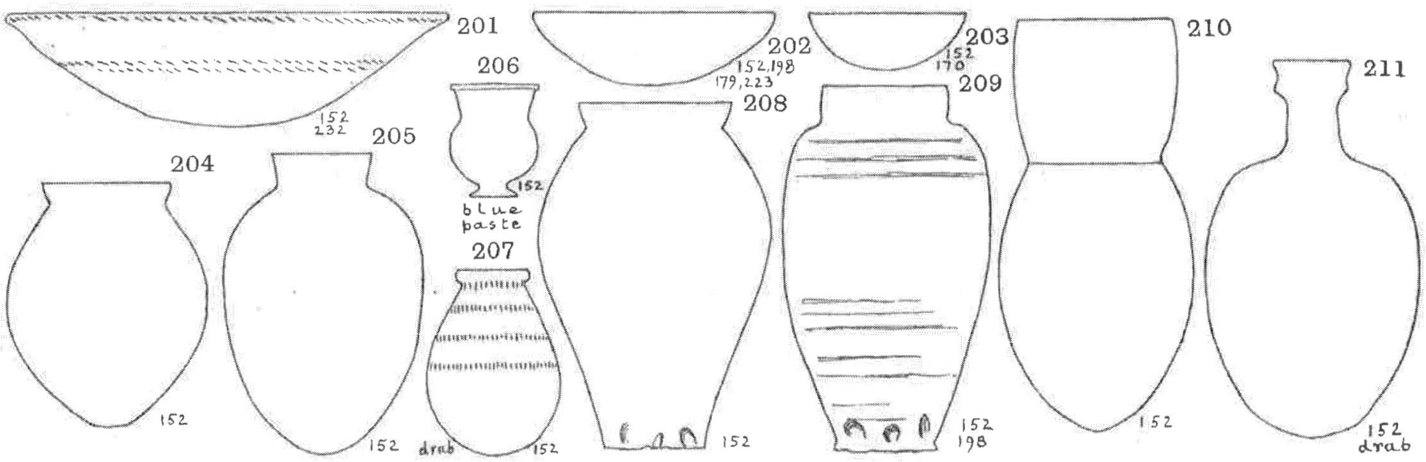

GROUP OF HATSHEPSUT, PL. XXIII, 19.

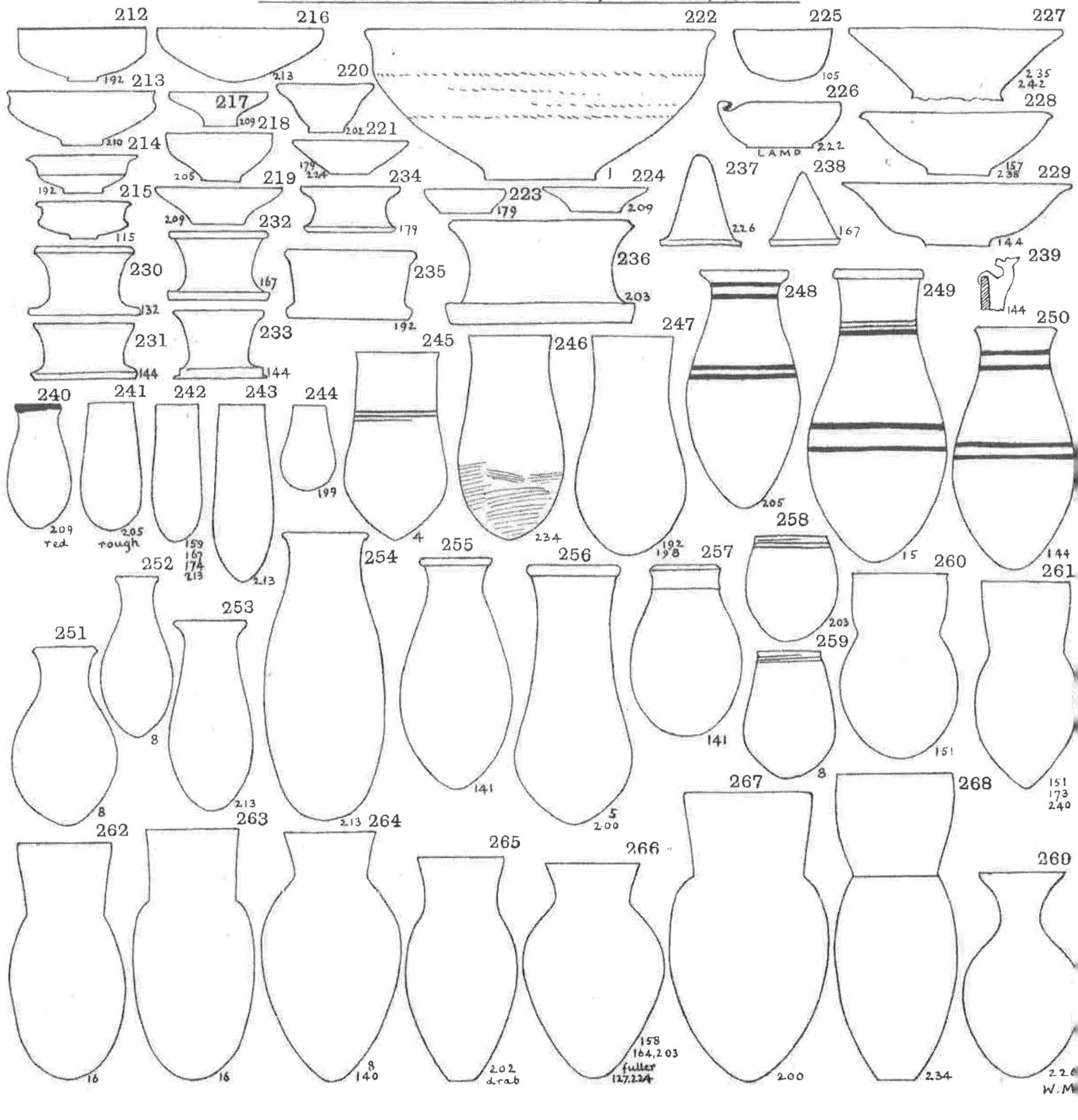

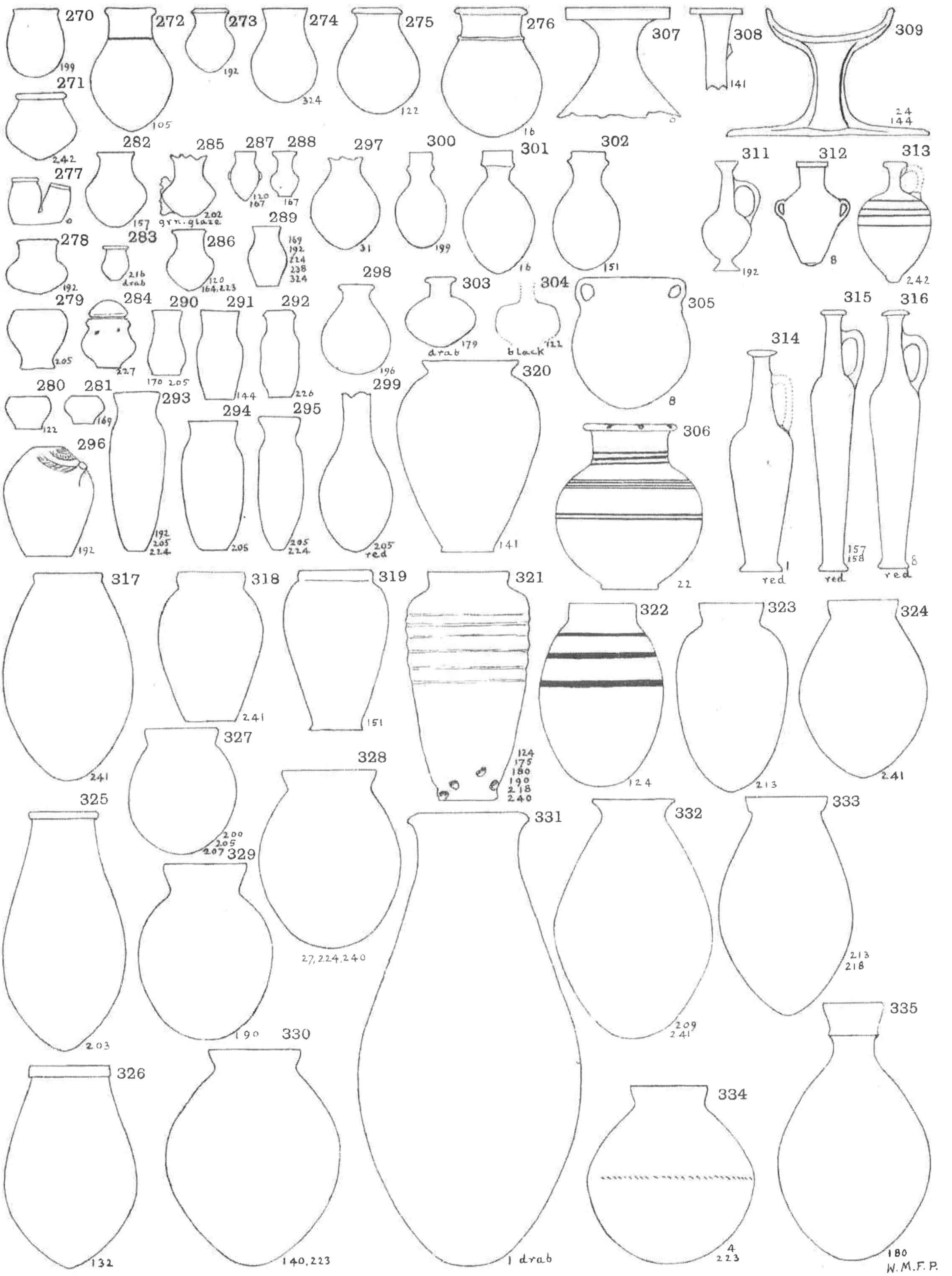
270 271 272 273 274 275 276 277 278 279 280 281 282 283 284 285 286 287 288 289 290 291 292 293 294 295 296 297 298 299 300 301 302 303 304 305 306 307 308 309 311 312 313 314 315 316 317 318 319 320 321 322 323 324 325 326 327 328 329 330 331 332 333 334 335
grn. glaze
drab
black
red
W.M.F.P.

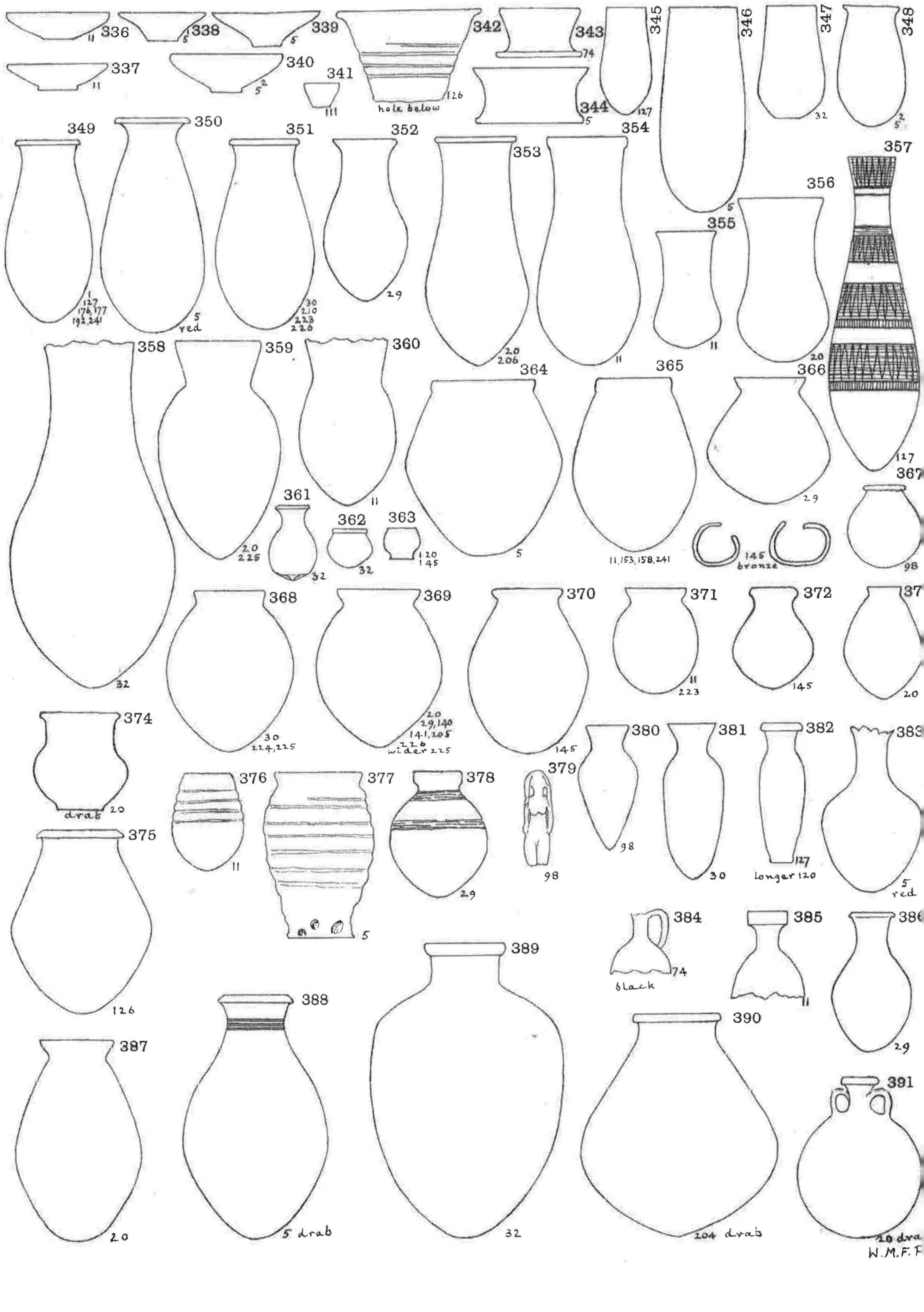

336 11
338 5
339 5
342
343 74
345 127
346 5
347 32
348 5²
337 11
340 5²
341 111
126 hole below
344 5
349 1 127 176,177 192,241
350 5 red
351 30 210 223 226
352 29
353 20 206
354 11
355 11
356 20
357 127
358 32
359 20 225
360 11
361 32
362 32
363 120 145
364 5
365 11,153,158,241
366 29
145 bronze
367 98
368 30 224,225
369 20 29,140 141,205 226 wider 225
370 145
371 11 223
372 145
373 20
374 drab 20
375 126
376 11
377 5
378 29
379 98
380 98
381 30
382 127 longer 120
383 5 red
384 74 black
385 11
386 29
387 20
388 5 drab
389 32
390 204 drab
391 20 drab
W.M.F.P.

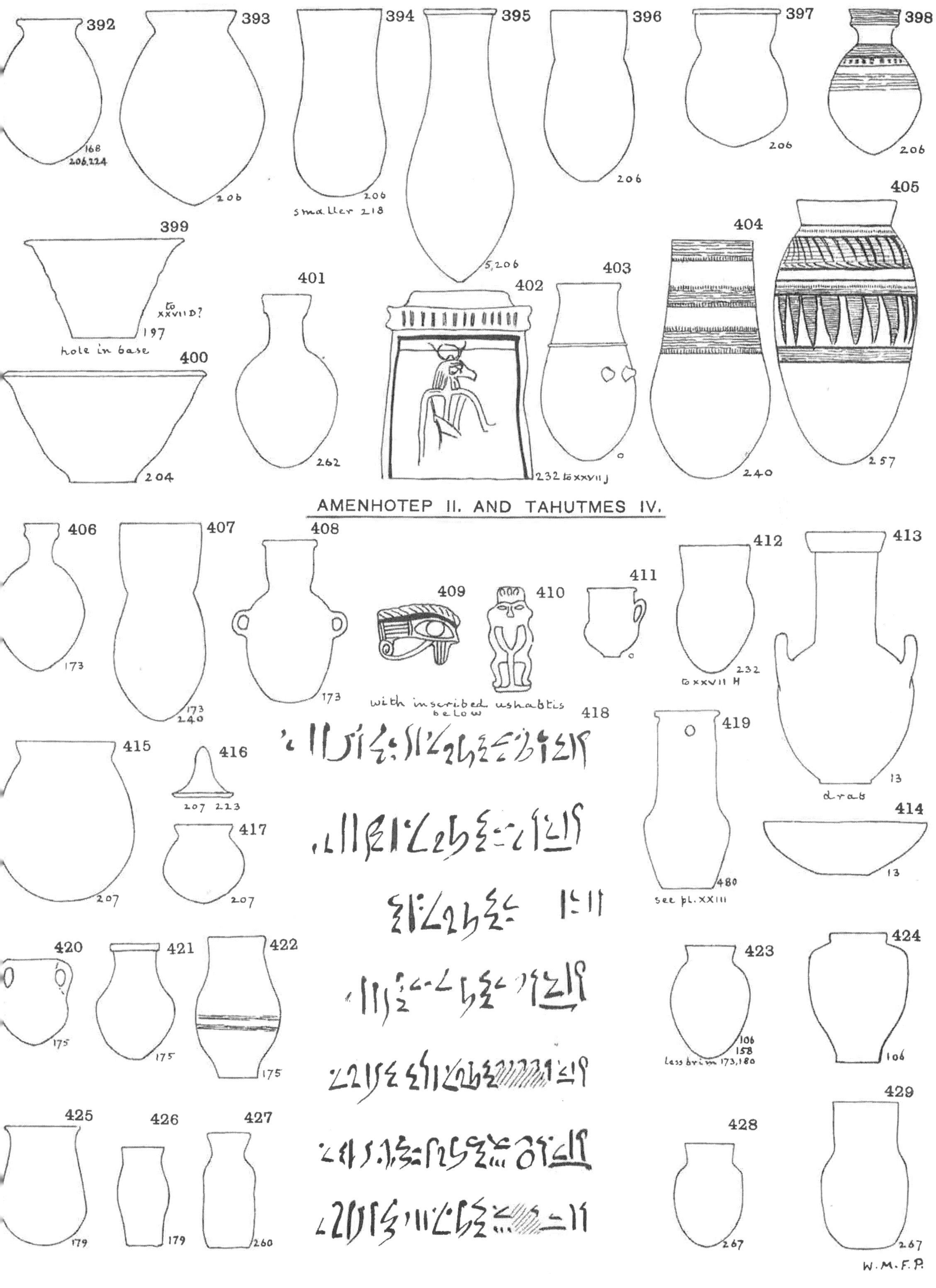
392
168
206,224
393
206
394
206
smaller 218
395
5,206
396
206
397
206
398
206
399
to XXVII D?
197
hole in base
400
204
401
262
402
232 to XXVII J
403
405
404
240
257
AMENHOTEP II. AND TAHUTMES IV.
406
173
407
173
240
408
173
409
410
with inscribed ushabtis below
411
412
232
to XXVII H
413
13
drab
414
13
415
207
416
207 223
417
207
418
419
480
see pl. XXIII
420
175
421
175
422
175
423
106
158
less brim 173,180
424
106
425
179
426
179
427
260
428
267
429
267
W.M.F.P.

Tomb	Up to Tahutmes I Forms	Tahutmes III	Up to Tahutmes IV	Later
1	3, 23, 24, 25, 50, 52	222, 314, 331	338, 349	
2	16, 17, 24, 28, 29, 36, 46, 47, 48, 57, 75, 129, 181, 200		340, 348	
4		245, 334		
5		256	338, 339, 340, 344, 346, 348, 350, 364, 377, 383, 388, 395.	
7	20, 164			
8		31, 257, 252, 259, 264, 305, 312, 316		
11			336, 337, 354, 355, 360, 365, 371, 376, 335	
13	114			413, 414
16	80	262, 263, 276, 301		
17	7, 13, 22, 38, 52, 87, 123, 180			
20			353, 358, 359, 369, 373, 374, 387, 391	
21	1, 4, 21, 23, 49, 53, 59, 79, 81, 91, 121, 124, 135, 149, 151, 156, 157, 158, 161			
22	3, 5, 15, 24, 26, 30, 43, 47, 52, 57, 60, 62, 74, 77, 78, 80, 85, 114, 115, 116, 117, 131, 132, 140, 143, 144, 146, 147, 163, 175, 179, 182, 187			
23	6, 23, 24, 37, 40, 48, 79, 81			
24	3, 52	309		
27	114	328		
29			352, 366, 369, 378, 386	
30			351, 368, 381	
31	20	297		
32			347, 358, 361, 362, 389	
74			343, 384	
106				423, 424
105		225, 272		
120	41, 108, 137, 138	286, 287	363	
122		275, 280, 304, 306		
123	21, 52, 159, 173			
124		321, 322		
126			342, 375	
127		266	345, 349, 357, 382	
132	3, 21, 52	230, 326		
135	3, 26, 34, 35, 52, 100, 101, 159, 186, 196			
139	4, 25 rough. 7, 21, 155			
140		264, 330	369	
141	10, 25, 52, 59	255, 257, 308, 320	369	
144	17, 53	231, 233, 229, 239, 250, 291, 309		
145			363 370 372	
147	58, 83			
151		260, 261, 302, 319		
152		201, 202, 203, 204, 205, 206, 207, 208, 209, 210, 211		
153	52, 68, 99, 106, 113, 189, 191, 193		385	
157		228, 282, 315		
158	14, 52, 88, 126, 136, 152	266, 315	365	423
159	21, 91 lower, 166	242		
160	9, 52, 140, 167			
161	59, 71, 81, 126, 190			
162	61, 82, 98, 119, 173A 176			
163	32, 52, 134			
164	68, 82, 98	266, 286		
165	11, 21, 42, 50			

Tomb	Up to Tahutmes I	Tahutmes III	Up to Tahutmes IV	Later
166	22 rough, 52.			
167	20	232, 238, 242, 287, 288		
168	59, 105, 120, 154, 166, 168		392	
169		281, 289		
170	8, 52, 89, 107, 125, 148, 159, 165	203, 290		
173	193 poorer form	261		406, 407, 408, 423
174	20, 50, 52, 53, 55, 70, 103, 118, 122, 142 148, 171	242		
175		321		420, 421, 422
176	18, 21, 53, 65, 90, 94, 95, 96, 176, 195		349	
177	2, 25, 45, 50, 54, 109, 128, 148, 194		349	
178	25, 110, 112, 126, 130, 184			
179	21, 82, 114	202, 221, 234, 223, 303		425, 426
180		321, 335		423
190	52 small, 147	321, 329		
192	4, 11, 21, 53, 91, 122, 135, 139	212, 214, 235, 247, 273, 278, 289, 293, 296, 311	349	
197	10, 160, 399			
198		202, 209, 247		
199		244, 270, 300, 327		
200		256, 267		
202		220, 265, 285		
203		236, 258, 266, 325		
204	3, 20, 52, 132		390, 400	
205	20, 52	218, 241, 248, 279, 290, 293, 294, 295, 299, 327	309	
206			352, 392, 393, 394, 395, 396, 397, 398	
207		327		415, 416, 417
208	21, 33, 52, 56, 86, 133, 188			
209	22	217, 219, 224, 240, 332		
210	52; 115+187 coarse	213	351	
211	21, 52, 63, 97, 111, 145, 192			
212	39, 44, 178, 198			
213		216, 242, 243, 253, 254, 323, 333		
217	21, 50, 52, 69			
218	21, 67	321, 333	394	
220	3, 86, 127			
223	4, 16, 20, 22, 25, 26, 50, 52, 53, 72, 73, 86, 90, 91, 104, 107, 141, 148, 169, 170, 172, 183, 184, 193, 199	202, 286, 330, 334	351, 371	416
224	20, 59, 91, 174, 193	221, 266, 289, 293, 295, 328	368, 392	
225	26, 93, 185		359, 368, 369	
226	3, 13	237, 269, 292	351, 369	
232	178	201, 402, 412		
234	178	246, 268		
238	3, 21, 41, 69, 102, 153, 197	228, 289		
239	23, 59 taller, 193			
240	12, 27, 67	261, 321, 328	404 mixed?	407
241	113	317, 318, 324, 332.	349, 365	
242		227, 271, 313		
324	52	274, 289		
267				428, 429

Single-pot Tombs, for reference to alabaster, &c.

Tomb	14	26	109	110	111	115	125	136	137	196	216	222	227	235	257	260	262
Form	84	56	66	162	341	215	150	26	51	298	283	226	204	227	405	427	401

The presence in one tomb of forms in different dated columns, shews that such form lasted through two or three periods, though the drawing is not repeated in the plates of each period. In such cases the forms which best shew the period are underlined.

W. M. F. P.

3

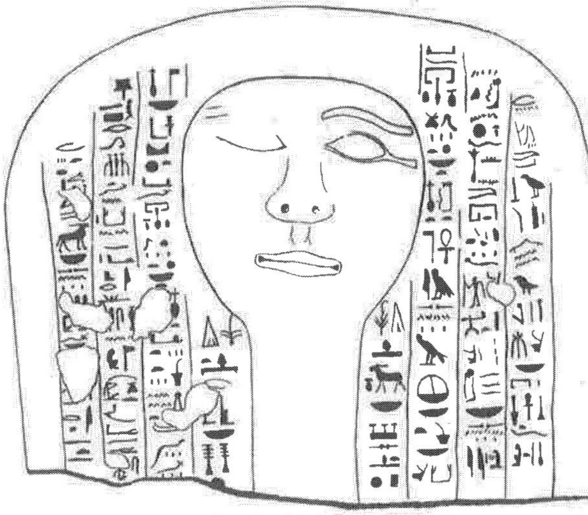

1

2

4

W. M. F. P.

Verso.

Recto.

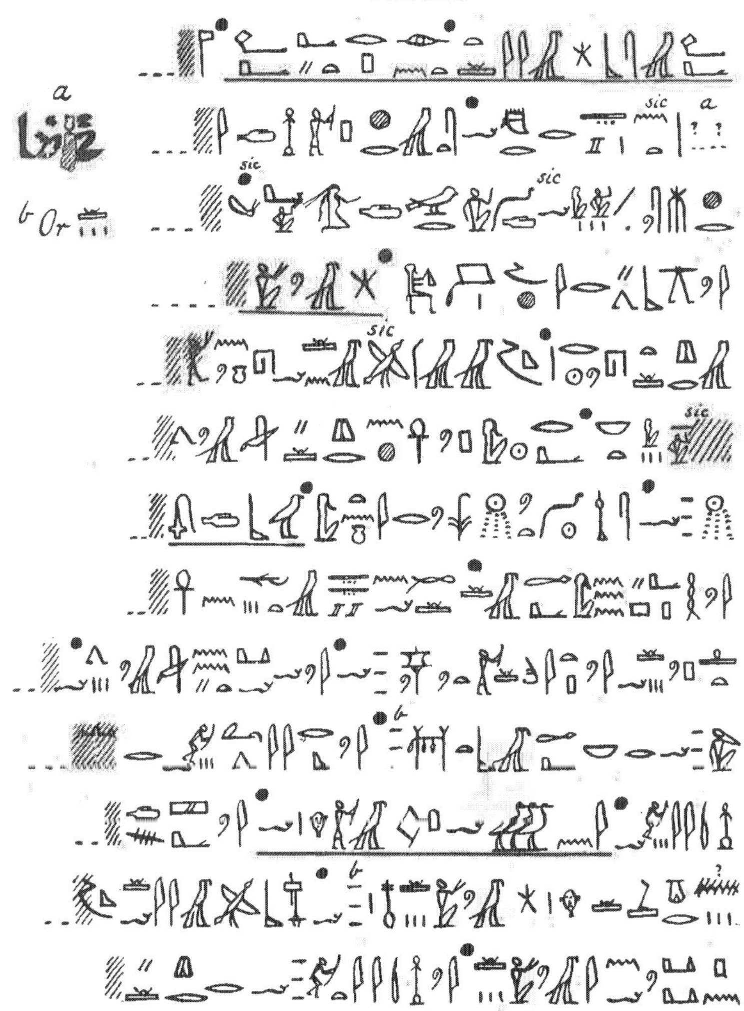

A. H. G.

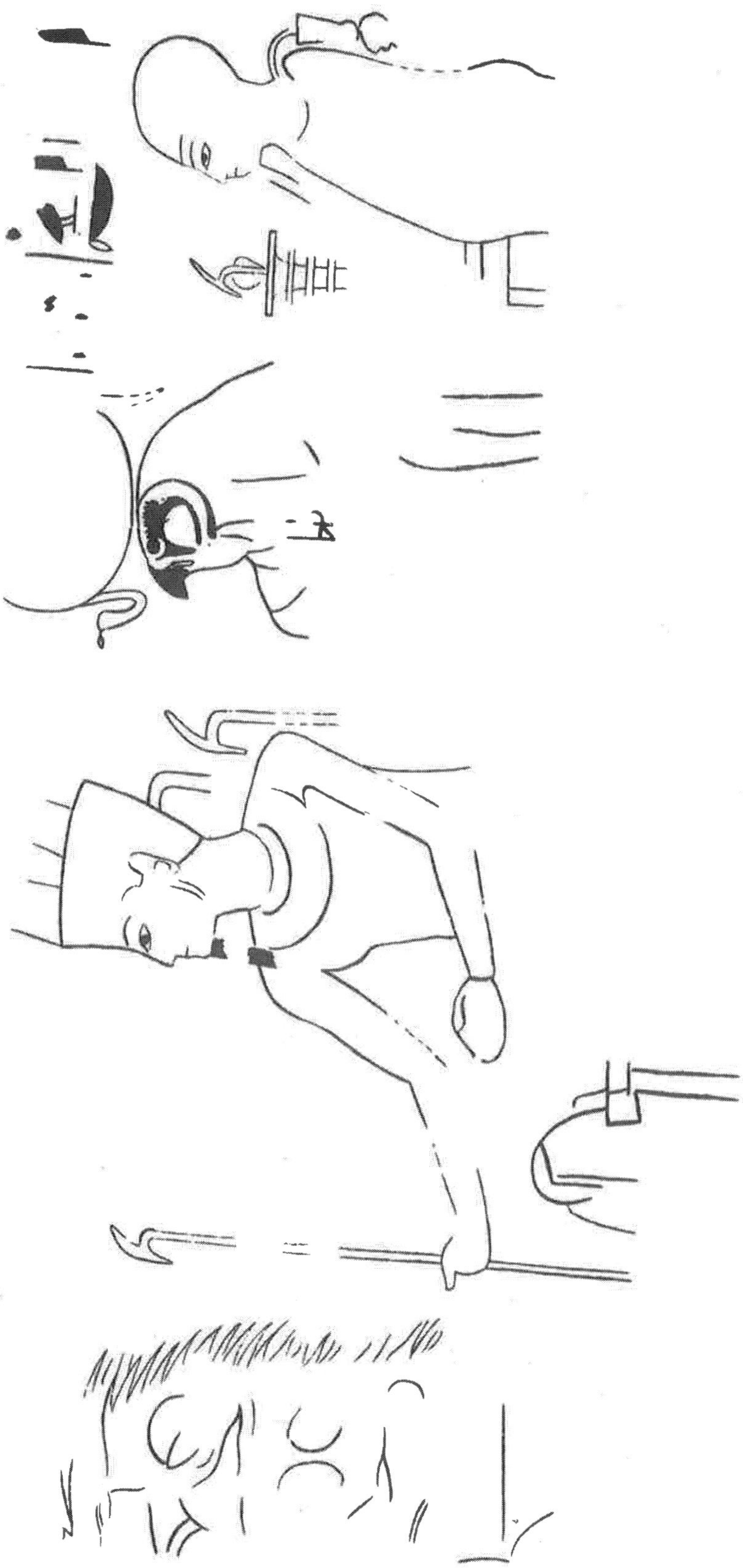

GLAZED VASES. EBONY SPOON HANDLE

SET OF AMULETS.

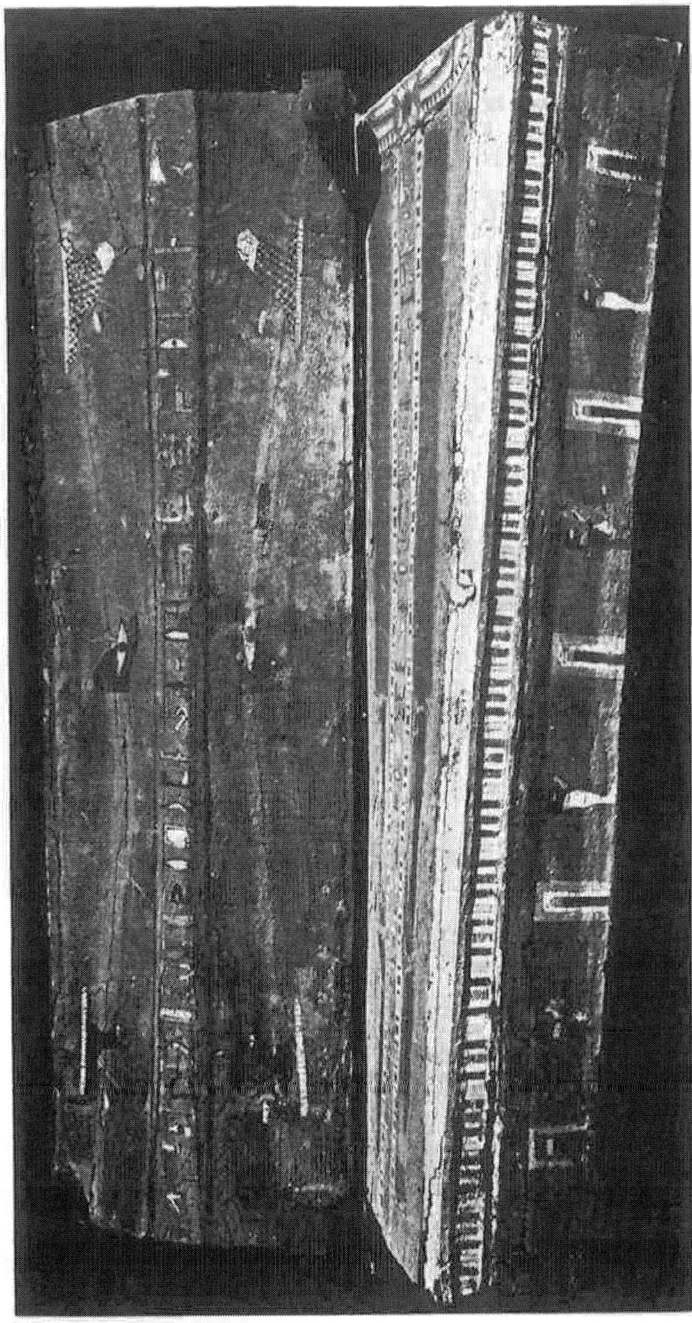

OUTER CASE. INNER COFFIN. BODY COFFIN.

CANOPIC JARS OF IMHOTEP.

COFFINS OF AMENREKHSU DAUGHTER OF ZEDHER.

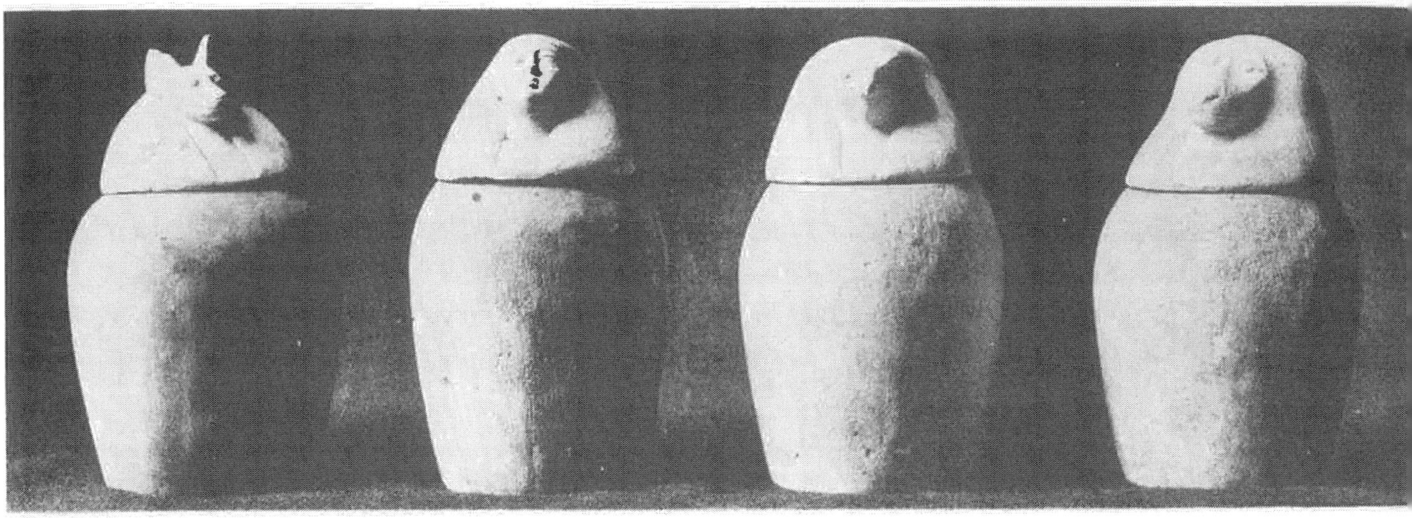

E. WALL OF N. CHAMBER.

ENTRANCE HALL, PIT, AND N. CHAMBER.

W. WALL OF E. CHAMBER.

W. SIDE DOORWAY N. OF ENTRANCE HALL.

W. WALL N. OF DOOR.

N. REVEAL OF DOOR.

S. REVEAL OF DOOR.

W. WALL S. OF DOOR.

F.P.
F.F.

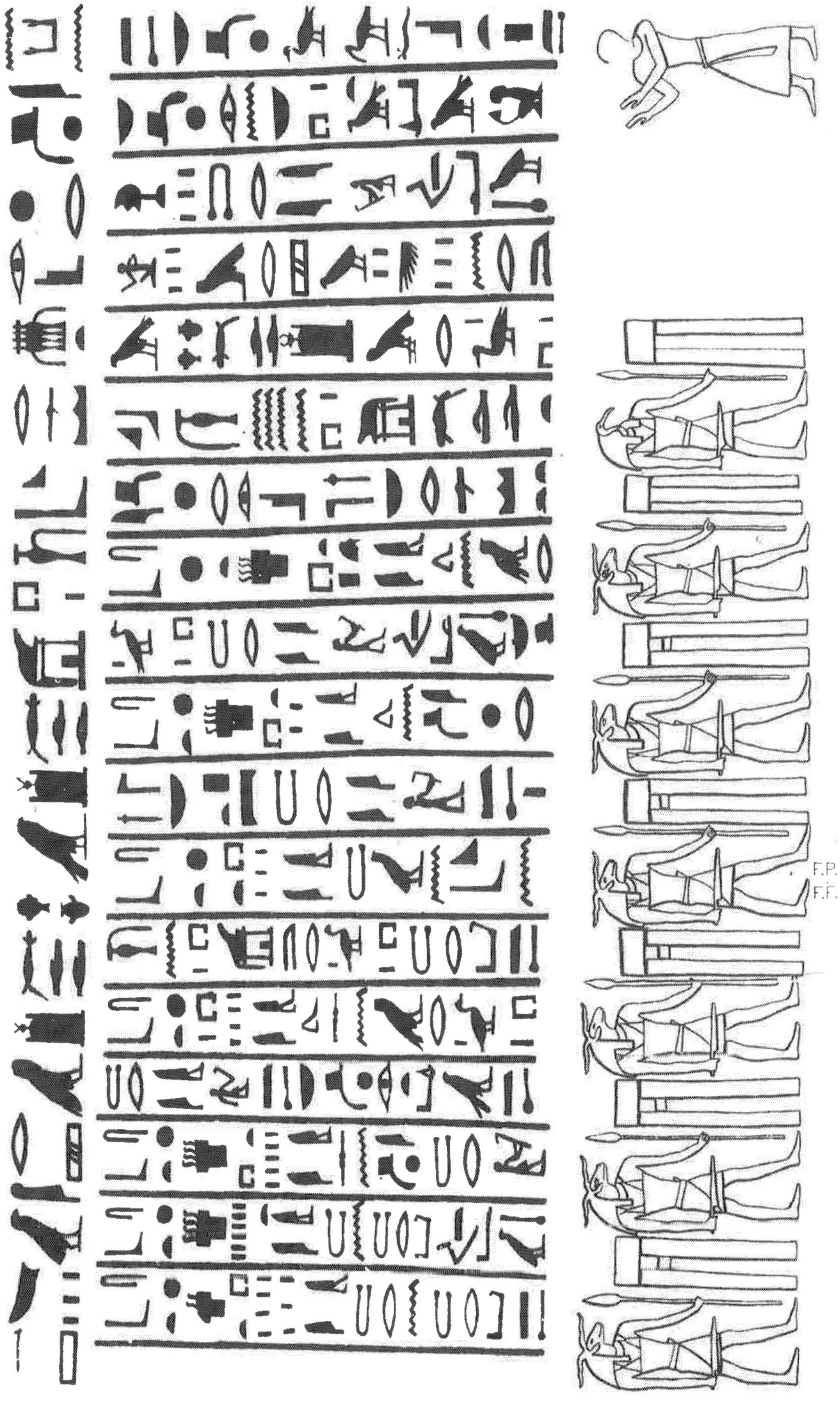
F.P.
F.F.

S. SIDE OF W. CHAMBER.

EAST SIDE OF N. CHAMBER.

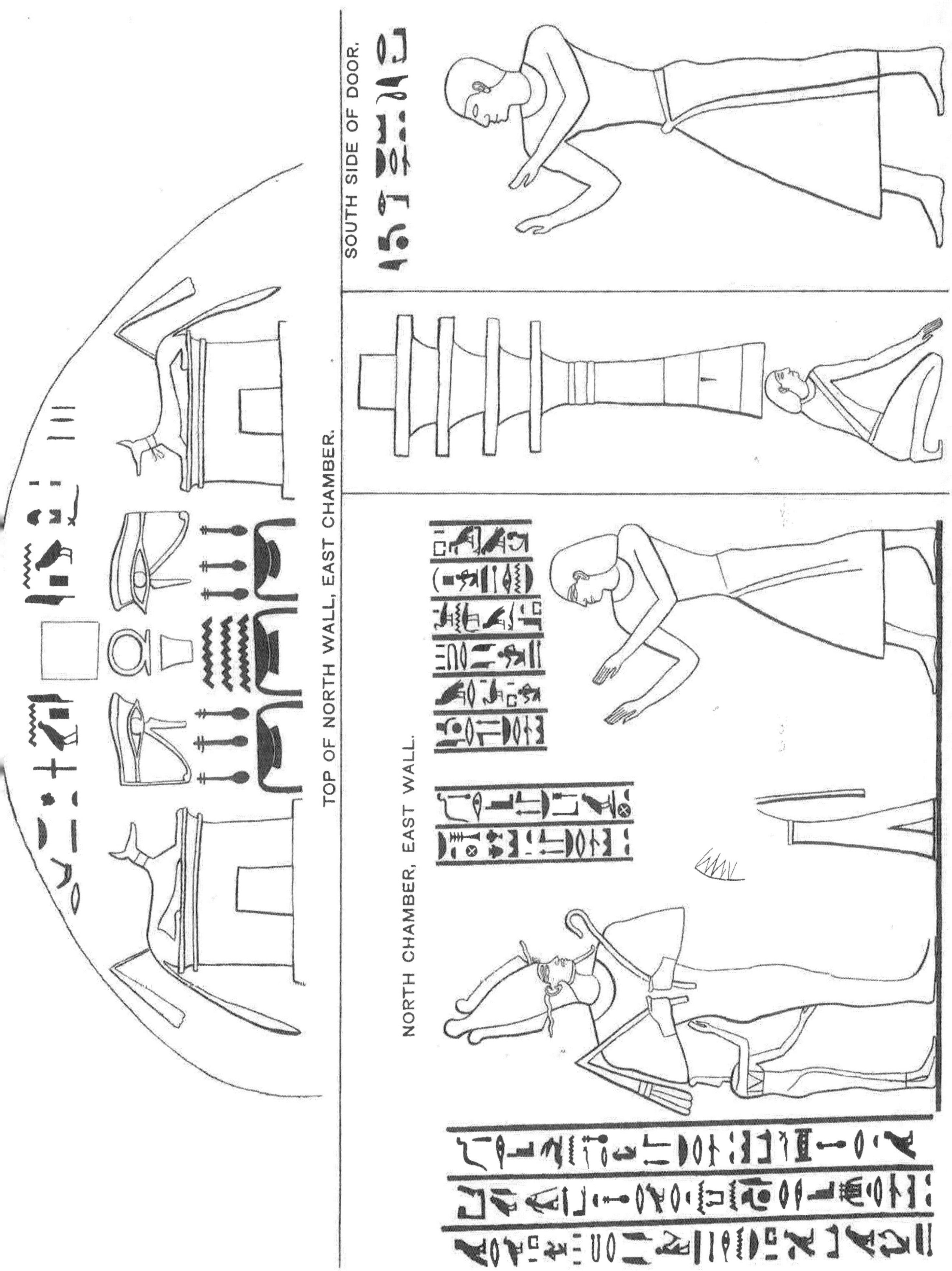
TOP OF NORTH WALL, EAST CHAMBER.
SOUTH SIDE OF DOOR.
NORTH CHAMBER, EAST WALL.

1:10 GIZEH. TOMB OF THARY: NORTH CHAMBER; SOUTH HALL. XXXVI c.

EAST SIDE OF SOUTH HALL.

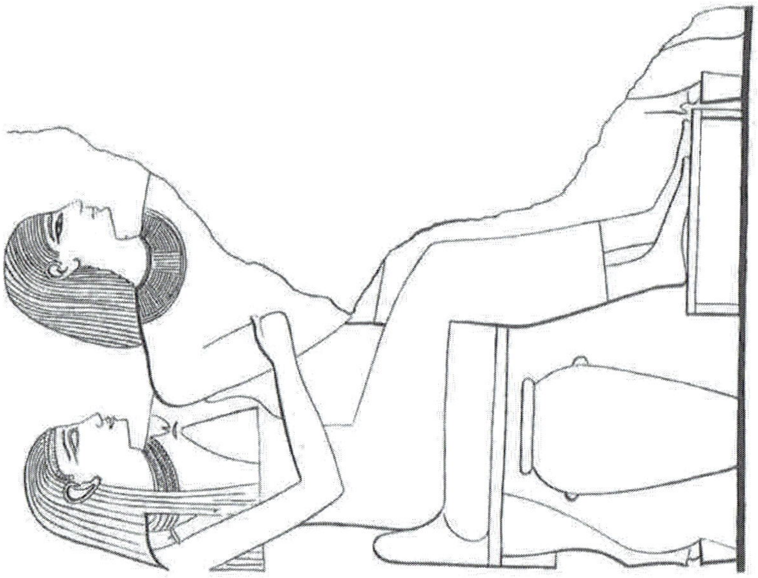

NORTH SIDE OF NORTH CHAMBER.

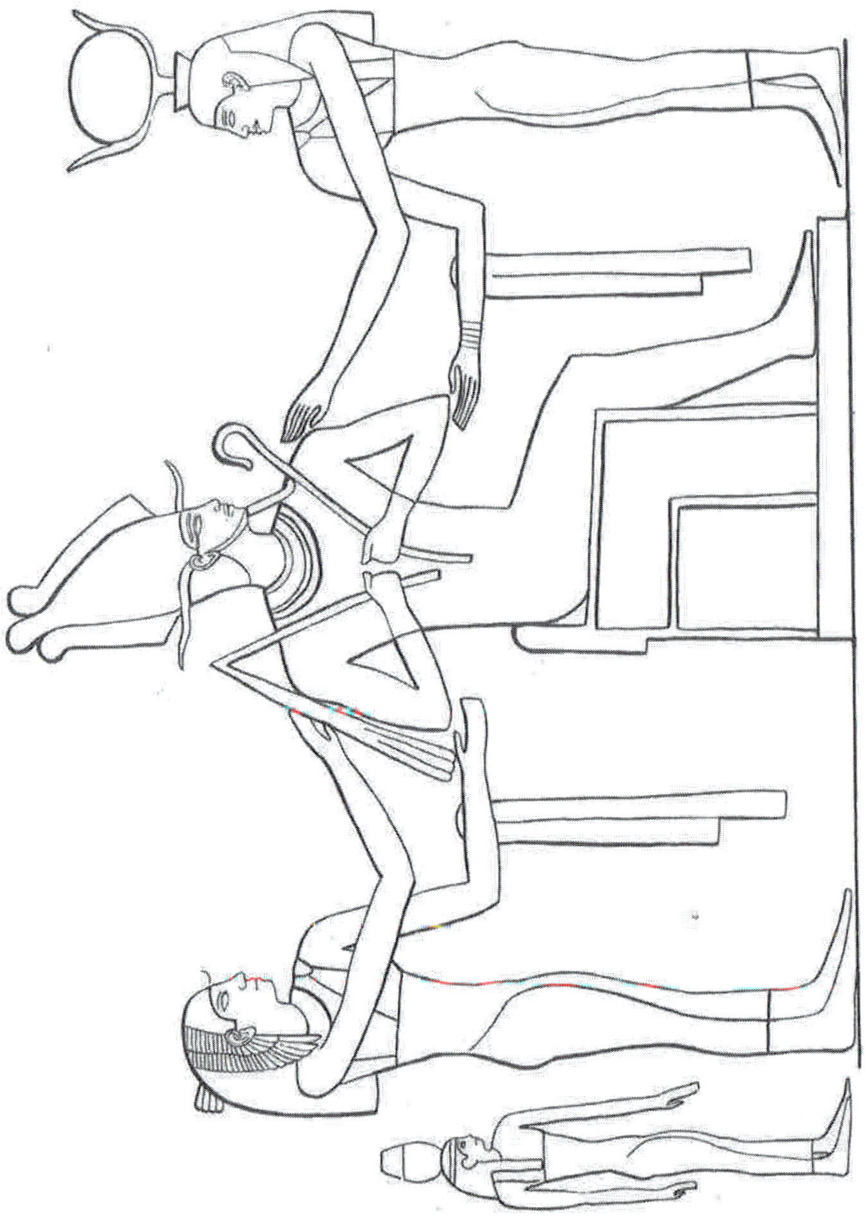

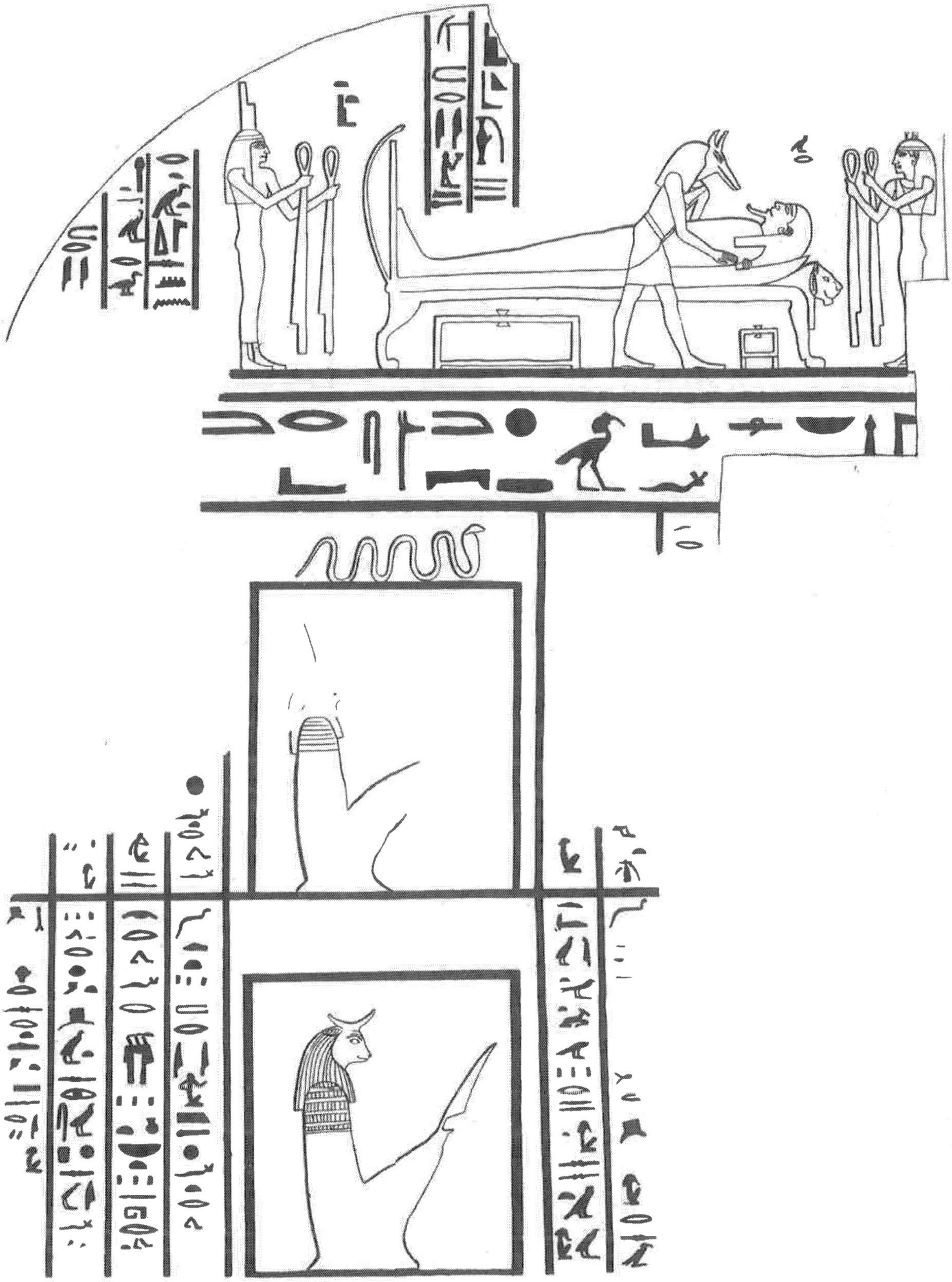

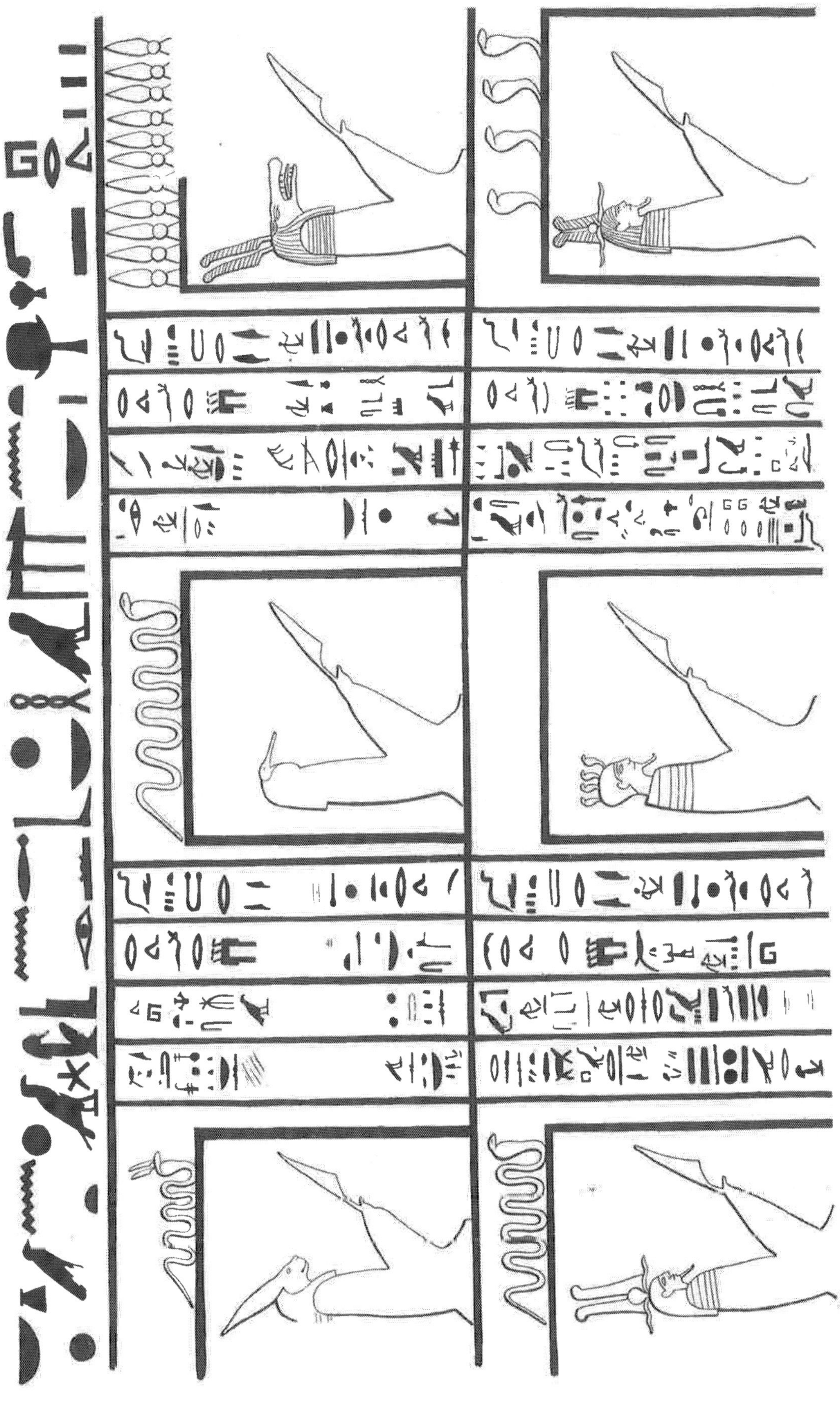

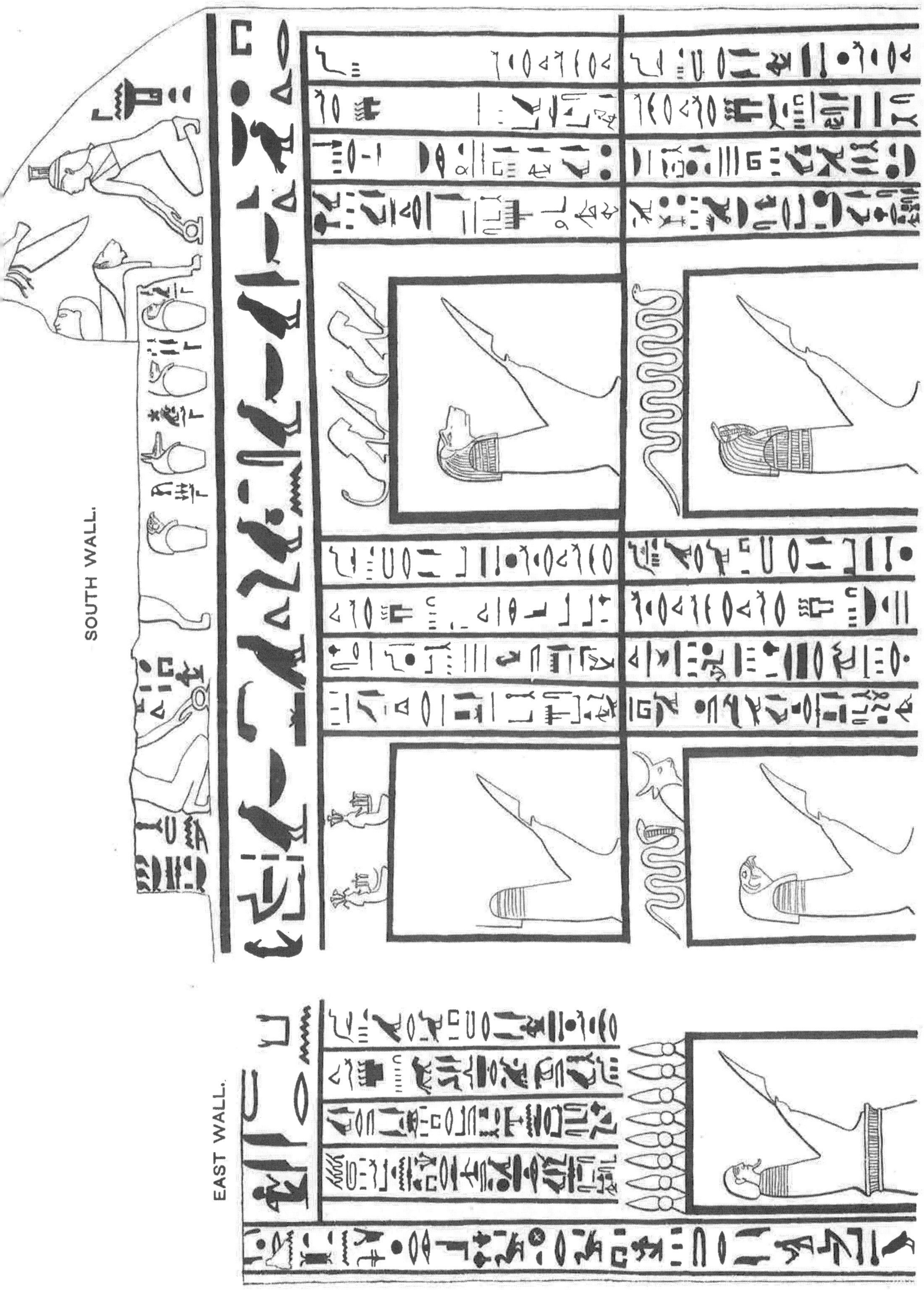
SOUTH WALL.
EAST WALL.

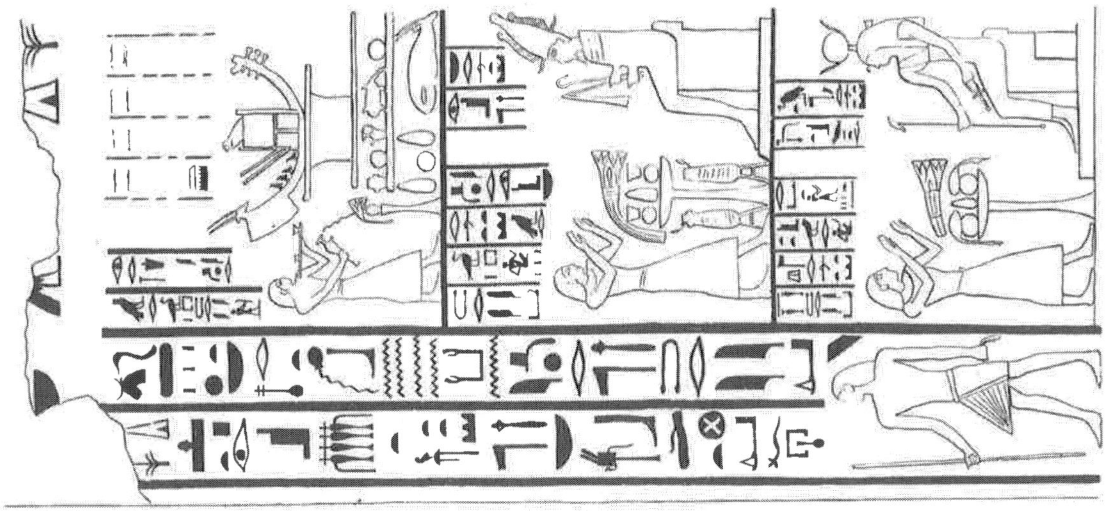

MID HALL, E. WALL, S. HALF.

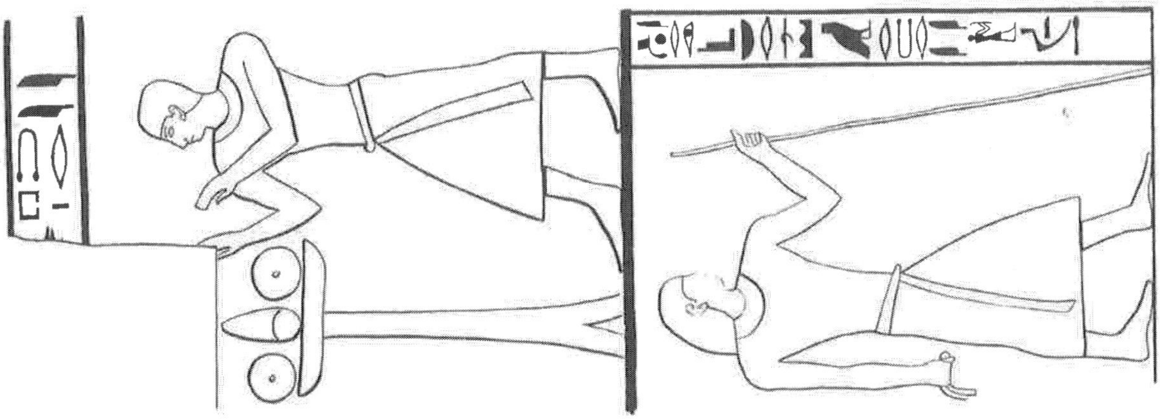

S. HALL, E. SIDE OF DOOR.

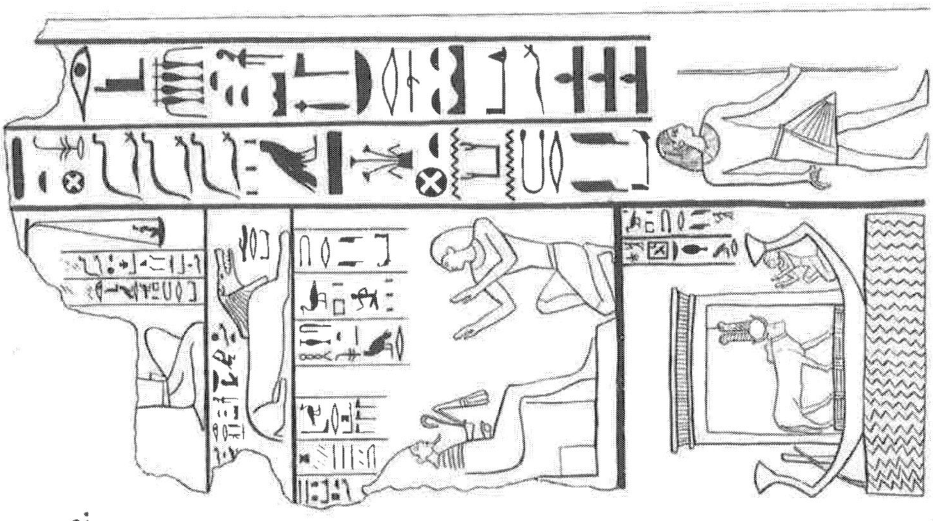

MID HALL, W. WALL, S. HALF.

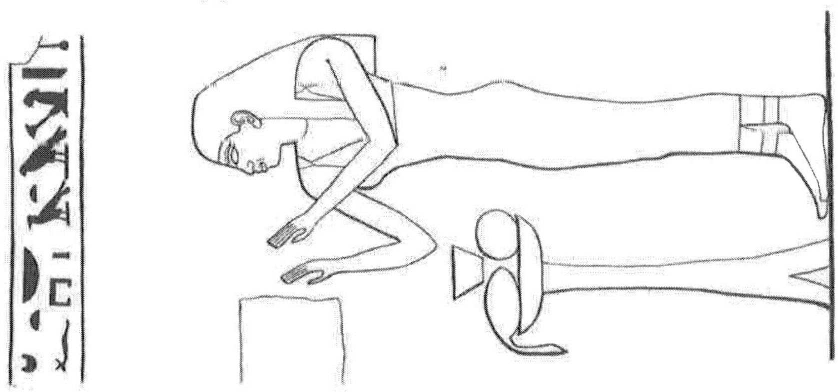

W. CHAMBER, S. SIDE DOOR.

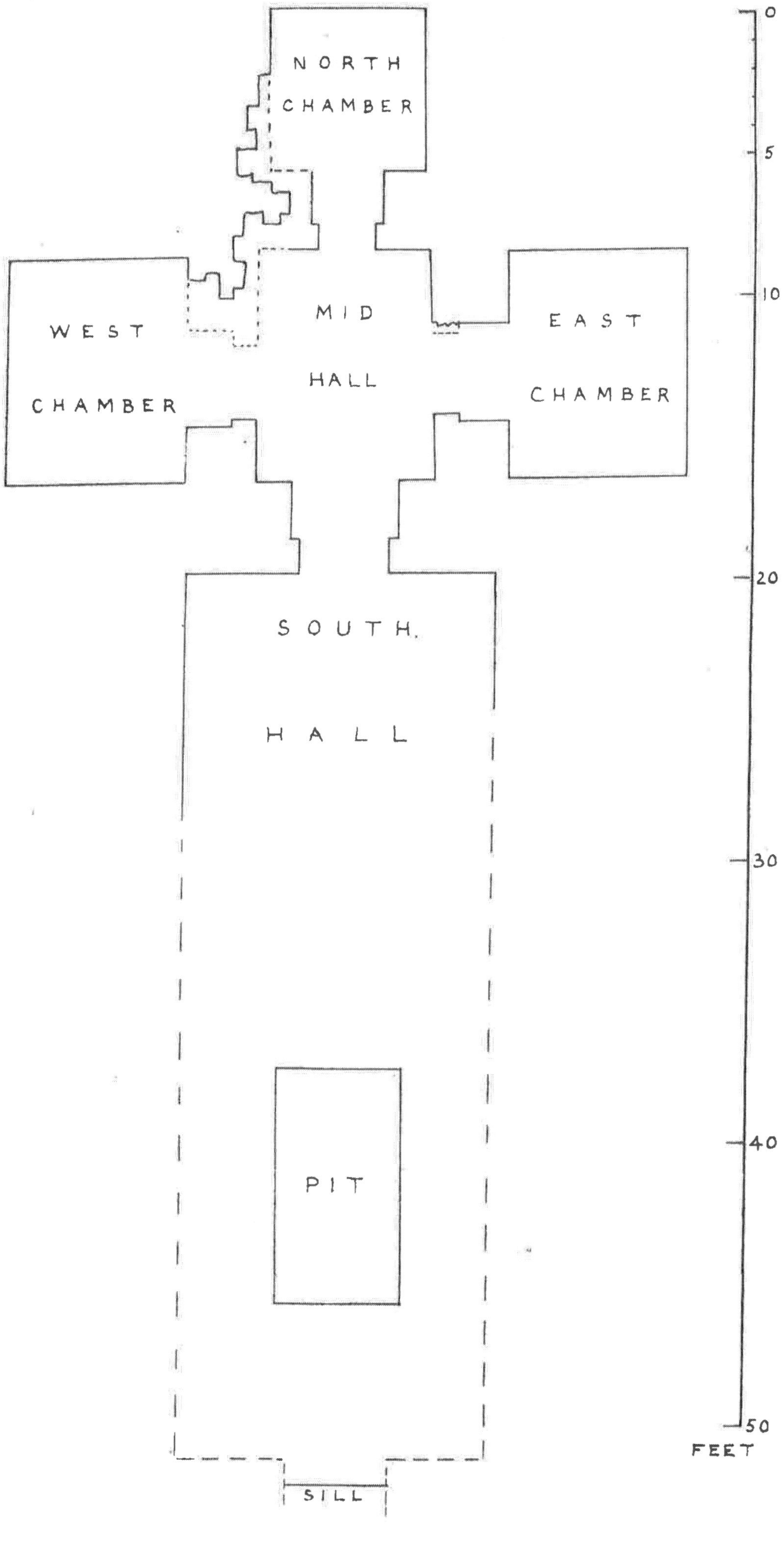
NORTH CHAMBER
WEST CHAMBER
MID HALL
EAST CHAMBER
SOUTH. HALL
PIT
SILL
0
5
10
20
30
40
50
FEET

CHOACHYTES PETOSIR SON OF PETEHARSAMTO.

CHOACHYTES ANKH-HAPI, ANKH-HAPI SON OF PETEHAPI, HORUS.

CHOACHYTES PATO, PESEKH....., TAMIN.

PAINTED CRYPT. ROMAN.

UNNAMED COFFIN.

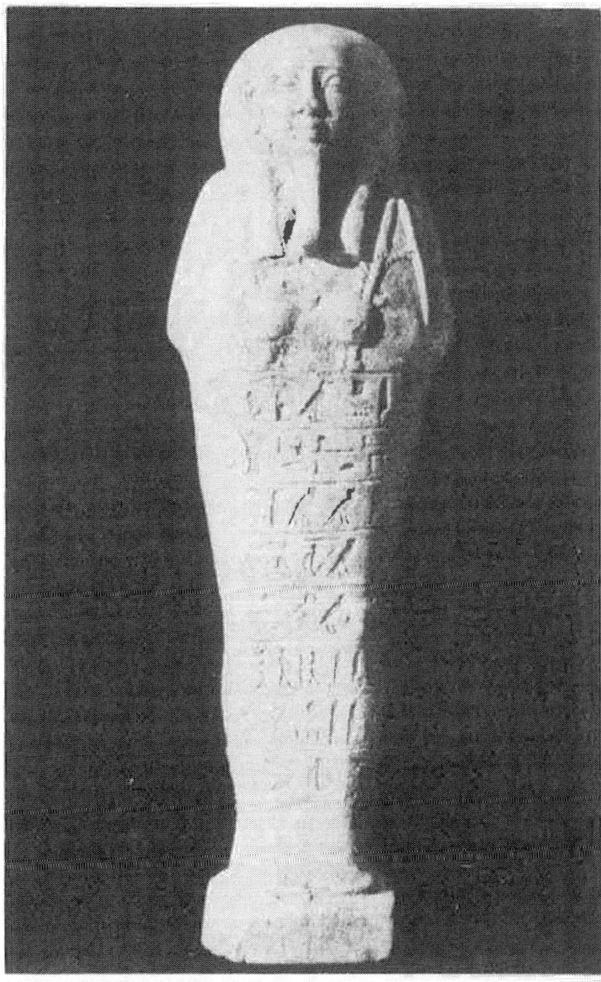

USHABTI OF BA-HOTEP-UR.

RIFEH. ROMAN FURNITURE AND COPTIC CARVING (1-12); BALYZEH, COPTIC (13-16).

DEIR BALYZEH, SOUTH WING.

DEIR BALYZEH FROM OUTSIDE WALL.

DEIR ZOWYEH, NOW OCCUPIED.

DEIR BALYZEH, SOUTH OUTER WALL.

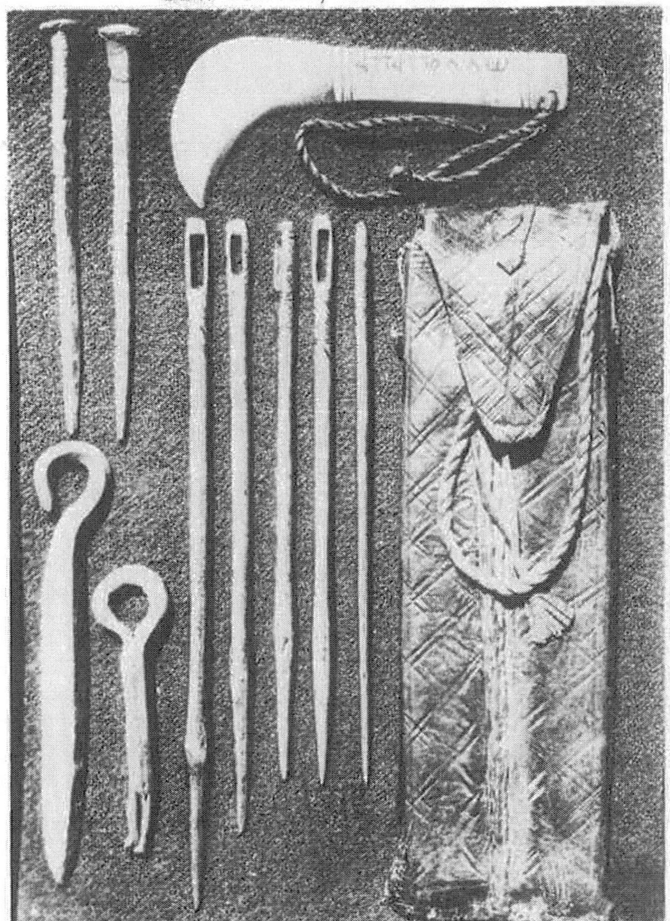

DEIR BALYZEH. SET OF TOOLS IN POUCH.

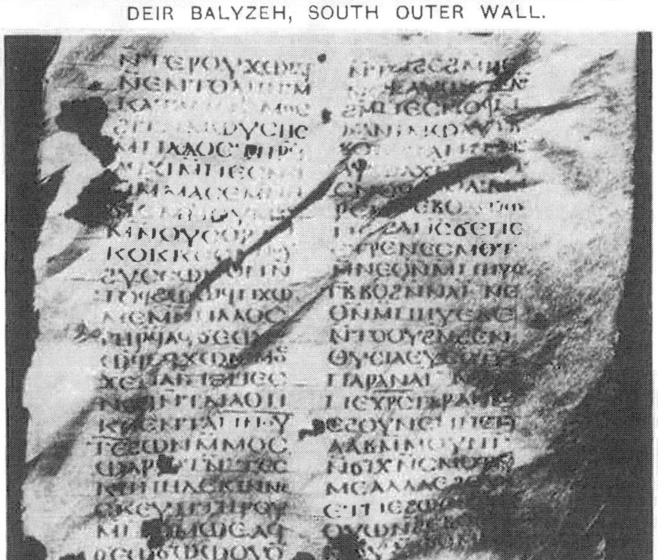

HEBREWS CHAP. IX. BALYZEH.

CLEARED ROAD ON TOP DESERT.

HUT ON TOP DESERT, SEE PL. VIII.

1

2

3

4

5

6

8 7 9

10

11

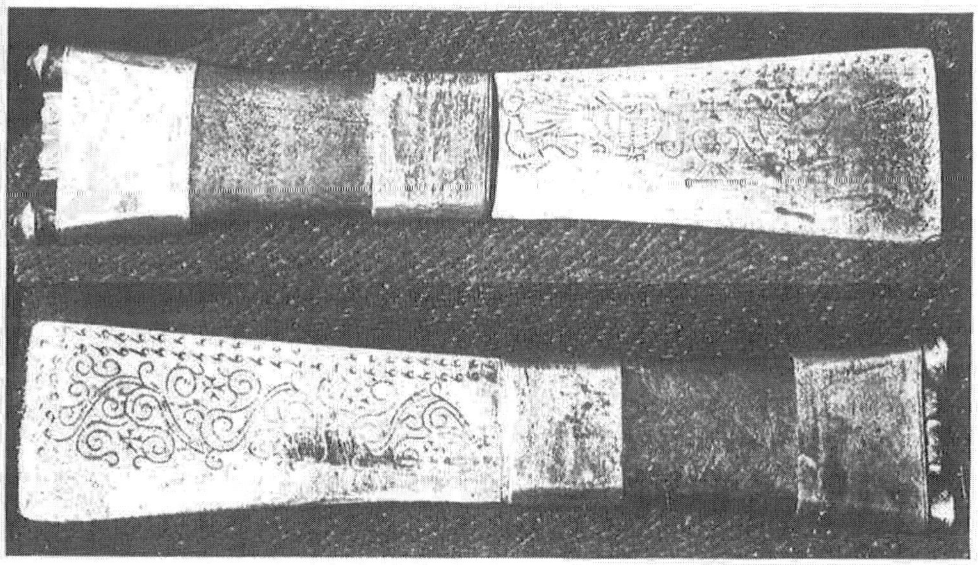
12

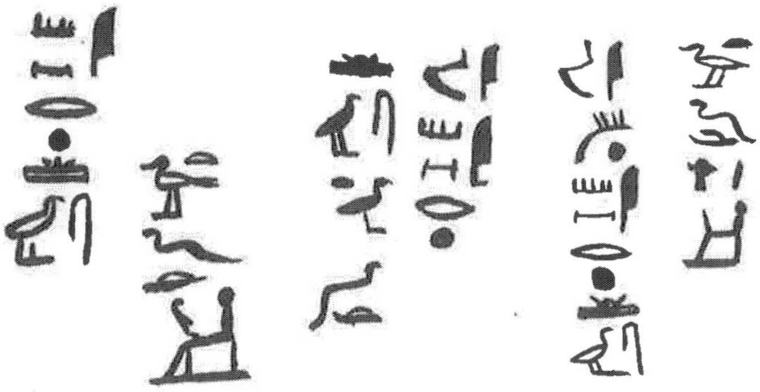

Outer Box Inner Box Body Coffin
Inscriptions of Amen-rekh-su, Pl. XXXI A.
W.M.F.P.

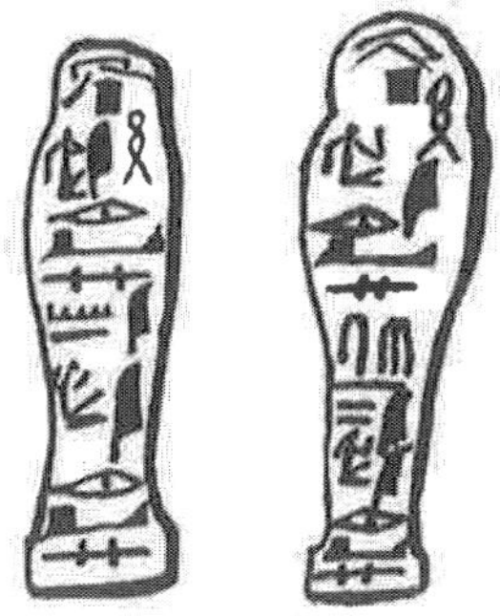

Ushabtis of Hapa-ardus
F.F.

Ushabti of Ptahmay.
Painted Limestone. F.F.

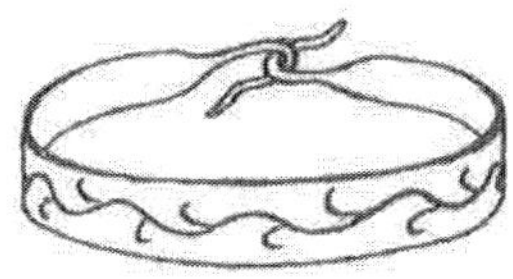

Silver bracelet. Rifeh.
F.P.

W.M.F.P.

QANADLEH. F.P.

BALYZEH. F.P.

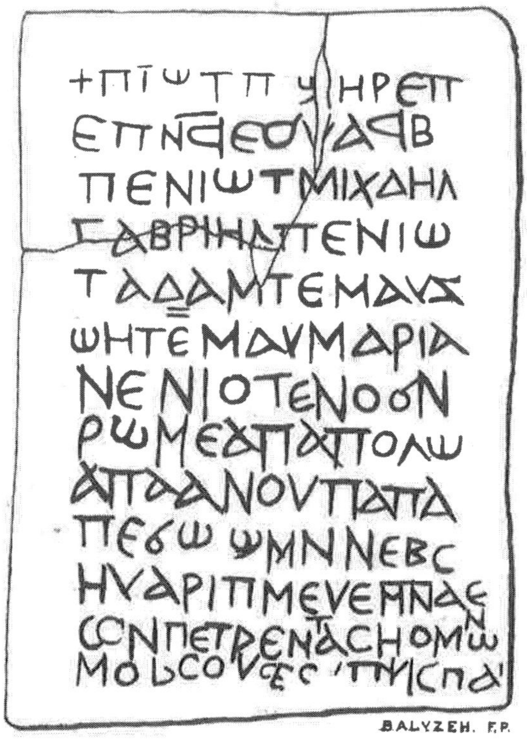

BALYZEH. F.P.

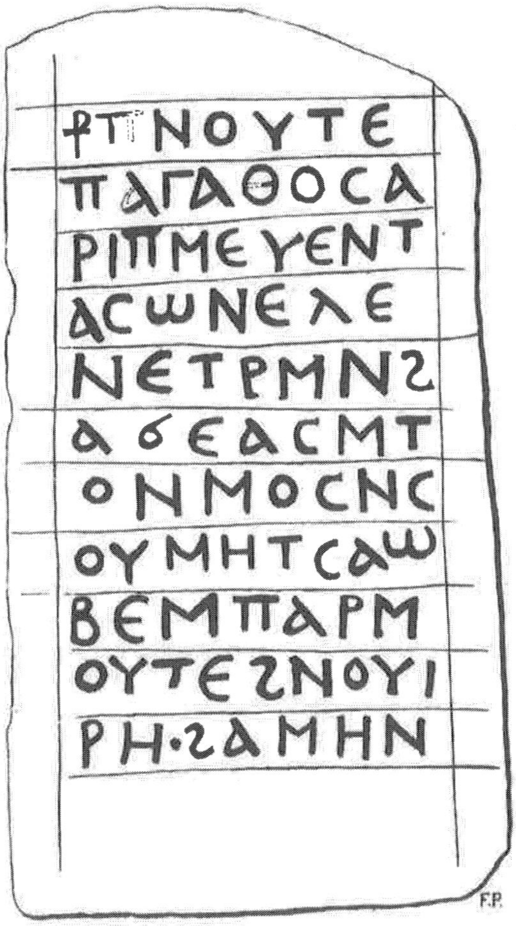
ⲫΠ ΝΟΥΤΕ
ΠΑΓΑΘΟCΑ
ΡΙΠΜΕΥΕΝΤ
ΑCΩΝΕΛΕ
ΝΕΤΡΜΝϨ
Α ϬΕΑCΜΤ
ΟΝΜΟCΝC
ΟΥΜΗΤCΑΩ
ΒΕΜΠΑΡΜ
ΟΥΤΕϨΝΟΥΙ
ΡΗ·ϨΑΜΗΝ
F.P.

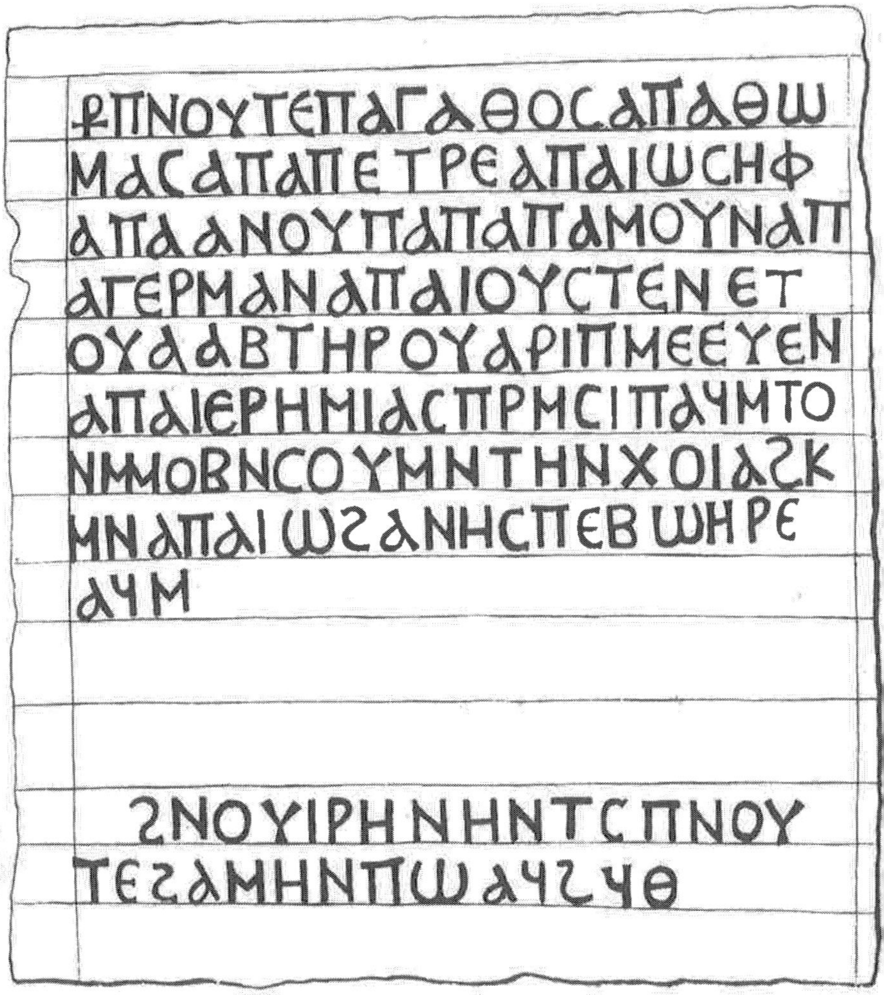
ⲫΠΝΟΥΤΕΠΑΓΑΘΟCΑΠΑΘΩ
ΜΑCΑΠΑΠΕΤΡΕΑΠΑΙΩCΗΦ
ΑΠΑΑΝΟΥΠΑΠΑΠΑΜΟΥΝΑΠ
ΑΓΕΡΜΑΝΑΠΑΙΟΥCΤΕΝΕΤ
ΟΥΑΑΒΤΗΡΟΥΑΡΙΠΜΕΕΥΕΝ
ΑΠΑΙΕΡΗΜΙΑCΠΡΜCΙΠΑϤΜΤΟ
ΝΜΜΟΒΝCΟΥΜΝΤΗΝΧΟΙΑϨΚ
ΜΝΑΠΑΙΩϨΑΝΗCΠΕΒΩΗΡΕ
ΑϤΜ
ϨΝΟΥΙΡΗΝΗΝΤCΠΝΟΥ
ΤΕϨΑΜΗΝΠΩΑϤϨϤΘ

E.M

+ΠΙΩ ΤΠϢΗ
ΡΕΠΕΤ ΝΔΕ
ΤΟΥΑ ΒΠΕΝ
ΕΙΩΤ ΑΜΜ
ΝΝΕϢΗΡ ΕΤΗ
ΡΟΥΑΡΙ ΠΜ =
ΕΥΕΝΠ ΑCΟΝ
ΤΡΜΤ
ΛϤΜ
E.M.

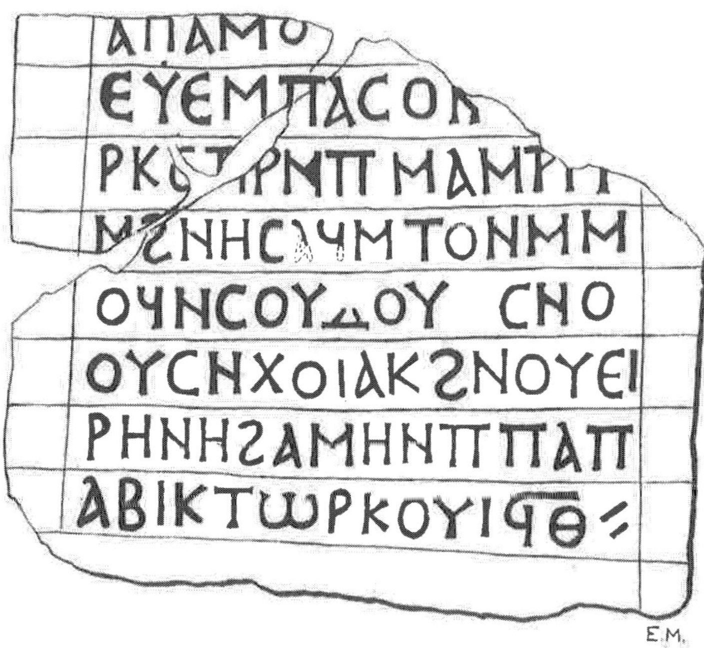
ΑΠΑΜΟ
ΕΥΕΜΠΑCΟΝ
ΡΚΕΤΡΜΠ ΜΑΜΡ
ΜϨΝΗCΑϤΜΤΟΝΜΜ
ΟϤΝCΟΥΔΟΥ CΝΟ
ΟΥCΗΧΟΙΑΚϨΝΟΥΕΙ
ΡΗΝΗϨΑΜΗΝΠΠΑΠ
ΑΒΙΚΤΩΡΚΟΥΙϤΘ =
E.M.